STEELHEAD

FLY ANGLING

GUERILLA FLY-ROD TACTICS

MICHAEL GORMAN

STEELHEAD
FLY ANGLING
GUERILLA FLY-ROD TACTICS

MICHAEL GORMAN

FAP

FRANK AMATO PUBLICATIONS

DEDICATION

Jason Mariner has come a long way since he first sat in one of my fishing classes at OSU in 2004, a freshman from Phoenix, AZ who had never seen a steelhead. Since then, his passion for steelhead angling and his considerable skill in locating and catching them are second to none. This book is dedicated to Jason, whose help in bringing this work into being was immense. As a fishing companion, confidant, fishing model, a man willing to endure my photographic direction and squeeze the shutter release buttons on my cameras hundreds of times, Jason was always happy and willing to assist me. He acted as my copy editor, and offered his suggestions and insights as this book was being written. Whether it's figuring out where and how to fish a new steelhead river, boating treacherous whitewater, bushwacking challenging terrain to reach pristine steelhead water, or watching my back in a street fight, Jason Mariner will always be my first choice, the best wingman on the planet.

Frank Amato Publications, Inc.
P.O. Box 82112, Portland, Oregon 97282
503.653.8108 • www.amatobooks.com

Photographs by the author unless otherwise noted.
Illustrations by Dave Hall
Fly Plate Photos by Jim Schollmeyer

Cover Design: Tony Amato
Book Design: Kathy Johnson

Printed by Kings Time Printing Press Ltd.
Printed in China
Softbound ISBN-13: 978-1-57188-479-4 • UPC: 0-81127-00321-1
Hardbound ISBN-13: 978-1-57188-485-5 • UPC: 0-81127-00330-3
1 3 5 7 9 10 8 6 4 2

CONTENTS

Introduction

WARNING! THIS BOOK IS NOT FOR THE FAINT OF HEART,
the politically correct, or those easily offended. It is strictly
for those wanting the "down and dirty" about overcoming
the challenges inherent to the sport of fly-fishing and
catching a steelhead on a fly rod.

The author teaching fly-casting at Oregon State University.

You may disagree with some of my aggressive strategies in a competitive steelhead environment. And, yes, if you are a mature adult, you may be inclined to groan and roll your eyes occasionally as you course through these pages. Irreverent and offensive attempts at humor are in the mix, too. In addition to hardcore information about finding and catching steelhead, the text is replete with my editorial comments, and not only about steelhead fishing. If you decide to proceed, you have been warned! My conscience is clear.

My Story

It took me seven years of dogged persistence to catch my first steelhead. It was another three years before I finally landed one on a *fly* rod. In order to protect my credibility as an "expert" angler and guide, I usually don't reveal this to my clients until they have actually caught a few steelhead with me. In a good year, my guests will combine to land more than 500 steelhead. In fact, I have had scores of clients who landed steelhead on their very first day of fishing for them. So, I guess I've learned a few things over time, mostly by the hard, long route.

Learn from my mistakes. My initial steelhead strategy was a losing one: learn it all by yourself through trial and error. My observations over more than thirty years of pursuing steelhead indicate that this is a very popular path for many beginners, vainly hoping a steelhead will have a Seizure of Silliness and bite their hook. I call this *The Edison Strategy*.

When I was a kid, my local library had a single book on steelhead fishing and it was filled, apparently, with sleeping gas. Every time I opened it, the book put me to sleep. Video-tape technology was many years into the future, and if sportsmen shows existed where knowledgeable anglers shared their fishing secrets, I did not know about them. My local sporting goods store owner/clerk/fisherman was on the other side of useless. And, unfortunately, I had no steelheading veterans in my circle of fishing companions. We all fished trout. Thus, it was trial & error for seven long years.

If you are persistent enough in the trials and errors of *The Edison Strategy*, you—like me—will eventually discover all the flies that don't catch fish, all the angling methods that don't appeal to them, and all the fishing holes on the river that don't hold compliant steelhead. Once all these are discovered, what remains are enticing flies, effective methods, and worthy fishing holes. There is a silver lining until you get there. In seven years, my casting technique became excellent because no steelhead ever interfered with my casting *practice*.

Thomas Edison made famous the strategy that I adopted. He was searching for an appropriate filament for the incandescent light bulb. He tried more than a thousand (!) different materials until he tried a strand of carbonized cotton, which did an adequate job. This discovery took him years. Before the discovery, when a friend remarked that he continued to fail, Edison pointed out that, on the contrary, he had learned more than a thousand materials that *didn't* work. So, in essence, he could scratch these off his lengthy list. Lemons into lemonade. Similarly it took me most of a decade to discover my "carbonized cotton".

I chose the trial & error tactic for a variety of reasons, none of them very good. These included money (lack thereof), ignorance, stubbornness, naiveté, underestimating my quarry, and an overestimation of myself. Because of the frustration and wasted time inherent in this game plan, I don't recommend the strategy. This book will shave years off your learning curve if you are a struggling beginner. Even if you are a steelhead veteran who wants to get better at locating and catching more of these fish on a fly, I'm confident you will glean some strategies that will add to your success.

I've come a long way since my first attempts to catch a steelhead. For more than three decades, I have guided Oregon rivers for these intriguing fish, logging more than 120 days on steelhead rivers in a typical year. On top of this, I have taught fly-fishing and steelhead fishing credit classes at Oregon State University in Corvallis since the late 1980's, and continue to do so as of this writing.

Important fly-fishing lessons illustrated by real-life steelhead stories are a large part of what you will read in every chapter. Just like every question my students and clients throw at me about "Why do you do it this way?" or "Why is that small detail so important to success?" I attempt to back up my answer with an experience I've lived or witnessed. There is little consensus among steelhead experts about which flies, methods, equipment, knots, wind direction, moon phase, and hat color are best for catching steelhead. This is part of the fun. I have some strong opinions born of experience, but I am open to discovery, re-evaluation and change. And, if I ever write a revised edition of this book, I will change, no doubt, a few of these opinions as the steelhead teach me more. However, until then, I'm giving you what I've gathered and processed in pursuing steelhead, trying to trick them into biting my hook.

This Book

I have tried to create a bare-knuckles field manual. It takes you out of the steelhead fishing schoolhouse and throws you into the foxhole. This book is intentionally short on inconsequential fluff and high on effective planning and preparation. It's lacking in steelhead fly-fishing history, devoid of discussion about fly-fishing pioneers and current "masters", and almost completely wanting in eloquent wet flies and their complicated designs. You won't find instructions about how to cast 200 feet. Others have presented all these much better than I could. My intent is not to cover well-traveled ground in writing about fly-rod steelheading. My intent is to give you a map, a canteen, a shovel, a "weapon", and a good plan to accomplish the mission—catching a steelhead on a fly rod.

Sometimes the topics discussed herein aren't pretty, artful, or genteel. Not all anglers and river users you will encounter while fishing are generous and courteous. The vast majority of quality public waters are overcrowded and the anglers there fiercely competitive. It doesn't matter how good your flies are

A late-run winter steelhead lies in the shallows for a quick photo before release.

and how far you can cast a beautiful tight loop if you can't find a place to fish, or you are relegated to water that has already been pounded today by three other anglers as skilled as you. I address these very significant issues.

This book will not be your Grandpa's primer on fly-fishing for steelhead on the uncrowded streams of the Olden Days. The successful steelhead fly-fisher of the 21st century has to have a comprehensive plan, a well-thought-out strategy when he or she goes fishing. It's challenging enough to locate, approach, and coax a steelhead without much appetite to bite your fly. However, add to this numerous other anglers competing with you for that very same fish, and the difficulty of the challenge increases exponentially.

Make no mistake, I will be laying out in the pages that follow effective flies, methods, and equipment that have produced thousands of steelhead I've caught or netted for my guests. (And, *thousands* is not an exaggeration in a span of more than thirty years.) In addition to the 'where' and 'how', and 'with what', I'll help you lay out a game plan to enhance your odds and enjoyment of catching a steelhead on a fly rod, just like a skilled, intelligent guerilla on an important mission.

My Perspectives

Much of what I write is from a dual perspective: I am both a fly-fisherman and a fly-fishing guide. Even when guiding, I am fishing…through my clients. I fish in these situations by proxy. When you think about it, the challenge of a good guide is to be able to fish *through* his guests. I must effectively convey to the angler how to cast accurately, achieve the proper presentation of the fly, detect the strike, set the hook, play the steelhead, and successfully slide it into the net or onto the beach. As I teach the details of effective steelhead fly-fishing to others, it reinforces the importance of such attention to details for my own fishing. If I really want to learn something well, I try to teach it successfully to others.

So, when I relate many stories in this book as I wear my "guide hat", do not let that cause you to lose sight of learning a valuable *fishing* lesson, even though you are probably not a guide. It's irrelevant.

And, since most steelhead fly-anglers do not fish from a boat, but on foot, do not lose sight of my lesson for you just because many of my stories take place when my guests and I are in a boat. For my personal fishing, I am usually on foot. Solitude in my personal fishing is important. Locations that are inaccessible to boats are my preference. Boat traffic can greatly diminish my enjoyment (and success) when I personally hunt steelhead. I am, also, willing to blaze a trail where there is no trail, in order to separate myself from other bank anglers. I try to avoid the easily-accessed walk-in locations.

I truly think I can improve the ease of understanding essential details critical to locating and catching steelhead. So, approach this as a fun-to-read technical manual. This book aims to be more entertaining and humorous (I hope) than any other book on the subject of steelheading with a fly, or any other angling method for that matter. I choose to take a more aggressive, opinionated writing slant toward the pursuit of the most worthy fish that inhabits freshwater. If you are open to such an approach for chasing the West's greatest game fish, then it is time to put on the spurs, saddle up, "cowboy up", and ride with me in pursuit of steelhead for the next 18 chapters.

CHAPTER 1
Getting Rooted in Steelheading Reality

CONSISTENTLY SUCCESSFUL STEELHEAD FISHING,
especially with a fly rod, is not easy. The fish, the conditions,
other anglers, and your lack of smarts, experience, and determination
can all conspire to beat you. Unless you address all of these issues,
and many others, you cannot often succeed.

Combat Zone.

Upon returning to freshwater, silver-sided steelhead eventually revert to their rainbow trout coloration.

To be successful in any endeavor—love, career, athletics, and fishing—you had better have a good plan. When it comes to steelhead fishing, I know most anglers do not. I see supporting illustrations on most of my fishing days. I know former steelhead-fishing wannabes and former steelhead guides who did not have a good plan, and this is the reason they are *former.*

One of the projects to be completed by all of my fishing class students at Oregon State University is to go fishing during the term, and write a summary of their outing using the guidelines that I have provided for them. Having read thousands of these summaries in more than 20 years of teaching, it is clear that very few students go with a plan. They do not check the weather report or the river levels; have no rudimentary checklist to remember all of their fishing gear and accessories; underestimate the needed number of flies and expendable necessities, such as tippets and leaders; have no contingency for alternative fishing locations; and, are shackled by unreasonable time restrictions.

Creating a successful steelhead-catching plan starts with the determination to *have* a plan. Begin with a notepad or computer document: where, when, what, how, why or why not, and what the heck can go haywire. Review all portions of the plan carefully. Because the conditions and circumstances have endless combinations of possibilities, prepare to make adjustments.

Your plan must include dealing with the unexpected. Steelhead fishing and Murphy's Law are constant companions. A rod may break. Your waders get a serious leak. You bury a barbed hook deeply in your thumb. A local fishing club has their annual outing on the section of river you plan to fish. You are an hour from home and have forgotten your fishing license. The deep-fried burritos from last night's dinner are ominously churning and burning. Did you leave the oven on?

If you think you have a comprehensive, good fish-catching plan, here is a simple way to check it. Pretend that you will receive the Reward of Your Dreams—the girl (or guy), the gold, or the goodies—IF you can successfully hook and land a steelhead tomorrow. If you visualize enjoying your potential prize, you will find many ways to improve and fine-tune your plan.

Steelhead are the most magnificent fish to inhabit our Pacific Northwestern rivers, and those of British Columbia, Alaska, and the Great Lakes Region of the U.S. Most fly-rod steelheaders would state this unequivocally. The adrenaline rush and sheer joy of hooking these silver denizens causes many of us steelhead junkies to endure and overcome numerous trials.

I have observed that many fly-anglers, especially the 20- and 30-somethings, can quickly evolve into being steelhead specific. Once having landed a few steelhead, for some anglers, other species can fade into indifference. Steelhead are a drug. They can become the sole focus of daydreams, planning, and virtually all outdoor activities when rivers are fishable. In the Pacific Northwest, this seems like a growing epidemic with the advances in fishing tools, media communications, and increased knowledge of flies and techniques. It seems to me that too many anglers will not let jobs, families, or college homework stand in the way of their steelhead fishing pursuits. More and more often, I find anglers on steelhead rivers on Tuesdays and Wednesdays, hoping to find less crowding. Instead of being at work or in class, they are on the water, harassing steelhead on some of my favorite rivers.

There is a significant price to be paid for consistent steelheading success. Notice here, again, I have carefully used the word "consistent." Even a blind bowman will hit a target occasionally. Having tried steelheading with a fly, many fine anglers decide they cannot or will not pay the price for consistent rewards. As I said earlier, overcrowding and rude behavior head the list of causes for surrender on readily accessible public rivers. Are you willing to adopt some strategies that will *eventually* encourage you to persist? The "encouragement" I am speaking about is catching more steelhead. If you are, let us start by dealing with more hard facts of reality.

First, consider the *ideal* world: a chicken in every pot, a beautiful, loving woman for every good man who desires one (and vice versa) and, magnificent, uncrowded steelhead water filled with willing fish for all who would cast a fly.

As for the *real* world, I will not comment further about poultry and companionship, but I do know something about steelhead reality on public waters. It is too often crowded, rude, competitive, and even occasionally, hostile. So, for the list of adverse steelheading realities, which follows, "other anglers" will rank at the top of the heap.

MG's "Top 12" Obstacles to Your *Consistent* Steelhead Fishing Success

1. Other anglers who want to fish the same fishing waters you do.
2. Lack of knowledge and experience. There is a learning curve.
3. Lack of persistence and determination to succeed. You must be willing to pay the price to "win".
4. Unhealthy attitudes: impatience, anger, greed, attempting to control the uncontrollable, know-it-all arrogance.
5. Inability to locate productive steelhead water.
6. Lack of *effective* fly-fishing techniques. Each technique is composed of small details, some quite subtle. Little details, correctly executed, often make the difference between success and failure.
7. Limited access because of private property or terrain. Inadequate equipment, including rod, reel, line and *chest* waders.
8. Inadequate equipment, including rod, reel, line and chest waders.
9. Fly selection.

10. River conditions constantly changing.
11. Temperamental steelhead that do not need to eat on their spawning migration. Most refuse to bite on any given day. Sometimes, it seems, ALL steelhead will refuse to bite.
12. Other river users such as rafters, kayakers, powerboats and jet skiers may drift through or patrol your fishing water.

On any given day be prepared to deal with a combination of the challenges listed above, not just one. For example, the weather and river conditions can hinder your angling efforts. To this stew, add trying to tempt wary fish that have little or no appetite. Moreover, you are trying to fool the fish with a *fly*, a fake morsel on a hook that does not have the smell, texture, or taste of a real food item that a steelhead might actually want to eat.

You are surrounded! Come out with your . . .

You are inexperienced, so you aren't even sure which patterns would be best for the conditions, let alone how to skillfully present the fly to the fish. If these are not enough, what few fishable spots you find to fish already have other anglers in them. You are relegated, then, to secondary locations, further decreasing your odds of success.

So, how are you doing with handling The Truth at this point? Are you getting a feel for the need for a tough mindset to succeed in this game? It is interesting how so many fly-fishing steelhead how-to books ignore confronting some of these realities, and helping the reader formulate a strategic game plan to effectively deal with challenges. The typical books of this genre focus on casting, fly patterns, gear, famous rivers, and paying written homage to too many steelheading "gods" they have known. It is similar to preparing a soldier for battle by only *talking* about weapons, munitions, how to fire a rifle, and famous old soldiers. Ignored are survival tactics in a hostile environment, concealment, adjusting to the unexpected, and hand-to-hand combat.

In the balance of this chapter, I want to focus mainly on the items #1 and #4 from my Top 12: other anglers and unhealthy attitudes. The other obstacles are addressed in chapters that follow.

The vast majority of the time your greatest obstacles to angling success are other river users, primarily other fishermen. Besides limited access, which tends to concentrate

Keegan Warrington. Fish on! Now what? Nearby boats can present a problem with an out-of-control steelhead.

once they've made it to said bridge, the steelhead don't seem to wander too far. Experienced anglers know this, so they take up their stations where the fish congregate and linger.

The return of the great majority of migrating hatchery steelhead to a single release point, I will vehemently maintain, has altered social behavior for the worse. Rude, aggressive conduct is too often the social norm, as fishermen resort to virtually standing on top of each other. And the state Departments of Fisheries wonder why more people do not buy fishing licenses each year!

It seems to me that too many in the fly-fishing culture try to be meek and proper to the steelhead boors who will not hesitate to cast into anyone's little piece of water. The Meek may inherit the earth, but not prime steelhead water.

anglers in the prime areas available, crowding is exacerbated by the fact that it is convenient for fish and wildlife agencies to plant steelhead smolts at a single release site. The young fish imprint not only on the particular river in which they were released, but, also, on the near proximity of the location where they were dropped into the river. If the release site is at Fish Creek Bridge, the returning adults will tend to congregate in the vicinity of Fish Creek Bridge. Some will be intercepted in the lower reaches of the river as they move upstream, but

Personal Space

Though I restrict myself almost exclusively to fly-fishing now, my steelhead fishing roots were potted in fishing with

For some, an opportunity to meet new friends on the river. For others, perhaps an irritation.

Flotilla on the Siletz River. Mind if I fish your water? A resourceful angler must learn to effectivelyt deal with crowds.

worms, salmon and steelhead roe, crayfish tails and sand shrimp. If I had to catch steelhead to feed my family, I would use a hook with bait on it. I have experienced good success with virtually all steelhead fishing methods. However, I am of the opinion that most fly-rodders, over time, have formed a definition of Personal Space. The majority of my broad fly-angling circle think that another fisherman who positions himself close enough to you to cast over your fly line—and is willing to do so—is too near, invading your Personal

Space and fishing water. Would you cut in line at the movie premier or the lunch line without permission? Like any other civil interaction, courteously wait your turn, or go elsewhere. Even though most fishermen, of ALL stripes, will not so blatantly violate your elbow room, a significant minority will. Again, the policy of single-site release of hatchery steelhead exacerbates this.

I know many fly-anglers who refuse to pursue steelhead because the environment can be socially unpleasant. Alterna-

I go about my mission, but I am fully armed. My "weapons", if you will, are my wits, determination, experience, and resourcefulness. This does not exclude me from being a nice guy. It is possible to be both an amiable human being and aggressive angler. The key to this balance is to be *subtly* aggressive, not overtly so. Most of the time.

As hard as I may try to fly underneath the radar when I fish or guide, there are times I get involved in "justified confrontation". This has naturally led to a little unwanted (I think) notoriety. But, sometimes you have to speak up. If some interloper parks his person or watercraft so closely that they fish the water my guests or I can comfortably reach from our position, I will usually call them out on it. It's too bad that other anglers so offensively put upon will not do the same, which reinforces this "trespassing" behavior. This uncivil conduct then, sadly, becomes the acceptable norm.

Another common ungentlemanly maneuver I frequently encounter occurs when I, or one of my guests, hooks a fish in the general vicinity of other anglers, be they on foot or in a boat. Often, I must temporarily move the boat from the position at which the fish was hooked into quieter water at the river's edge. My intention is to return to the original anchored spot to try to tempt a second fish. Your exact position as you fish can be extremely important. Too often, as another angler who has watched us at the time the fish was hooked—and knows we will most likely want to return to that fishing position once the battle with our fish has been resolved—steps in or drops anchor at the exact spot we wish to return to. It is like having a great seat in a packed movie theater, excusing yourself for a bathroom emergency, only to find someone else in your prime seat who will take offense when you try to reclaim it. You, I think, are justified in gently, but firmly, stating your case and standing your ground in the theater, and on the river. Brace yourself to be switched from being the offended to the offender. I find it best to speak quietly, slowly, and with conviction. Never resort to name-calling, even if the other party does. This is throwing gasoline on a fire. If any kind of confrontation—justified though it may be—causes you anguish, wish the intruder well and move on.

For you boaters, I have another unpleasant scenario I experience constantly. It happens as I am fishing a long piece of likely water, drifting flies through the prime areas as I slow my boat in the current. Another boat passes. As it does, one of two things may happen: One rude, the other ruder.

In the lesser case, the other boat may steer wide of us, but the anglers in it will cast into the water we are obviously fishing or will be fishing in the next few seconds. I have had such anglers cast over my line or that of my guest, tangling our line with theirs. Unbelievable!

In the ruder situation, a boat will pass me, sometimes actually drifting the craft directly over the water we are fishing. I always say something in this situation.

tively, if they do stay with it, they may be content to cast into a single pool all day. For the mellow roamers I encounter, they seem content to fish through runs that were pounded by good fishermen who preceded them. I admire, and strongly encourage, this very accommodating behavior. I sincerely hope they hook the occasional steelhead to reinforce their good behavior. As for me, I am on the move. Stick and run, stick and run.

I view steelhead fishing—time to roll your eyes—very much as gentlemanly warfare. I can be friendly and smiling as

Surf's up! Wading anglers beware, here comes the tsunami.

The more common, ruder scene is to have a passing boat give us wide berth, but, then, immediately cut to our side of the river to begin fishing only a couple of boat lengths in front of us. I can usually see this stunt coming, and head it off. As the boat passes us, the oarsman will look back to gauge the distance between him and us. That's my clue he is thinking about cutting back to our side of the river to cut us off. When his head turns and he canters his boat for the cutback, I push on my oars to move my boat quickly downstream. When the oarsman looks back again to see how much distance there is between us—Surprise!—he finds my boat near his stern, and I am looking him square in the eye. He has no place to go but farther down river—how embarrassing. If I do this to the same pirate boat several times during the day, or over the course of several days, it is amazing how they soon learn not to try such a maneuver with me again. No words are exchanged. None needed.

Incidents like these are too common. You will encounter them, too, both on foot and in a boat. Too many anglers will not think twice about trying to catch steelhead almost under your rod tip. If the need arises to speak with another angler violating your space, anticipate it. As best you can, blunt the emotional impact, which is sure to follow, with a little conversational rehearsal before the inevitable situations arise.

I had an elderly philosopher fishing friend, Wade Meeker, who said to me, as he looked down, shaking his head slowly, "People…they're a tacky lot." So, make like a Boy scout: Be prepared. Just like death, taxes, and tangled lines, insolent encounters on steelhead rivers are a certainty.

Bad Students, Bad Attitude, No Pudding
"If you don't eat your meat, you can't have any pudding."
—From *Another Brick in the Wall Part 2*, Pink Floyd

I have discovered, and had it reinforced many times, that my attitude plays much in my success. Obstacle #4 from my Top 12: There is a correlation between bad attitudes and poor fishing results. Conversely, a happy, humble, open-to-learn angler can and will catch more steelhead.

There are essential cornerstone attitudes I had to adopt, and suggest you do too: 1) a sincere willingness to learn while overcoming poor habits and incorrect notions. 2) an even attitude or outlook, a determination to put aside emotions that get in the way of learning and enjoying the fishing day. Finally, 3) overcoming the pressing *need* to catch a steelhead. Such a need is an open-arms invitation for Murphy's Law to manifest itself.

We Don't Need No Education
Recently it was impressed upon me, *again*, how difficult it can be for "experienced", know-it-all fly-fishermen to be successful at catching steelhead. Invariably, most have a gross overestimation of their steelhead knowledge and fly-fishing skill. Things are further complicated by their stations in life. They are "order-givers", unable to take suggestions; suggestions that are critical for them to catch a steelhead. Because these are domineering decision-makers in their occupational and family life, their ability and willingness to learn are severely hindered.

In the fly-fishing realm, if they have succeeded in catching a few suicidal steelhead on previous outings, these people mistakenly believe they know how to effectively fish for steelhead. These "easy" fish have led them to believe that there is little more to learn. If they do not catch fish, it's due to the fly pattern, the moon phase, the water conditions, lack of fish, or the guide they have hired. They cease to consider that they may have more to learn.

A prospective client who wanted to fly-fish a particular river with me to catch his first winter steelhead on a fly rod contacted me. As I always do, I queried the man about his fly-fishing experience and that of his fishing companion. He recounted many of the rivers he and his friend had fished, and assured me he and his bud were "very accomplished casters". Upon hearing the "accomplished casters" part, an alarm bell immediately went off in my head. In thirty years of guiding, I have come to know that many experienced fly-anglers are prone to an overblown assessment of their angling skills. Too many are not inclined to take instruction in the minute details necessary to be a consistently good steelheader, especially in the winter season. In essence, they have shut down their willingness to learn anything they do not already know, or *think* they know. Most often, if I receive a subsequent call from them to fish with me again, I refer them to someone else.

In attempting to catch fish that are few in number, that do not need to eat on their spawning migrations, ascending rivers where the competition from other anglers is fierce, success—like the devil—is in the details. Scores of tiny details. Ignoring just one little detail can be the difference between hooking a steelhead and not even realizing there was a willing fish on your last cast. Or, if the steelhead strike does come, the fisher missed the fish because his rod tip was in the wrong hook-setting position. Maybe the reaction to the strike was too slow, there was an incorrect adjustment in the fly-reel drag, there was too much slack line on the water, or it is incorrectly assumed the fly was temporarily stuck on a rock on the stream bottom.

A Little Humility Can Mean Lots of Fish

Rewarded by his humility and willingness to learn, Salt Lake City George turned out to be a shining example of what an excellent student of fly-fishing can be.

George had dreamed of and read about steelhead for years. With no steelhead able to find passage from the Pacific Ocean into Utah rivers, he had traveled to Idaho the previous September to fish the famous Clearwater system for a chance to catch the fish of his daydreams. He related to me that he had had one strike, a very brief tug, in two hard days of fishing. And, now, six months later, he wanted to try it again.

Right from the start, I knew George was fishing well. He listened to and followed every direction I gave him for two days. He was as willing to learn as any student I ever had. He humbly complied with my reminders. Though George was an experienced fly-fisher, he put his bad habits aside and replaced them with those necessary to be an excellent steelhead angler. The casting technique, casting angle, rod position and line control were as consistently good as I have seen. And George

Simultaneous hook-ups. Greg Schuerger and author on a productive winter day on the north Oregon Coast.

never made a cast longer than 25 feet(!) for two days, eight hours a day. He didn't need to. After I precisely positioned the boat for him, he put virtually every cast where I suggested. I will trade distance for precision and control of the drift of the fly every time. Tangles were minimal and he never lost a single fly to a tree or river rock in two days. He maximized his fishing time in productive water.

On Day One, George solidly played five winter steelhead, landing three. The two escapees eventually threw the hook, winning fair and square. No break-offs. He topped off the day with the biggest steelhead I had seen all season. The big buck might have topped 15 pounds! As we took out at the boat ramp, I was concerned about how George would deal with Day Two. There was little chance a winter steelhead beginner could top these numbers. I related to George how thrilled I am when a fly-angler hooks two fish on a winter day, and he hooks five!

At the start of our second day, George hooked a bright steelhead within the first ten minutes. He played it perfectly. After it slid into the landing net, we got some good pictures, and the fish was returned to the river unharmed. I was ecstatic, but I wondered if we had seen our one and only fish of the day. Sometimes that's how it plays out in steelhead fishing. As far as I was concerned, though, George had already had a successful second day, having landed a magnificent, temperamental winter steelhead. He had beaten the odds. Down the river we went.

George cast as I coasted the boat slowly through a couple of productive stretches. Nothing. With an upstream boat coming down on us hard, I brought the boat to a virtual halt backferrying hard on the oars without dropping the anchor. With

the approaching boat no more than a hundred feet above us, George's fly line halted in its drift. He set the hook as I said, "Pull!" There was a throbbing response in the tight line as he lifted the rod tip. George began to play his second fish of the day. When he guided the steelhead into the landing net, Day Two went from a success, to a BIG success. Moreover, whether he wanted it or not, George had an envious audience who watched him as they drifted by while he landed the prize.

For the next hour and a half, George fished well in likely water but there was no cooperation from the steelhead. Several more boats had passed by. They were fishing hard with bait and lures in the same water we would eventually search with flies. Part of a good strategy, then, is to focus on those areas that they may have overlooked. I need to discover and fish such locations in a competitive environment in order to give my anglers the best chance to hook fish, seeking a hidden oasis in the desert.

We soon found such an "oasis" with a biting fish. George got what appeared to be a good hook-set, but the fish quickly escaped. That's fishing.

Float, float, float. Cast, cast, cast. We continued on, occasionally catching distant glimpses of the anglers preceding us. We approached a fallen tree in mid river that had toppled in a winter storm and found a temporary home as the river level had dropped. The easy, logical place to pass the obstruction is on the left, so, of course, we made a tight squeeze on the right side. I knew of a little stream bottom depression that sometimes held a willing steelhead. And, it did that day for George. He made all the right moves to land his third fish of the day. Life on a steelhead river doesn't get any better than

Keep that rod bent against the fish! Steve Severson finds a willing biter, while wife Joann enjoys the show on the Siletz River.

A little creative photography adds to a successful steelhead day.

this. George was a good guy, a willing student, and justly rewarded…again.

We found two more overlooked biting steelhead, and George hooked and landed both. Six hooked, five landed were the totals on Day Two. For the trip, George, who had never hooked a steelhead before his trip to Oregon, tallied eleven fish hooked, with eight steelhead landed! And, as I mentioned before, he never cast more than 25 feet to do it.

Clean Slates Are Best

As each term begins at Oregon State University, I pose a question in each of my classes: "How many of you have never caught a fish on a fly, or maybe, not even held a fly rod in your hand before?" A majority of the students will raise their hands. I follow this with a statement and a second question: "Those of you who have never fly-fished, or who have done very little, have a very large advantage over those in here who are experienced. What is this advantage?" Eventually, one brave and smart student will raise his or her hand and get the answer to the riddle. Beginners are clean slates. They have not incorporated bad habits into their fly-fishing techniques, and they have an open mind when it comes to learning what it really takes to catch a trout or a steelhead on a fly.

Steelhead Pay No Heed to Need or Greed

I am not superstitious, but I do observe some unexplainable correlations. They have to do with a spoken desire by the steelhead angler and the response—or lack thereof—by the fish. Two statements make me wince whenever I hear them because I know the inevitable result.

Statement #1: "I *need* to catch a steelhead." Ouch! This guarantees the angler who utters this will not land another steelhead the rest of the day. You can bank on it. Fish may be hooked, but none will be landed. Murphy's Law will rule the rest of the day for this fisherman, manifested in all manners of tangles, miscues, mysterious break-offs, and Houdini-like escapes by the fish.

Statement # 2: "I just want to land *one more* steelhead." I have had angling guests who have experienced stellar fishing days, landing five or six steelhead for the day. This is "lights out" fishing. Many fishermen would be thrilled to land this many steelhead for the *season*. But, a "greedy" angler has doomed himself to be a little (at least) disappointed when "just one more" fish is not landed. It's as if he has no recollection that he may have already had the best fishing day of his fishing life. As best you can, be happy to have landed one of these fabulous, elusive game fish. If you land more, consider each steelhead as a fortunate bonus to your day.

In both cases explained here, the fishing partner of The Doomed may very well catch fish, as long as they, too, have not spoken either of the two aforementioned statements.

If you are wondering if there is a way to undo or neutralize the curse, I have not discovered any. An apology to "the fishing gods", chanting the statements in reverse three times, and human sacrifice will all fail.

A Parting Thought

When it comes to Luck, I believe in it. Take all you can get in Life and in fishing. Strange thing I've discovered about Luck: the more I learn, the more relaxed my outlook, the harder & smarter I work, the luckier I get.

As part of your Master Game Plan to catch steelhead, formulate a way—I just told you what works for me—to get lucky.

CHAPTER 2
You Must Know Your Quarry
Life Cycle, Spawning Migration, Physiology
and Behaviors of *Oncorhynchus mykiss*

AS A STEELHEAD HUNTER,
the more you know about your quarry,
its life cycle and behavior, the better
your odds of catching one.

When do steelhead enter their home rivers to spawn? More specifically, where exactly in your rivers will you find them? When do they bite best? When do they not bite, and why? How keen are their senses? How do environmental factors—light, temperature, water clarity, flow changes, etc.—affect them? Generally, what are their likes and dislikes? How can you effectively use this information to catch a fish? This chapter is an attempt to acquaint the reader with a comprehensive overview of the steelhead from fertilized egg to adulthood; from the time they begin, until the rendezvous with the angler casting a fly.

One more obstacle for steelhead to overcome. Spillway flanked by power-houses, Bonneville Lock near right, Columbia River. Photo courtesy of U.S. Army Corps of Engineers, Portland District.

The Lesson Begins

Whether a steelhead angler realizes it or not, he is pursuing wary survivalists, fish so attuned to their environment they were able to beat great odds to stay alive while the vast majority of their comrades who began the journey with them perished.

From the beginning, many steelhead do not make it to term as fertilized eggs buried in streambed gravel; many more die as young juveniles trying to survive in their birth stream for two years; even in adulthood—during one, two, or three years at sea—predators and starvation exact their toll. The best and the luckiest make it. These elite survivors, through their individual instinct, strength, speed, reactions, awareness, stamina, and luck, have evaded death from predators, hostile environments, dams, starvation, pollution, disease, high-seas fishing nets, and fishermen. Most that remain are no one's fools willing to grab the first baited hook, shiny lure, or pretty fly they encounter. Even some of the oft-maligned hatchery steelhead have survived life's trials up to this point, successfully reaching their stream of release.

Whether natives born in the river system or those of hatchery origin, all steelhead prove fabulous and worthy game for any angler pursuing them. It is always with a sense of awe that I look at any steelhead caught by my guests or me. Just like the fish, we have beaten the odds to trick one into biting a fly. The fish in hand has evaded death and capture for years—for its entire life—to arrive at the single moment where you or I are fortunate enough to find it on the end of our fishing line. An amazing encounter when you pause to think about it.

A steelhead (*Oncorhynchus mykiss*), taxonomically classified with the Pacific salmon, is an anadromous rainbow trout. An anadromous fish is one that is born in fresh water, spends its early adult life in salt water, then, returns to fresh water to spawn. By contrast, resident rainbow trout never leave their freshwater homes. Being a resident or a migrant is largely due to genetic inheritance. As a fish, if your parents were steelhead, odds are great you, too, will find the ocean someday.

The timing of the steelhead spawning migrations into the rivers and streams of western North America—their range spanning from central California north through Alaska—vary widely. Some rivers have one spawning run; others have two. Some have both a winter and summer; others, spring and fall runs. In addition to run-timing variations, a wide spectrum of life-cycle minutia will boggle anyone trying to remember all the possibilities. "The life history of the steelhead trout varies more than that of any other anadromous fish regarding the length of time spent at sea, the length of time spent in freshwater, and the time of emigration from and immigration to freshwater." (Barnhart, R.A. 1986)

Rather than getting caught up in a morass of details about the exact timings of spawning migrations, precise time ranges of actual spawning, incubation durations for the developing steelhead eggs, freshwater duration for the juveniles, and

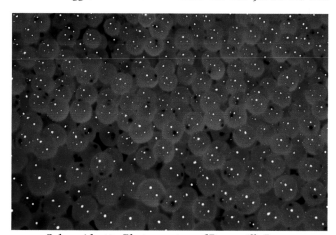

Salmonid eggs. Photo courtesy of Bonneville Power.

smolt migration, I am going to speak in generalities about the "typical" Oregon steelhead. This, because Oregon is where I do most of my fishing and guiding. Just know that tremendous variations of the steelhead life cycle exist in its expansive geographical range. There are rebel steelhead outside the main portion of the statistical Bell Curve in all stages of the "typical" life cycle that will prove to be exceptions to my generalizations.

The Dance of Life Begins

As spawning time nears, steelhead adults enter tributaries of the main river, or swim to the upper reaches of the main stem. Those entering tributaries tend to swim farther up than chinook or coho salmon in order to find cool spawning areas with smaller-sized gravel. Once the fry emerge from the gravel, they survive and thrive in cool streams that have: "1) good streamside vegetative cover to keep the water cool and provide plenty of leaf litter for growing the insects that steelhead eat, and 2) lots of wood and boulders in the stream to create riffle-pool complexes with plenty of places to hide and rest." (Fitzpatrick 1999) In those tributaries where flows tend to recede and warm with the advance of summer, the young steelhead drop into the main river.

In my part of the Pacific Northwest, spawning is, typically, February through May. It is during this period that a female steelhead will pair up with a worthy buck for the Dance of Life. As spawning time nears, the female steelhead selects a, a depression, by turning on her side and swishing her tail vigorously. A typical nest is one to two feet across, and several inches to a foot deep. The hen deposits no more than a quarter of her eggs in the nest. As the female expels her eggs, the buck releases sperm in a milky matrix that washes through the eggs, ideally fertilizing all.

Once her male suitor has fertilized the crop, Ms. Steelhead moves upstream of the eggs to excavate another nest. In a model of natural efficiency, as the hen creates the second nest she is covering the first. The Dance continues as more nests are created, the eggs are laid and fertilized, and the female steelhead is finally emptied of her precious cargo. The collection of these four, five, or six nests is referred to as a *redd*.

In his book, *Steelhead Fly-fishing and Flies*, Trey Combs suggests a twelve-pound female may lay 10,000 eggs. In general, adult female steelhead contain about 2,000 eggs per kilogram of body weight. (Moyle 1976) One kilogram is approximately 2.2 pounds, so about 2000 eggs per 2.2 pounds of body weight.

There is a species survival advantage for not depositing all the eggs in a single nest. If any of the eggs go unfertilized, a fungus can invade that egg, then, eventually, spread to destroy the entire nest. Because they are physically isolated from one another, the fungus from an infected nest will usually not be able to spread to the next.

Having deposited her entire egg supply, the spent female, now known as a *kelt*, is finished. She will eventually resume feeding, rebuilding her strength, and make a move to the ocean again. Once the last nest is covered, her spawning work for this year is complete. She will now go her own way and the mating partner, his. Unlike the Pacific salmon that die soon after spawning, a spent steelhead can survive. With a lot of luck, these fish will return to this stream next year to repeat this procreative drama.

The male, like his counterpart of the human species, complicates matters for himself. He is capable of spawning with other females. Instead of being satisfied with one successful mating encounter, the male now seeks out another ripe female. Maybe he finds one; maybe he does not. It may be necessary to fend off more potential suitors with the same plan. In addition to the exhausting rigors of spawning, an embattled buck may be torn and wounded by other would-be boyfriends.

Between the wounds and physical exhaustion, the buck may not be able to survive the return to the ocean. He may very well die in the stream of his birth. There's a lesson here somewhere for us all, guys.

Buried Alive

The buried, fertilized eggs develop and undergo a metamorphosis over the next two to three months. Slowly, the egg starts to "morph" into a tiny fish. In several weeks, the egg has a small fish head and a small fish tail with a relatively huge belly that is the shrinking egg. At this stage, the developing steelhead is referred to as an *alevin*. Having provided the infant steelhead with nourishment up to this point, the egg will eventually be entirely absorbed. The completion time for the final absorption of the egg depends on water temperature, taking longer in colder water. Then, the luckiest, most determined little steelhead will wriggle, zig, and zag through the maze of interstitial spaces in the gravel to make it into the wide-open expanse of the stream. Here, they must now seek out food items on their own to sustain themselves and grow. Most of a survivor's siblings may not make it; buried forever, never emerging from where they were "hatched".

The tiny survivor, then, must search for food while at the same time not becoming a meal for a larger predator. And, many

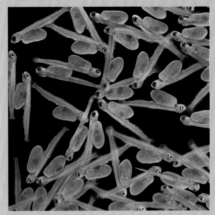

Salmonid alevin. Most will likely make it to adulthood. Photo courtesy of Peter Steenstra, U.S. Fish and Wildlife Service

more of his baby steelhead comrades who've made it this far will not survive their first few weeks in open water, having been eaten, starved, or swept to their deaths, unable to find shelter in raging winter river flows. For those that do make it through their first year in the river, many will not see their second.

Newly emerged tiny steelhead swim freely, exploring their spacious, dangerous environment. Initially, the tiny fry school in quiet protected portions of the stream, usually along its periphery. Here they are sheltered from strong currents and predators as they forage for food items. Their diet consists mostly of small aquatic insects, and the occasional terrestrial. In the first weeks as free-swimming roamers, the mortality rate can be very high, and largely determines the size of the surviving class of a given river for that year.

If their luck at surviving continues, the fry that beat the odds will stay in their home stream here in the Pacific North-

A young steelhead displaying parr marks. Most Pacific Northwest steelhead juveniles will be in their home stream for about two years before journeying to saltwater.

west for one or two years, continuing to mature. Over the next few months, the tendency to school with its siblings disappears. Most juveniles strike out on their own for a solitary existence.

With growth, physical features and markings on their bodies become more evident. At this point, they are *parr*, characterized by large, oval-shaped markings on the fishes' sides. For the next one to three years—usually two—the parr steelhead focuses on food and survival. Driven by their inherited instincts in the spring of their second full year, most steelhead

North Pacific Gyre, the offshore destination for many of our West Coast steelhead. Photo courtesy of NOAA/Dept. of Commerce.

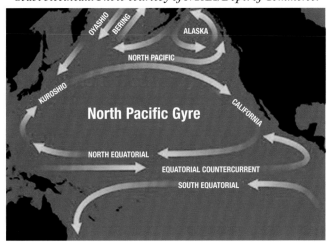

smolt, usually at a size of four to eight inches, and begin their downstream journey to the ocean.

In the spring, responding to their biological urge, the young steelhead start migrating downstream which will eventually lead them to the Pacific Ocean. For some in the lower portions of coastal streams, the journey is short, maybe a few miles. Those in the heart of Idaho may have to traverse many streams and rivers, journeying almost a thousand miles to reach the Pacific. It is on this journey where these smolt must face even more trials waiting downstream of them—dams, fishermen, more predators, disease, injury, and potentially lethal high water temperatures to name a few. Again, most of those that actually begin the trip toward saltwater will not make it in typical years.

For the lucky ones that make it to the ocean, the journey in the salt has just begun. Our little Pacific Northwest adventurers make their way hundreds, if not a thousand miles or more, out into the Pacific Ocean to spend a year or, more typically, two, in the very general vicinity of Alaska's Aleutian Islands. Some British Columbia and Alaskan fish may spend three or four years.

Those migrants of extreme southern Oregon, south of Cape Blanco, and those from California Rivers, stay much nearer the coast in the Pacific. All have answered some instinctual and environmental cues that take them to their marine stations. Here they feed, they grow and they frolic until their genes prompt them to return to their home stream as sexually mature adults.

Trading A Rainbow For Chrome

Besides an internal adjustment to its marine environment, an important exterior physiological change has occurred as the steelhead heads to sea. The body's coloration is continuing to change for the sea-going rainbow trout when entering the saltwater environment. The hint of a red lateral stripe of its early freshwater life has faded to silver even before leaving fresh water, as have the rosy hues of the gill covers. These changes progress, until lost are the spots on its lower sides and belly. Instead, the back is charcoal with a hint of blue or olive. The sides become chrome bumper silver. The belly is snow white. All of these serve good adaptive purpose: the fish is difficult for predators to see. Spied from above, the steelhead's dark back blends with the dark ocean

Krill are utilized as a major food source for steelhead in the Pacific. Photo courtesy of NOAA/Dept. of Commerce

depths against which it is viewed. The silvery sides of the fish reflect its surroundings like a mirror. Eyed from below, the white belly helps camouflage the fish against a bright sky backdrop. Consequently, it is much more difficult for us two-legged predators to spot a fresh-run steelhead when it enters the river than a fish that will revert, with time, to its original rainbow trout colors.

Time to Go Home

After two years (for most) of accelerated growth and the building of fat reserves, our sojourners respond to their inner clocks, heading in the general direction of their freshwater homes. Steelhead begin navigating toward their natal stream of origin by, apparently, celestial and electromagnetic means. Iron-bearing structures in some of the body's cells orient the returning fish with an indication of the magnetic North Pole to aid in its navigation. Once near the coastline, the steelhead relies on its keen olfactory sense to detect the trace elements' "fingerprint" of its home stream. Like a bloodhound following the trail, the fish locates the stream of its birth (or release, if of hatchery origin), and the upstream ascent begins. The fish that started its epic travels at four to eight inches tipping the scales at a few ounces will return home usually at 23" to 30", weighing four to ten pounds, as determined by the favorability of its ocean environment, the abundance of food, and its genetic growth potential.

A few special fish—most from British Columbia rivers—will grow extra large by remaining in the marine environment for three or four years. It is ocean time that produces the

largest steelhead, some exceeding twenty-five, or even thirty, pounds. The largest fly-caught steelhead weighed in at just over 33 pounds. It was taken in B.C.'s Kispiox River in 1965. The largest steelhead ever caught on rod, reel and line was in salt water off the coast of Bell Island, Alaska: 42 1/2 pounds. A young boy trolling for salmon inadvertently caught it.

Run Timings

Some Oregon rivers have runs of *summer* steelhead that enter fresh water May through October, with a few rebels arriving earlier or later than this general range. When is a summer-run actually a fall fish is open to interpretation. Alaska and British Columbia have runs that are better defined as "fall" run fish. To confuse the issue further, in the Pacific Northwest we often see an overlap of late-run winter steelhead with early-arriving summer steelhead. Ditto for late-run summer fish and early-run winter steelhead.

A summer steelhead arriving in its home river in May or June may dawdle for six to eight months before yielding to the spawning urge. Amazingly, the fish do not need to eat between the times they enter fresh water until after mating. Their ocean-grown fat reserves are adequate. However, as steelhead anglers will testify, you can induce the occasional steelhead to dine. It is difficult to ascribe this to any one reason. Perhaps

Nehalem River mouth, Oregon. Adult steelhead returning from distant points in the Pacific will seek out their home streams in which they were reared, an amazing navigational feat. Photo courtesy of U.S. Army Corps of Engineers, Portland District.

we have triggered an autonomic eating response. Think of being at a Sunday morning deluxe buffet. Even though absolutely stuffed, many of us will eagerly succumb to dessert. So, too, a steelhead without hunger pangs *may* be led into temptation. Most will probably exert self-control, but not all. That's our kind of fish.

Winter steelhead in the Pacific Northwest are those, generally, returning home from late November through April. The time between freshwater arrival and spawning is usually much shorter than that for most summer steelhead. Their activity level, compared to summer-run fish, is less enthusiastic in pursuit of a fly due to the colder water temperatures. (More about this later.) Just as some of our Oregon rivers have only summer steelhead, some streams have only winter-run fish. A third group has both summer and winter steelhead.

Steelhead may return and successfully spawn annually several times, though the odds against this are high. Rigors of spawning, injury, disease, dams, treacherous river passages, natural events, predators, and fishermen take their toll. A hardy British Columbia steelhead hen was determined—through scale analysis—to have returned to her home stream for the sixth time. (Combs 1976) What a special fish! In most "normal" years, the return rate of would-be second-run returning adult steelhead is less than 10%.

I Thought My IQ Was At Least Average

Even though they have a brain the size of a pea, as I recounted in the Introduction, it took me seven years to catch my first steelhead. I was an excellent young trout fisherman when I began my steelhead quest: skilled caster, athletic, determined, and resourceful. However, I could not hook a steelhead to save my life. This was a bit odd to me since I often fished with other less-experienced anglers who would occasionally land a steelhead as I stood beside them. Over my fruitless years, I even "coached" several rookies who had never fished steelhead before into hooking and landing a fish!

As I personally began to experience fish-catching success, my confidence in locating and hooking steelhead grew. However, no matter how many I hooked, I learned to maintain some degree of humility. In the early years of my success, the fish beat me many more days than I succeeded in hooking one of them. I gave them—and still do—high marks in survival intelligence. So, I was a bit taken aback by the remark of one of my fishing acquaintances. I have a guide friend, I'll call him Glenn, who maintained, "Steelhead are the stupidest fish that swim." Yeow! At this, I

Some falls are insurmountable for migrating steelhead, marking The End of the Line.
Photo of Shoshone Falls, Snake River, courtesy of Karthik Chinnathambi

am thinking, "What does that say about *my* intelligence when I can't catch one on many days?" I protested Glenn's remark to him. He invited me fishing to prove his contention.

We fished three different rivers on three different days. He was the guide. I was the "client". We used his flies. I stood where he told me, and cast where he instructed. I moved when he said "Move"; and changed flies at his command. Glenn fished hard, too. Three rivers in three days. Seasonal prime time. Fished with focus. The result: not a single strike! Neither of us got a sniff from the "stupidest fish that swims." I did not know which I felt more: amused or vindicated.

Despite their minimal cranial capacity, the steelhead that return to spawn are survivors: the fittest of the fit, the wariest of the wary. In polite disagreement with my friend, I re-

Negotiating the falls. Natural obstacles can sort out the weak from the strong, or the strong from the strongest.
Photo courtesy of the Bureau of Land Management.

iterated that these returning voyagers are nobody's idiots. We have fish surviving a perilous youth, scrounging for food, hiding from hungry bullies, fending off parasites and disease, and dodging dam turbine blades. The vast, vast majority of their siblings never even made it to the ocean, let alone survived all the saltwater hazards to grow and thrive. They are special in the extreme when you consider that only one or a few out of a hundred make it back to their rivers of birth to challenge your fishing skills and wits. A steelhead is truly a worthy adversary.

Whereas much of our brain mass can be devoted to "higher endeavors", such as creative thought, pondering choices, and planning our next vacation, the fish's little bit of gray matter is totally focused on survival and procreation. A steelhead is not concerned about finding the TV remote control or playing with his friends. Its prime directive is, "What must I do to survive today?" If he or she cannot find the right answers *every day*, or runs into some bad luck, they are removed from the gene pool. Just like the Marines looking for a few good men, Mother Nature is constantly selecting only a few exceptional steelhead. All others will meet the Grim Reaper.

Acute Senses

The three most important senses of steelhead the astute angler must concern himself with are smell, sight and movement/vibration detection. Let's address these one at a time.

Spawning steelhead instictively seek out the proper depth, current velocity and rock and gravel size to provide maximum survival opportunities for the young. Photo courtesy of NOAA/Dept. of Commerce

Smell

Once in the ballpark vicinity of its stream of origin, a steelhead finds home base by discerning through smell the unique "scent" of its birthplace. The "scent" is very faint, perhaps a few distinct molecules mixed with millions of others! The parking lot oil on your wading shoes, the cat pee on your waders or the sunscreen inadvertently rubbed from your hands to your fly may put off, even startle, a willing fish. Always be thinking about what alarming underwater odors are washing downstream to the fish below.

An old, now-deceased, angling friend told me many years ago about L-serine, a natural chemical found in human perspiration and natural body oils. He maintained this is repugnant to fish. Subsequent internet research corroborates this; and, streamside observations of other anglers demonstrate the same belief that human scent can be significantly repellant to steelhead.

While surfing the internet, I found the following. Some of it may be abbreviated and paraphrased with reference to the author, Marv Taylor.

A chemical called L-serine. The smell on your hands. I remember as a youth outfishing my father and his angling cronies on almost every trip we made. It got so bad it was embarrassing to my father's friends. Initially, Dad thought it was great. But when his fishing buddies quit inviting us on their fishing trips, my father suddenly found ways to avoid taking me along. At first I feared it had something to do with body odor...or bad breath. I now believe it had more to do with the odor on my hands (or lack thereof) than anything else.

Dad and I tried an experiment some years later at a popular western Idaho trout lake. I baited Dad's hook, he baited mine. He caught fish, I didn't. When we later baited our own hooks, things returned to normal. I caught more fish than he did.

Technically, L-serine falls into the category of compounds known as amino acids. The fact that amino acids have a high solubility in water reinforces the problem, because fish thus have the opportunity to detect this chemical.

While scientific studies have not confirmed my "positive" L-serine theory, I strongly believe it does exist. In his book, The Scientific Angler, author Paul C. Johnson writes, "Every time a fisherman casts and retrieves his line and lure, he leaves an invisible smell track. All humans have

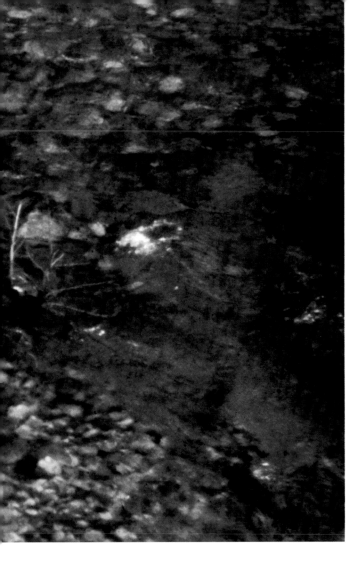

some level of L-serine in their skin oil; everything a fisherman touches contains a chemical remnant of L-serine plus anything else he may have had on his hands.

"What else?" Johnson writes. "Plenty: gasoline and motor oil, suntan oil and sunscreen, bug repellent, and nicotine, for smokers (my father was a heavy smoker), are all potential negative smell track generators.

Johnson goes on to describe the most common negative, neutral, and positive smell tracks. Every angler would do well to memorize this list.

Negative Smell Tracks: L-serine (human skin oil), nicotine, petroleum and derivatives (gasoline and motor oil), suntan lotions, bug repellents, chemical plasticizers added to soften plastics, and perfumed soaps. Neutral Smell Tracks: Alcoholic beverages, anise oil, natural vegetation (grass, leaves), human urine, chlorinated water and treated septic water, soda pop and fruit juices, nonperfumed soap and biodegradable detergents.

Positive Smell Tracks: Fish extracts, including herring oil, baitfish guts, fish slime (can also be a negative if the slime originates from a species offensive to the game fish being sought; e.g., the slime of a northern pike is negative to many species), natural bait (including juices from

worms, frogs, crawdads, leeches and maggots), milk and some dairy products such as cheese, and human saliva.

An old time walleye guide described an experience he had observed on a top lake in Canada: Neither member of a husband and wife team had even had a bite during a morning of fishing. They went in for a shore lunch. Almost immediately when they went back out on the water after eating, the wife started catching walleyes.

The husband, using an identical line, lure, and technique, never got a strike. They began discussing why. It was finally determined that the only thing they had done differently, was she had smeared Oil of Olay on her face to prevent windburn. He tried it...and began catching fish.

What's in the stuff? Among other things, natural turtle oil.

For several years I've been routinely washing my hands several times a day when I'm fishing; with a good neutral (non-perfumed) biodegradable soap. Even if I "might" have a positive L-serine on my hands, I'm still not about to take any chances.
—Marv Taylor, from "Smell Tracks" internet posting

I see a growing number of steelhead and salmon guides who wear latex gloves all day. They do so since they are constantly handling the baits and lures for their fishing clients. They are moved to such an extreme convinced that scent matters, especially to anadromous fish, survivors that have successfully navigated the last leg of their journey home by their very sensitive noses. Apparently, latex gloves are an effective barrier to human scent.

Wash Up Before Dinner...And Fishing, Too

A fisheries biologist friend of mine, Jay Nicholas, was the chief architect of *The Oregon Plan*, a comprehensive living document of guidelines for improving the survival of salmon and other anadromous fishes in Oregon. This plan was crafted in response to the drastic decline of many native salmon stocks in Oregon. Then-governor John Kitzhaber commissioned the study, believing Oregonians could better help their fish than the federal government. Jay is a smart guy and an accomplished steelheader, so when he speaks I listen closely. He told me an interesting story. It seems a steelhead guide acquaintance, skilled and knowledgeable, had all of his clients wash their hands immediately before they would begin fishing. This, so the procedure could be overseen by the guide to make sure it was done properly. The guy was a fanatic, but if it meant one more fish in the boat during the fishing day, that made for happy clients who will return, and tell their friends, too.

I am a stickler about sunscreen and insect repellent. These chemicals are strong smelling and long lasting: an extremely bad combo. For myself, I apply these at home or at the motel and wash my hands thoroughly with soap before leaving. I apply sunscreen or repellent to the back of my hands by placing a dollop on the back of one hand and spreading it with the back of the other hand. If additional applications are needed on-stream, I suggest taking a couple of minutes to massage the hands with in-stream vegetation, mud and sand to mask the smell. I will do the same to a contaminated fly or lure. Even after these precautions, it may be best to replace a "ruined" fly.

Whenever I suspect a fly has a fish-repelling scent, I will massage it in a mixture of stream mud, sand and aquatic vegetation. If these are not readily available, I smear the fly with the slimy algae coating of a river rock. Another scent that seems to have a neutralizing, if not enhancing result is fish body slime rubbed on a fly. In the natural course of handling and releasing a fish, slime adheres to my fingers. Before I rinse them in the river, I may rub my digits on a possibly tainted fly. It can't hurt.

Also, I do not use fly tying head cement on my subsurface steelhead flies. The nasty ingredients contained in this liquid glue *will* clear your sinuses. I am sure they may do the same for an offended steelhead. Even though I have tailed many steelhead caught with flies tied using head cement, I wonder how many more I may have caught if without it.

Most of the time I have two clients in my drift boat when I am guiding. When things are going according to plan on trout fishing trips, both anglers are catching fish on a regular basis. On a number of occasions over the years, I have observed one angler's number of strikes drop to zero while his partner continues to catch fish as before. It's time to pull to the bank, "wash" hands, and change flies. Every time this has happened the fishing success then resumes for *both* anglers. If resident trout are this sensitive to repugnant scent you can safely assume that a far-ranging steelhead that must find its home with its nose will be at least as fickle.

A dry-fly angler might wonder about the scent put on a floating fly by some of the noxious floatants used to waterproof a fly and retard its sinking. I use floatant regularly myself. The reason the fish are not concerned is that they are in the downstream "vapor trail" of the fly only for a brief instant as they rise to intercept it. The fish are usually holding much deeper than the surface currents that carry the smell over the heads of the fish.

I think it important that you be aware of a steelhead's keen sense of smell, and some of the more common ways a fly can become "contaminated." Precautions are simple once you are aware of potential problems with scent. Little preventative measures may, I believe, translate into more fish hooked during a season.

Vision

Steelhead have great vision, so a stealthy approach to exposed fish-holding areas is important. One of my favorite games, particularly in small coastal streams in the winter, is to cast to visible fish. Experience has taught me to wear a camouflage jacket, stay low, stay behind the target and cast sidearm. Once

I am seen—even if the fish does not immediately dart for cover—the game is over.

A fish in shallow water, or holding high in the water column, has a greater scope of the surroundings above the water line, a larger cone of vision for things external to the water. A stealthy approach is demanded of the angler to accommodate this. Crouching or kneeling positioning, minimal movement, clothing colors that blend with the surroundings, and sidearm casting may all be essential. Remembering that fish face into the current, the fisherman should move toward his position from downstream of his quarry.

Jackets, tops and shirts that are red, yellow, or white cause me to wonder about possibly discouraging a steelhead to bite. These are hi-vis colors that may draw attention to an angler,

Steelhead have excellent visual and olfactory senses to assist them in survival and navigation.

resulting in startling or, at least, alarming a steelhead. Though a red garment makes for eye-catching photos, I request that my clients avoid this color, and the others, too. A red cap will provide enough pizzazz. Though I have had clients wearing bright clothing catch steelhead, I always recommend colors that blend with the dominant background. An angler wearing my taboo colors may catch three steelhead, but I wonder if he could have hooked one or two more dressed in neutral tones.

Vibration

The lateral line is a sensory organ that runs along the side of a fish, and act as sensitive "ears". It detects vibrations and movement. Vibrations may convey a number of different things including, but not limited to, "food," "enemy," or "unknown, but probably dangerous." The lateral line is also particularly temperature sensitive. It prompts the steelhead toward water temperatures that are nearer its preferred range of 50 to lower 60's degrees Fahrenheit.

Careless, noisy wading, or banging around in an aluminum drift boat will announce to the steelhead your arrival. Because water is a denser medium that air, underwater sound carries much farther, and the volume does not diminish with distance as rapidly. Wary steelhead will go to High Alert. A fish in an alarmed state is not likely to bite your fly.

The keen senses of survivor steelhead should cause you to wonder. They certainly plant questions in my mind. During the seven years I struggled to catch my first one, I wonder how often I blew opportunities due to my lack of knowledge about the sharp acuity of a steelhead's senses of sight, smell, and "hearing". Even today, I wonder how many more fish my steelhead clients could have / should have caught if only willing fish had not seen them. I will never know, but now, I do have awareness.

It is actually a bit unsettling to consider how many steelhead are startled out of a biting mood because insufficient homage is paid to their sharp senses. Their importance can easily be discounted by anglers—me included—when a few steelhead are hooked and landed during the fishing day. We can be lulled/trapped into believing our stealth and scent precautions are adequate. Personally, my day is made when my clients or I catch a few steelhead. We hooked three today. But, we might have hooked six, if only we had accorded greater respect to the steelheads' keen senses. Maximum fishing effectiveness starts with awareness. I am convinced I can never be too careful about human or repugnant scents, visual detection, and fish-scaring noise as I wade or move around in my boat.

Estimating A Steelhead's Weight

There are three factors that, in large part, determine the eventual length and weight of a steelhead: the abundance of marine food items (primarily small fish and crustaceans), the length of time spent in the marine environment, and its individual genetic potential. In the case that a caught fish is to be released, whether of hatchery or wild origin, you might want to know how much the fish weighs. Since very few anglers carry appropriate scales with them, a couple of key measurements will help you estimate the steelhead's weight.

You can apply a couple of equivalent mathematical equations for determining a steelhead's weight in pounds. You need two measurements in inches: the length and the maximum girth. The latter is best taken so the measuring tape touches the leading edge of the dorsal fin as it is carefully wrapped around the fish. In addition, because the girth has such a great bearing on the final answer (it is squared), be accurate to the fraction of an inch.

If you are not carrying a cloth or soft plastic tape measure, use a section of leader material to make the measurements. Cut them as the measurement is made. Accurately measure these pieces of cut line at your convenience.

Steelhead size estimation: 0.00133 x length in inches x girth inches squared = approximate pounds.

Mathematically, this equation is the equivalent of $(l \times g2) / 750$ = approximate pounds.

For a cruder but quicker estimation of the weight for fish from 24 to 35 inches, subtract 19 from the length. The remainder is approximate weight in pounds.

Example: 27" length - 19 = about 8 pounds

Steelhead Activity & Behavior and Water Temperature

Let me make another generalization: summer steelhead are more active, more aggressive, than those of winter. It has to do with water temperature. Fish are cold-blooded creatures. Their body temperature assumes that of its environment. Given a choice, steelhead will choose water that measures, roughly, be-

A water-resistant vinyl tape measure is a handy tool for a steelhead angler.

tween 50 and 60 Fahrenheit. This is a very common range in our Northwest streams June through October. Late November through April, upper 30's to mid 40's can predominate.

With some exceptions, you must put your fly right on the nose of a winter steelhead to interest it. Numerous sight-fishing opportunities over the years tell me this is so. Six inches from an interested steelhead may be too far for the fly to entice it.

Fly-fishing for aggressive summer steelhead offers satisfying thrills that cannot be found with any of the other methods. The hard grab of a wet fly presented on a tight line downstream gives you the sensation of being unexpectedly struck by lightning, only in a euphoric, not a hair-raisingly painful, way; or, watching the big head of a rising steelhead pierce the surface as it intercepts a skating dry fly has no freshwater parallel. I always recommend that my students and clients have their hearts checked by a cardiologist before trying this. This scene CAN stop your heart! Every time I bear witness, I still cannot believe what I am seeing. Talk about addictive.

Summer steelhead will chase a fly. They will track it across the current. They will swim to the surface from six feet deep to eat a fly sometimes. However, much of the time these fish will not budge, no matter the fly, the presentation, or the depth. Lockjaw. Bad attitude. Like a stubborn five year old at the dinner table.

This segues into my next point: migrating steelhead do not need to eat. They are healthy and active living on the fat supply created in the ocean. A steelhead entering a stream in June has the health and energy to forgo food until after spawning in January, February or March the following calendar year. The spawned-out *kelt* will then start looking to dine. As they re-coup and make their way towards the sea again, feeding habits and diet will closely approximate those of the resident trout in the river.

So, why will a fish that does not need to eat bite a fly, chase a lure or swallow bait? I like to use an analogy here. Imagine yourself during your last Sunday brunch at a fine restaurant. Odds are good you ate too much. The food was excellent and you wanted to make sure you got your money's worth. Maybe even a little more than your money's worth. When you know a single bite more will make you burst (visions from a scene in Monty Python's *The Meaning of Life*), you spy this fudge cheesecake with cherry-cream topping creation. You shouldn't. You must. You will. I am sure some steelhead do the same thing. Lucky for us.

A Guide Story – How Low Can You Go?

As I remarked earlier, steelhead have great vision. One of my favorite games, particularly in small coastal streams in the winter, is to cast to visible fish. Experience has taught me to wear a camouflage jacket, stay low, stay behind the target and cast sidearm. Once I am spotted, even if the fish does not immediately dart for cover, the game is over.

My buddy Phil was desperate to catch a winter steelhead on a fly. This prompted a little adventure on Oregon's North Coast. We went to a favorite small stream in January during a cold snap during which it had not rained for more than a week. Low, clear water and spooky fish are what I expected and, indeed, these are what we got.

There are advantages and disadvantages to low water. The opportunity to visually locate and cast to holding steelhead is a tremendous plus when the stream is a trickle. Additionally, there are fewer prime holding areas for the steelhead to station themselves. These holding spots are more obvious, more defined at reduced flows, which translates into an easier time locating the fish. At lower water, most, if not all, of the prime holding lies can be approached by a determined hunter in chest waders. Such wading apparel also allows access to both sides of the river when your course is steered by dense brush, high sheer banks, and private property.

There are a couple major disadvantages to reduced river levels. Steelhead that have beaten tremendous odds, surviving the perils of youth in fresh water and predation and attendant hazards of the marine environment have very keen senses: sight, "hearing", and smell. Extreme stealth is required to be a successful fly-angler here. Slow, quiet movements and a low profile

are keys. Stand too high or wave your rod tip overhead and you will be seen. Shuffle the stones or stumble while you approach, and you will be detected. Once alerted, though you may still be able to watch a holding steelhead, they will refuse to bite.

When Phil and I stalked our way up the river, we were careful to move slowly and quietly. (You do want to move upstream because fish face *into* the current.) As we came upon a likely tailout I spied three fish finning ever so slightly to maintain their exposed, but undisturbed, positions. As Phil moved up beside me, the trio darted towards deeper water near the head of the pool upstream.

With Phil remaining stationary for the time being, I circled away from the water in order to approach their suspected position from the side while keeping an extremely low profile. In fact, I approached on my hands and knees to the elevated gravel bank overlooking the pool. This would have been an interesting scene to a wandering observer who happened by. My stealth was rewarded. I managed to see the three fish now huddled in faster, deeper water. This would actually be a better holding area for Phil to approach when he prepared to cast to our quarry.

It is important to let the fish settle in and settle down once they have been alarmed. Initially they will not bite. Time must pass for them to shake their worries. In the meantime, I had Phil retrace my circuitous path so that he could see his eventual targets. He actually one-upped me in the stealth department: he slithered on his belly as he moved onto the high gravel bank. Then, like a dog smelling a pheasant goes on point, he elevated to all fours, studying the pool from his hands and knees until he spotted the steelhead.

Once he had backed quietly from his poolside position, Phil rejoined me at the tailout, well out of view of the fish. We double-checked his terminal gear. The leader and fly were as they should be. No nick in the line, and the hook point was sharp. I had tied on a baby pink Glo Bug bearing a fluorescent green dot in its center. This very same pattern enticed my very first winter steelhead.

Under my direction, Phil made his approach to fishing position. Crouched, with a snail-like pace, Phil moved upstream along the river's edge, barely getting his boots wet in ankle deep water. Once he got within reasonable casting range—25-30 feet—it was time for the dance to begin. Keeping the rod tip low, casting sidearm, I asked Phil to make his first cast purposely short. He was a dutiful student. The idea here is to prevent the possibility that the angler will cast farther than he realizes, inadvertently alarming the fish as the line splashes on or above their position. The game would be over before it had begun.

There is also the chance that even a short cast may draw the attention of one of the fish to the fly, even though it had landed well behind it. Do not underestimate the vision and crazy behavior of a rebel steelhead.

Of the trio of steelhead sighted, the fastest and most determined was, also, the smallest. This chrome rocket charged the egg fly on the first cast. In a blink, it made an aggressive interception, virtually hooking itself. Phil did an adequate job of playing the steelhead and eventually brought it to hand. My friend had his first steelhead and a lifetime memory.

Even if you plan to "dispatch" a hatchery fish for the home BBQ, something is wrong with you if you do not feel a little reverence when you hold a captured steelhead in your hands. If you ponder, even briefly, what this fish has gone through to return to the exact point where your paths have crossed, and it grabbed your hook, you cannot help but be a little bit wonderstruck. The steelhead has unknowingly timed its life efforts for this eventual encounter with you, perhaps its *final* rendezvous with its destiny. This fish has cheated death for years, facing and overcoming life-threatening challenges every day of its life until you caught it. The steelhead can be both food… and "food for thought".

References

• Combs, Trey, *Steelhead Fly-fishing and Flies*, Frank Amato Publications, 1976
• Moyle, P.B., 1976, *Inland Fishes of California*, University of California Press, Berkley, p. 405.
• Barnhart, R.A. 1986. *Species profiles: life histories and environmental requirements of coastal fishes and invertebrates (Pacific Southwest - steelhead.* U.S. Fish & Wildlife. Serv. Biol. Rep. 82(11.60). U.S. Army Corps of Engineers, TR EL-82-4.
www.nwrc.usgs.gov/wdb/pub/species_profiles/82_11-060.pdf
• Fitzpatrick, Martin, *Coastal Steelhead Trout: Life in the Watershed*, Cooper Publishing, 1999.
• Marv Taylor, from "*Smell Tracks*" internet posting

Merganser ducks are fish-eaters that take their toll on young steelhead.

CHAPTER 3
Steelhead Fly-Fishing Equipment Essentials

ASPIRE TO BE A MEDIOCRE
steelhead angler? If not, know that, for the long run,
well-chosen, high-quality fishing tools will significantly add
to the number of fish you hook and land.

Fred Mueller, Rogue River. Photo assist from Tom Ahlers

Be it a battle-tested soldier preparing for battle, an athlete readying for a high-stakes contest, or a skilled carpenter building his dream home, each will use excellent tools to accomplish their ends. If you think these examples are a little extreme because you view steelhead fishing with a fly as a "casual" endeavor unworthy of your best preparations, then your angling success will fall short of your potential. When *successful* steelhead fishing for most mortals is typically measured as one and two fish hooked for the day, the line that separates fish hooked from no fish hooked in a day can be extremely fine. In a day where I may make a thousand casts (2 casts/minute X 60 minutes/hour X 8 actual fishing hours = about 1,000 casts), I may get 2 strikes (0.2% return on casting investment) or 1 strike (0.1 % return). Factor in the days where no fish are hooked and your return on time investment is drastically smaller.

There is an old adage, which states: "Even a blind squirrel finds an occasional acorn". The same applies to steelhead. Many fly-anglers can claim they landed *one* steelhead on a fly. Accidents happen. If an angler meets with a couple of such accidents he or she may very well be led to sincerely believe they have an adequate grasp of what it takes to catch a steelhead, including an adequate rod, reel, line and leader under most circumstances. It's a little like playing the slot machine, winning a couple of jackpots, then believing you know how to win the money on a consistent basis. Anyone who underestimates the importance of well-chosen angling gear for steelhead will be disappointed. Usually sooner than later.

The rod that does not present the fly at the necessary distance is a weak link in the system. The reel that does not smoothly release line at high speed with a streaking fish will break your heart…more than once. The floating fly line that does not float, or will not shoot through the rod guides for long distance when needed, will cost you fish-hooking opportunities. Sinking lines that sink too quickly, or not quickly enough, translate into missed chances. Leaders that are too long/too short, too heavy/too light, or too visible are problematic.

The insidious trap with all these is that the unsuccessful fisherman may blame his lack of success of hooking a steelhead on unwilling or absent fish. The problems may lie, instead, with the equipment that either did not get the fly to the steelhead's distant vicinity, or did not present the fly in a convincing drift at the necessary depth.

The Angling Samurai's Sword

The Samurai of 12th-17th century Japan epitomize a warrior's dedication to the art of lethal combat. The stakes of their profession were about as high as they come: life and death. (For steelhead addicts, the stakes are *almost* the same!) The painstaking craftsmanship and quality extremes that forged the Samurai's swords are legendary. These weapons had to be sharp, lightweight, and virtually unbreakable and unbendable. These are a difficult mix. In addition to being the difference between living and dying, the samurai's swords were

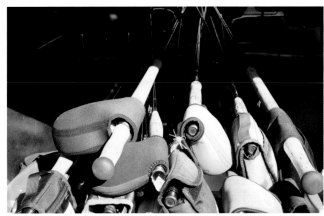

A steelhead angler can never have too many rods.

extensions the warrior's honor, ego, and pride. If the samurai was defeated, but not killed, he might use his own sword to check out eternity.

Though I would never fall on my own rod at the end of a fruitless fishing day, I do see some tempting steelhead fishing parallels here. When the river is crowded with rude anglers and fishing guides, I *almost* feel like I am locked in mortal combat. Besides my wits and bad attitude, the fly rod is the tool that can inflict wounds on the opposition. If my clients or I can cast a fly where others cannot, or will not, in order to hook a fish, we have won a minor "battle". A quality fly rod has done its intended work. And, just as the samurai preferred to fight on foot, the *wading* angler is particularly dependent on a *comfortably* long-casting fly rod.

A fabled battlefield for wading anglers that immediately comes to mind is Oregon's world famous North Umpqua River. If you are fascinated with the possibility of eating humble pie for breakfast, lunch and dinner, journey to this stream! In the 33 miles of fly-only water, a drift boat cannot be used. Shore-confinement or wading are your only approach options. With an excess of smooth, grease-slick bedrock on much of the stream bottom, this river challenges even the most surefooted. Wade a little farther to put your fly nearer that distant submerged boulder…now, get ready to swim.

Further emphasizing the need for a samurai fishing tool, high summer finds some of the best long-line casters in the West vying for the Umpqua's choicest steelhead runs at dawn and dusk. The demeanor astream may *seem* gentlemanly for the most part, but there is definitely a competitive atmosphere. What you lack in raw casting prowess needs to be compensated for by casting a magnificent fly rod to reach the distant fish.

When looking for the right steelhead fly rod for you, my Samurai friend, the number of choices may seem overwhelming. Your first test will be patience, Little Grasshopper… Search and cast before you buy.

Fly rods come in a variety of lengths and "line weight" designations. Let's consider each with our end goal to find the ideal steelhead fly rod for you.

Six to 16 feet is a range of rod lengths that you may encounter in a well-stocked fly shop. The length of a rod does not

A winter buck is beginning to change back into its rainbow trout colors.

directly translate into the size of the fish you will normally target with it. As an example, the typical 300- to 500-pound billfish is played on a fly rod of 8'8"-9'. The longest rods, those in the 12' to 16' range, are two-hand models typically used for steelhead and salmon that commonly run from 5 to 20 pounds.

For steelhead, the most popular lengths are 9'-10'. This range provides the *typical* steelhead fly-angler—man or woman—the optimum combination of casting ease, casting distance, comfort/minimum fatigue, and line control. For those using a specialty two-hand fly rod, 13'-14' seem most suitable.

The suggested fly line "weight" inscribed on the fly rod blank that indicates the appropriate quarry for a particular rod. When the rod is matched with its recommended fly line, the rod's performance can be maximized, and the fly most easily presented to a fish at a reasonable distance.

Fly line "weights" range from 0-weight through 14-weight. These whole numbers correspond to an actual physical weight of the tapered portion of a fly line, the first 30 to 40 feet. The unit of weight measure is a grain. 1 ounce = about 454 grains.

Following is a general summary of line weights/fly rods matched to the typical target species:

0- to 3-weight fly lines/fly rods: panfish and small to average trout

4- to 6-weight: typical trout rods

7- to 9-weight: typical steelhead, salmon, bass, and light salt water.

10- to 14-weight: big species salt water or mountain rescue

Now, let me remind you that the above classifications are accepted generalizations. I have landed 7-pound rainbows on a 3-weight fly rod, and I have captured 6" saltwater snappers on a 10-weight. However, it is usually best to select the appropriate rod for the particular species sought. There is no such thing as a "one-size-fits-all" fly rod. Get the appropriate tool for the job. The typical steelhead fly rod casts a 6-, 7-, 8-, or 9-weight fly line. For all-round general use, get an 8-weight.

Because fly-fishing is my business, I own many rods, including lightweight models I dedicate to steelhead fishing, some that cast a 5- or 6-weight fly line. Good steelhead rivers may be excellent trout waters, too. To add to my clients' fishing enjoyment, and to keep them alert, I always attempt to choose flies that both trout and steelhead will eat. The trout action allows me to be constantly coaching the clients about casting, line control, properly setting the hook, and playing the fish. Because steelhead strikes are usually few and far between, anglers—even experienced ones—can lose focus. When the strike comes they are, too often, taken by surprise, having been lulled into catatonia for lack of fishing action. The trout keep my anglers sharp.

One of the reasons I often use 5- or 6-weight fly rods is so that my clients can enjoy the tug of even a small trout. If they are playing 9" trout on an 8-weight rod, it's shooting pheasant with a deer rifle. Envision smashing a tiny spider with a sledgehammer.

A second good reason for using a trout rod on steelhead is that it is more difficult for a ham-handed angler to break off the fish. Imagine trying to break a bungee cord by pulling the ends in opposite directions. Not impossible, but not an easy proposition. The forgiving, shock-absorbing stretch cushions and slows the force. A hard-striking or fast-running steelhead will put a serious bend in a lightweight rod, but—like a stretching bungee—it is more difficult for the fish to impart the force of sudden impact against an easily bent rod than a heavier, higher-inertia 8-weight rod tip.

Two-Hand Fly Rods

I am observing a steady evolution in preference for steelhead fly rods. More and more anglers are using two-handed models. Such tools, with lengths most typically ranging from twelve to fourteen feet, have some very obvious advantages: minimal back-cast room required; in skilled hands, the potential for great distance; magnified mending ease and line control; and, less fatigue and arm strain afforded by the use of both arms while casting. All of these advantages contribute to covering more steelhead-holding water in less time with less effort. Because more water is potentially covered in a fishing day, this should translate into more steelhead hooked.

Think of a good two-handed fly rod as a fast, high-performance sports car. Such a car has the potential for high-speed thrills and fun, but a student driver will run into difficulties. A two-handed fly rod can move so much fly line so quickly the beginning caster can find him wrapped like a birthday present with a fly hook in his face. A little on-water instruction with a knowledgeable friend or instructor goes a long way toward getting comfortable with a two-hander.

As you research casting instruction for two-handed or "Spey" rods, beware of information overload. You will encounter so many casts with so many names it is easy to become overwhelmed and frustrated. I'll risk offending the experts when I suggest to beginners that—boiling the various casts down to their essence as I see it—virtually all casts here amount to a myriad of methods to position the fly line in order for the caster to, ultimately, perform a roll cast. In reading books, viewing DVD's, and watching instructors you will eventually encounter the Single Spey, Double Spey, Spiral Spey, Spiral Double Spey. Switch Cast, Snap T, Snake Roll, Turbo Spey, Jelly Roll, and even the Wombat Cast. If I might suggest, start by learning to roll cast well with a two-handed rod. The easiest cast for me to use and teach in most short- and medium-distance situations is the "Snap T" cast. After the beginner is familiar and comfortable with the basic roll cast and Snap T over both the right and left sides, he can add to his casting quiver.

Two-handed fly rods: Fishing weapons of mass destruction.

It is imperative that you cast a two-handed fly rod on water before buying or building a particular model. What may look pretty on the rod rack may not be a suitable fit for you. All rods have a distinct casting action, ranging from slow- and medium-action Traditional to the fast-action "European" type. If you are just starting out, I find the Traditional action rods by leading manufacturers are usually preferred. These seem to have a more comfortable, "forgiving" stroke for beginners and intermediate casters. As for length, I would suggest 13'-13 1/2' for your first rod. One that casts an 8-weight fly line is a good one for all-round use.

Have It Both Ways

If you are torn between getting a new one-hand rod and a two-hander, there is a compromise: a *switch* rod. This type can be the standard overhead cast of the standard fly rod, but also perform a more-than-adequate Spey cast typically done with the two-hand rod. Eleven feet is a very popular rod length, splitting the 9' of the most common single-hand rod with the 13'-14' of the most Spey two-hand models. Switch rods have an extended butt section south of the fly reel that allows for gripping it with the second hand as a Spey cast is performed. Whereas typical steelhead fly rods cast a 7-, 8-, or 9-weight fly line, some switch rods are designed to cast 4-, 5-, or 6-weight lines suitable for trout fishing. One might consider a 6-weight switch rod useable for both trout and summer steelhead.

Another BIG Fish Story

My client friend Chuck Frank was fishing with me on the Rogue River in the shadowed hours of a late-summer morning. Swinging a wet fly in a tailout Chuck got a jolting strike. The big fish that initiated the action refused to show itself, even after ten minutes. Our suspicions grew that this bully was a chinook salmon, not a steelhead. After I remarked this was a serious battle on a 5-weight fly rod, having little influence in tiring the fish, he informed me that he was actually using a 4-weight rod!

Now, it may be desirable to break off such a mismatch because the fight can consume a significant portion of the fishing day. In addition, while one angler continues in a prolonged encounter his fishing partner, confined to the boat, cannot resume fishing anytime soon. However, Chuck was cordially insistent that he wanted to attempt to land this fish. Certainly it would stand as a near-certain-unbeatable personal record for the wispy, straining 4-weight.

A gasp went up from the crowd when we finally confirmed the fish as a salmon. It was at least twenty pounds!

Chuck exhibited great patience, as did his fishing partner, Paul. Because the salmon refused to drop downstream through a perilous rapids, taking with it the entire fly line and most of the backing, it took about 30 minutes to net the fish. An amazing feat. The panting little fly rod reminded me of the little engine that thought it could. It did.

I anticipate some arguments about the ethics in the use of lightweight rods in pursuit of steelhead, especially after I recommended you consider an 8-weight. I have some "splainin'" to do.

First, my clients and I are fishing from a boat. I learned long ago that my time is better spent coaching and positioning my client friends than consuming a lot of time helping them in and out of my boat, and helping them wade into the perfect position to present their flies to holding lies. Inevitably, while I am helping one angler I must ignore the other who may be killing time waiting for my return. One or both may be unable to follow my fishing directions as soon as I leave their side. Add to these the possibility that one of my 75-year-old or 14-year-old clients loses his footing and starts bobbing down the river into dangerous water. Ever try to run through waist-deep water to perform a rescue? Ever try to swim to the aid of a drowning person while you are wearing waders? Now that's excitement!

Fishing from a boat, I am prepared to quickly pull anchor to pursue a runaway steelhead. My guys and gals can keep maximum pressure on the fish, tire it more quickly and land it sooner than if they had to pursue it on foot through a challenging rapids or fast chute. Being able to chase a fish allows for the advantages of a lighter rod. Here, I think I have cancelled the concern that with a light rod an angler cannot land a steelhead before it might be fought to the point of unrecoverable exhaustion.

However, won't you break a light rod on a big fish? Maybe, but participating as a guide or angler in the capture of several thousand steelhead I have never witnessed the breaking of a rod while fighting these fish. If you perceive jeopardy when a strong specimen puts a dangerous bend in your rod, merely drop the rod tip to a lower position toward the fish. You can minimize the bend to any degree you want, even to the extent where you position the rod horizontally, pointing it directly at the steelhead. Now, there is absolutely no bend and, now, you just felt the fish break your tippet.

Rod action—the extent to which a rod bends over its entire length with a big fish on the line—is usually chosen to suit the angler's casting comfort. A fast-action fly rod is one where, generally, the upper quarter to one third of it readily bends. A medium-action rod bends to its midpoint, while a slow, or full-flex, rod bends all the way to the grip. Each has its pros and cons. Each has its advocates and detractors. Most inexperienced fly-fishers think that a fast-action fly rod is the best choice. I am sure they think of such a tool as a high-speed sports car. Because the rod tip is powerful and recovers quickly to its unbent "resting" position quickly, the fast-action rod is capable of propelling a fly line at higher velocities, resulting in greater casting distance. However, just like driving a sports car at high speeds through the curves, timing and control can become overwhelming issues. Some casters can master the timing stroke and cast a long beautiful line. Others bully or mis-time the casting stroke rhythm of a fast rod, losing the distance potential. The fast rod will seem unmanageable and unpleasant.

There are occasions—low, clear water, for instance—where a light tippet is required to fool the steelhead. With a fast-action rod there can be a high-impact force imparted to the leader that can easily break off the fly. There may be too little "give" in the rod tip if the hook set is too forceful, little, if any, shock absorption. Even with more common 1X and OX tippets, an overly powerful response to a steelhead's strike will part the leader. A small bonus: a steelhead with a broken fly in its jaw will usually jump. So, at least, you will see the fish you might have landed.

In contrast to the tip-action rod, there is the slow or full-flex action. The casting stroke is much slower. An impatient caster may move the rod to and fro too quickly, not allowing the bending rod to reach the natural terminus of its flex in either direction. Calmed relaxation is a good mental posture with this action type. This is not the rod action for the hyper-active.

The longer, extended flextime of the slow-action rod allows a focused caster to better feel the bend of the rod. Also, the slow action accentuates the feel of the unfurling fly line, as it straightens out on the back cast. This signals just the right moment to move the rod tip in the opposite direction in the cast. An attentive angler has time to process and prepare for the next stroke to begin. This, I call a "forgiving" action. The slower flex allows better for imperfect timing—within reasonable limits—of the casting stroke. And, for those who may have fished quality bamboo or fiberglass fly rods in their careers, the slow action feels quite normal.

The possibility of breaking off a fish on the strike is reduced with a full-flex rod. Acting like a springy shock absorber, the impact of a solid hook-set against resistance is cushioned. While fighting a big fish, a heavy-handed angler who tries to turn a stubborn steelhead will have a lesser chance of a break off than an angler performing the same maneuver with a stiff, fast-action stick. It is the same effect as playing a steelhead on a lighter, more limber 5- or 6-weight fly rod.

The majority of fly rods will fall into the broad medium-action category, flexing most commonly down to its mid section. Take a fast-action and a slow-action model, and then split the difference. It is here that most fly-anglers will settle with their choice when it comes to selecting a fly rod.

I highly recommend that you cast any rod you consider buying. Even an expensive rod can feel "clunky", or heavy, or uncomfortable, or too heavy in the tip. The grip might look pretty on the display, but be too big or too small for your hand. Even if your casting skill is minimal, cast before you buy. Always take a rod for a test drive in the alley or on the lawn before plunking down your cash. Its appearance on the rack may have little bearing on the rod's feel and performance.

Examine the components on the rod: the cork grip, reel seat, the guides, the thread wraps on the guides, and the epoxy or urethane finish work on the wraps. The majority of the guides—usually twisted 's' snake guides—need to be made of *chrome-plated* stainless steel or some Space Age alloy. Do not settle for mere stainless-steel guides. They will wear with time, and more easily corroded if ever used in salt water. They may have to be replaced in a few years. Not an inexpensive proposition. If you do not know their composition, ask the guy or gal behind the counter. Read the manufacturer's literature. Also, count the number of guides tied on the rod, not including the tip top. On a quality fly rod there should be at least one more guide than the whole number of feet in the fly rod's length. Example: a 9' or 9 1/2' rod should have at least 10 guides. As the rod is flexed forward and backward during a normal cast, the line in the guides should mirror the flex. If the guides are too far apart because the manufacturer or rod builder cut corners on work time and materials to save money, the line will slap the rod blank during the cast, creating friction that slows the line as it slides through the rod guides. Casting distance is decreased. Additionally, when the rod you hold horizontally on the forward stroke as the cast is completed, the line sags between consecutive guides, again causing distance-killing friction.

More guides than I have recommended are not necessarily better. One rod manufacturer attaches *two* more guides than the whole number of feet in the rod length. No problem, but any more are certainly not needed, and will only add excess weight and stiffness to the rod.

Let me reiterate. Every fly-angler in the market for a new rod should cast a variety of lengths and weights. It's a little like test driving cars. One my look sporty and pretty, but drive like a truck with flat tires…on bumpy terrain…uphill…with a cross wind.

Just like an inexperienced driver can get a feel for the vehicle that suits him and his budget, an inexperienced fly-caster will feel an affinity for a rod that appeals. It will seem comfortable and pleasant to cast, even though the casting stroke is far from perfection. So to make a wise choice, put your pride aside and do some comparison casting. You will not know what suits you unless you compare. No matter your experience level, do this. It may preclude you saving a few bucks by buying that "deal" on the internet or in the bargain bin, but look long term. The right rod may be fished for a lifetime. If you amortize a few extra dollars over a lifetime, it can mean only a few pennies a year. Compare, and don't skimp on the cost. That way you will only have to buy right rod once.

Fly Lines: Welcome to the Land of Confusion

Here are some of the possible choices/variables you will deal with when selecting the fly line, or lines, for your steelhead fishing needs: taper, color, length, full floating, full sinking, floating/sinking combination, length of sinking portion, sink rate, quality level/price, and manufacturer. Combining all these variables will present the angler with more than 200 choices. Yikes! Unless you have a good reason backed by personal knowledgeable or experienced advice, I am suggesting that you consider using the lines I personally have found useful and effective. You will eventually need more than one. Different steelhead fly-fishing techniques require a few different fly lines. The more techniques you master, the greater the likelihood of steelheading success.

For most anglers getting started, the first choice in a steelhead fly line should be a high-quality, high-visibility, weight-forward tapered, floating fly line. A high-quality line lasts longer, casts better, floats higher and longer than a cheap fly line. As for a hi-vis color, you want to be able to see—approximate-

ly—where your fly is drifting as you fish it. I'm ahead of you here. Yes, fish can see color. However, it is not the fly line color that startles a fish, but the shadow and splash as the line lands.

In my opinion, a double-tapered fly line—which most beginners have heard of—is a specialty fly line with a couple of serious limitations for the majority of average steelhead fly-rodders, including casting distance limitations and overcoming the wind. A weight-forward taper, when properly cast, maximizes distance, performs better than a double taper in the wind, and does a better job of presenting heavy and air-resistant large flies at distance.

Use a floating fly line to present dry flies, shallow-running wet flies, and deep nymphs to steelhead. The floater is the most versatile fly line in your arsenal. The floater is also the easiest line to cast, mend, visually track, and pick off the water to re-cast. Make it your first fly line. My clients and I use a *floating* line more than any other line, by far.

Consider 10' or 15' sink-tip fly lines for your subsequent choices. I carry three, the main difference among them being the sink rate.

Sink rates are usually designated with a Roman numeral from I to VI, Type I or "intermediate density" being the slowest, sinking at a rate of between 3/4" to 1 1/2" per second, and Type VI the fastest, dropping at 8'-10" per second.

My sinking choices are a clear ("transparent") Type I Intermediate tip, a Type III tip, and a Type VI sink-tip. These enable me to reach steelhead at all reasonable depths and current velocities, ranging from slow, shallow water to fast, deep runs. I

have not found any advantages in having a sinking tip longer than 15'. Such lines are harder to manage, mend, cast, and detect the strike.

WF = weight forward taper	**WF-6-S**
6 = fly line/rod weight	**TYPE III**
S = sinking	2.50-3.50 ips
Type III = sink rate (2.5-3.5 ips)	90 ft/27 m
ips = inches per second	

Interpreting the information on a fly line box.

Fly Line Backing: A Crucial Insurance Policy

Peeling all the fly line from your reel during a panicked run is not a difficult task for most steelhead. As insurance, have 100 yards of braided Dacron backing knotted to the rear of the fly line. This material—I use and recommend 30-pound breaking strength in most situations—has virtually no stretch, is very strong for its diameter, and does not deteriorate significantly over time, as monofilament will. Do not even consider using monofilament. Exposure to sunlight over a couple of fishing seasons will greatly weaken it. Imagine your mono backing breaking as a steelhead swims down river trailing your expensive fly line with it. Like that image?

The Fly Reel: Brake Without Breaking & Smooth Under Pressure

Once a nasty steelhead is on the end of the line, the final scene in the drama—capture or escapement—is largely determined by your fly reel. The rod presents the fly to the steelhead, but the reel pressures the fish. A reel that does not release line very smoothly at high speed, even when the drag system is wet, is worthless to me. If an angler consistently hooked fifty steelhead in a day, the disappointment of lost fish due to reel malfunction would not be as intense. However, a biffed chance by most of us mere mortals who feel lucky to hook one or two steelhead in a fishing day is serious heartache. I would rather use a mediocre fly rod and an excellent fly reel than vice versa. Like I tell my students, "Put a star by this statement: get a GOOD fly reel!" Even if you are a natural-born skimper, do not frugal-ize on this piece of steelhead fly-fishing gear. I guarantee you will be sorry.

The drag mechanism in a fly reel adjusts the amount of resistance against the force of a steelhead pulling line off the reel. This pulling force varies throughout the battle in duration and intensity. The drag must *smoothly* and instantly adjust to these changes.

Examples of common drag designs include spring & pawl, caliper, and disc types. Disc drags are the most widely used in quality steelhead fly reels. Simplistically put, a smooth, flat surface on or geared to the spinning/turning spool of the reel works against a stationary flat, smooth surface on the inside of the reel frame. Drag (resistance against the pull of the fish) is increased or decreased as the angler tightens or lightens the

Doh! Proper drag adjustment is essential to prevent overruns and subsequent break-offs.

drag by means of a lever or knob on the reel. Too little drag and the fish feels no tiring resistance. Too much drag will cause the leader to break when the fish pulls hard or suddenly against the resistance. Experience gained through a little trial and error will enable the angler to discover what is too little and what is too much.

Frankly, I do not like spring and pawl reels for steelhead fishing, though I know some very good fly-fishers who love them and would use no other. They love to palm the spinning spool, and cherish the whirring scream of the instrument when a fish peels line from it. In the first case, I can precisely set my disc drag exactly where I want it to take the guesswork out of palming the drag, not risking a miscalculation resulting in too much tension on the spool rim, breaking the tippet. Secondly, it is rare that I want to draw attention to the fact that my clients or I have a steelhead on the end of the line. Click-and-pawl reels loudly proclaim, "Look at me! See where I hooked that fish? Come back here soon, and bring your friends." I have disengaged the clicking pawl in of my disc-drag reels, converting them to silent running.

Further insuring I do not show up on someone's radar screen while playing a steelhead, I sometimes strip line from my reel and lower my tip to remove any rod bend as a boat or car approaches. In certain situations, I would rather chance losing a fish than making it plain where a Sweet Spot may be located.

Woe Is Me, Bob Cratchit. What Do You Mean, I Squeak When I Walk?

As with all fly equipment choices, don't scrooge the reel, *especially if you do not have to*. I have an angling friend with a truckload of cash in the bank. Let us pretend he is a high-earning professional with a healthy six-figure income for many years, and has fared well in the investment world, too. Think million$. For years and years, he fished a tacky $30 spring-and-pawl fly reel. Yes, he landed fish on this obnoxious thing, but there is something *seriously* wrong with this picture. It reminds me of someone who drives an expensive Mercedes (and could probably even own the dealership), and decides to put re-capped tires without wheel covers on his vehicle. This is just sick.

Poor design or inferior workmanship may cause even an expensive disc-drag reel to fail on a fighting steelhead. Water—getting the reel wet—can create problems for faulty disc drags. In addition, because you are in the constant vicinity of water as you fish, eventually your reel will get wet or, you will fish in the rain. If water penetrates the minute space between the two drag surfaces in a disc-drag reel, "hydroplaning" may result. Just as steering and braking control in a car may be lost as it travels through standing water at high speed, wet drag surfaces in a faulty reel will lose the friction necessary to retain the necessary resistance battling a steelhead. The reel spool will spin madly as drag is lost, creating a hideous backlash tangle of line which will guarantee a break-off of the fish. Before you shell out $100-$300 dollars for a fly reel, extract a guarantee from the seller that the reel's drag *will* perform when wet.

Some drags are lousy when put to the test by a big fish even when they are dry and properly lubricated, if lubrication is required. Immediately return the reel to the seller. As best you can, resist being cajoled into sending it back to the reel manufacturer yourself. Let the seller of the item be responsible for packaging, handling and delivery charges if the item must go back to the manufacturer for repairs or replacement. Oops! Bought it through the mail or on the internet? Can you spell "time" and "hassle"? Consider dealing face-to-face with a local merchant. The service provided by a local fly-fishing, specialty retailer is a good investment. You might also receive some quality fishing advice as part of the deal.

Size matters. Virtually all modern fly reel models come in a variety of sizes. For instance, the Acme Wizbang series has four different sizes to best accommodate a broad spectrum of fly line size (line weight) and desired amount of backing. Your clue to the reel size appropriate for your particular fly line is the stated "reel capacity" in the owner's manual. If you have a WF-6-F fly line and want to back it on the reel spool with about 100 yards of 20-pound braided Dacron, select the Wizbang model that has the closest approximation to the capacity you need. It is rare that any given reel will have exactly the stated capacity you desire. Since most manufacturers tend to overstate the amount of backing that can actually be held on the spool, I suggest you choose a reel that is slightly too large over a reel that is slightly too small. Think in terms of buying shoes. With no size fitting perfectly, are you going to buy slightly larger, or slightly too small? If you have ever worn shoes that were too small, seek out and listen to comedian Steve Martin's "Cruel Shoes". You will relate.

The Down & Dirty About Leaders and Tippets

Veteran anglers, you may want to bear with me. Since you have a very tenuous physical connection between you and a hooked steelhead, the leader can make or break (bad pun) the outcome. There is a chance you may glean a tidbit of insight about these essentials. If it adds a steelhead or two to this year's catch, I would say it's worth it.

Starting with the obvious, the leader is the transparent segment of total fly line "system". To its end is tied the fly. Lengths range from three feet to twelve feet or more. Typically, I start with a 9' tapered leader, often lengthening it by adding

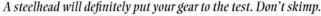

A steelhead will definitely put your gear to the test. Don't skimp.

Tippet. When in doubt, use second generation fluorocarbon.

tippet material. Final length may be 10'-11'. I tend to use the longer length when fishing nymphs; the standard 9' for wet flies and dry flies.

The profile of the typical out-of-package 9' tapered leader: 0.024"-0.0.21" at its heavy butt section, narrowing to 0.009"-0.011" over the next 7'. The final two to three feet of the leader, where the fly is tied on its end, has a uniform diameter. This taperless portion of the leader is the *tippet*.

A tapered leader's length is naturally reduced by changing flies or breaking the leader on a lost fish or casting into trees. To replenish the length, pull tippet from a spare spool purchased at your favorite sporting shop, and tie it to the shortened leader with a double surgeon's knot.

Leaders and tippets are available in an assortment of line technology chemistries: monofilament, copolymer, first-generation fluorocarbon, and second-generation fluorocarbon. Without getting too technical, know that monofilament leaders and tippets are cheapest and have the lowest breaking strength for their diameter; copolymer types are more expensive but up to 50% stronger; second-generation fluorocarbon lines are as strong as the copolymer varieties, have significant "invisibility", and are three to four times as expensive as the copolymer.

Distributors and wholesalers of leaders and tippet materials can choose from a list of variables to create unique leaders and tippets. Besides the general chemistry of the line, these variables include color, taper design (leaders), suppleness/stiffness, knotting strength, and abrasion resistance.

My Personal Choices, Leaders & Tippets

For dry flies and wet flies, I gravitate to a stiff leader butt section, and a very supple tippet. The stiff butt section makes for casts that lay out generally straight at all distances, even in a significant breeze. A supple tippet allows the fly to drift and swim more naturally in the current. Even when I am skating a dry fly on a tight line across the river current, I like the subtle bobbing and weaving of the fly allowed by a soft tippet.

For fishing nymphs and egg patterns along the bottom, I start with a tapered leader that has a smaller butt diameter, 0.021"-0.022", and is supple throughout its entire length. The fineness and softness are imperative to getting a good natural drift of the fly while fishing deep. As best as I can, I want minimal influence from the leader and tippet on my fly as it drifts down the river. Because fluorocarbon tends to be stiffer, I prefer a copolymer leader. I cut off the tippet portion of the leader and replace it with fluorocarbon tippet. In the tippet, I am sacrificing a little suppleness for invisibility. I always prefer a *second*-generation fluorocarbon tippet, no matter the leader. Second generation is stronger than first-generation tippet for the same money. Seems like a no-brainer.

Losing a steelhead to an unexplainable break-off is disheartening. When you witness these too often with a particular tippet brand name, it leaves a lingering bad impression. Not all second-generation tippet materials are the same quality. For knot strength and minimal mysterious breaks in the middle of a fish fight, I prefer one brand name above all others…so far. Readers are invited to contact me personally through one of my websites to discover my choice. Because new and better items come to market all the time, I may discover something even more to my liking in the future.

I admit to being addicted to fluorocarbon. It is the "invisibility" factor. This, I think, is imperative in clear water where wary steelhead are on high alert. Plenty of steelhead succumbed to my flies before the advent of fluorocarbon tippets and leaders. However, at the end of a lean or, heaven forbid, fishless fishing day, I do not want to wonder if a willing biter would have struck a hook if only I had used fluorocarbon. To remove this doubt is important. Even though fluorocarbon is expensive, it is a small cost in comparison to the much larger costs of my other equipment, including, rods, reels, waders, boat, and travel. I might use $2-$3 of tippet in a day. Keep perspective.

The key to getting the right combination of line extension during the cast coupled with an effective drift of the fly once it hits the water lies in the diameter of the tippet. For generally matching the tippet diameter to the fly size, use the following equation:

$$\frac{\text{Fly (hook) size}}{3} = \text{appropriate ``X'' number}$$

The "X" number found on a tippet spool and leader packaging is a reference to diameter. If you look closer at the

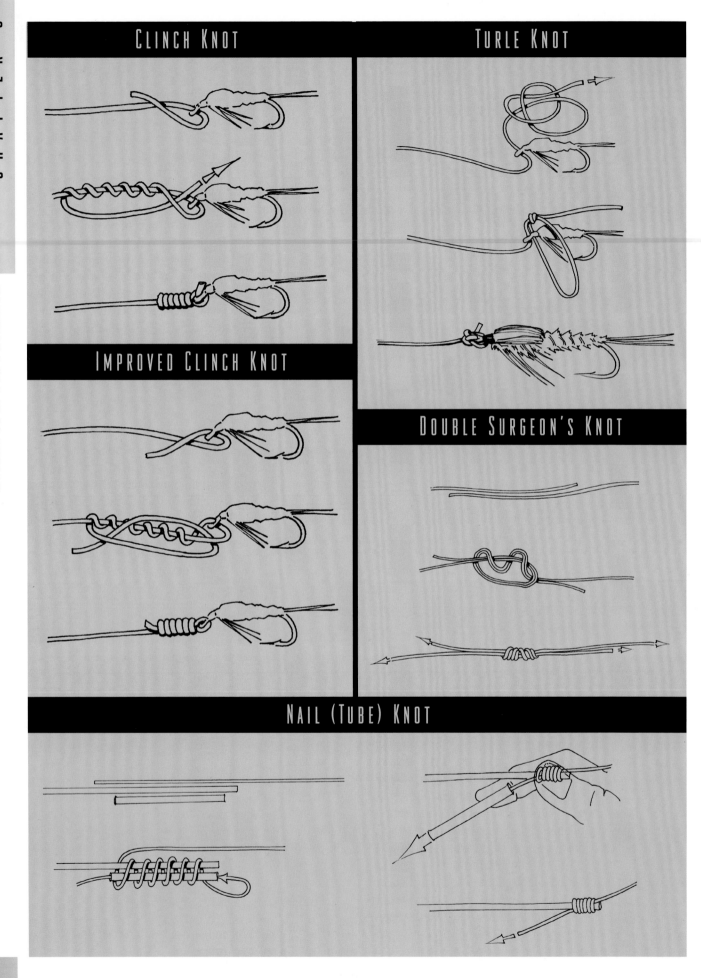

Clinch Knot

Turle Knot

Improved Clinch Knot

Double Surgeon's Knot

Nail (Tube) Knot

labeling, you will usually discover the translation into inches. Example: 2X = 0.009". Using the equation above for common steelhead flies, you will probably find 0X, 1X, and 2X tippets to be the most useful diameters.

In case you are new to this information, know that there is an inverse relationship between the hook size number and the actual physical size of the hook. That is, the larger the hook number the smaller the hook's measurable size, specifically the measurement between the main body of the hook (the shank) and the point of the hook. This is a measurement of the hook's *gap* or *gape*. Example: a #6 hook is larger than a #12 hook.

The "X" number and diameter measured in inches have an inverse relationship also. The larger the "X" number, the smaller the diameter. Example: 7X (0.004") tippet is a smaller diameter than 4X (0.007") tippet.

In tough clear-water conditions, I will often give up castability for a better drift and tippet invisibility. Instead of using a 2X tippet suggested by my mathematical formula for a #6 fly, I may, instead, use a smaller 3X or 4X diameter so there's a diminished chance that an eagle-eye steelhead won't be able to detect a line attached to my hook.

Putting It All Together: Knots

I rely on three knots to assemble or repair my line-leader-tippet-hook connections 99% of the time. If you prefer alternative knots, use 'em. For the specific mechanics of tying each, I recommend a book of knots or a quick internet search. Take a look on the next page at the schematic overview, knot tying instructions.

Any time backing or leader is tied to the fly line, the tube/nail knot is my choice. A tool or a small-diameter, rigid tube is a necessity. For joining leader and tippet material together in order to replace or extend the tippet, the double surgeon knot is simple, fast, and strong. Though there are many choices for tying a fly to the leader, I can quickly tie a clinch knot with frozen fingers in dim light.

In addition to knowing how to assemble and effectively use it, having good equipment will translate into better fishing success. Good tools are a pleasure to use, will endure heavy use, and land more fish than cheap goods posing as fly-fishing equipment. My recommendation, get the best gear you can reasonable afford. You are worth it, aren't you?

Jason Mariner, the steelhead-catching machine in action. The backpack allows for a long fishing day on foot. And, a splash of red makes for a little more interest in the photo.

CHAPTER 4

Locating Productive
Steelhead Water

ALLOW ME TO STATE THE OBVIOUS:

you cannot catch steelhead where they aren't.

Identifying specific locations in a river where steelhead hold to rest

on their upstream spawning journey is absolutely

crucial to angling success.

Jason Mariner ambushes a steelhead resting in a quiet pocket above mid-stream boulders.

Though most steelhead must swim miles and miles of a river's course, they must periodically pause on their journey. It is when the fish actually *stops* to linger for a time—minutes to days—that an angler has a reasonable hope of enticing the steelhead to strike. There is little or no interest from a fish on the move.

As for choosing specific resting stations, steelhead are fussy. They do not linger just anywhere. It is similar to a camper walking through forested mountains. When it is time to pitch a tent for the night, the location is selected with great care, considering the slope, the weather, cover, protection, and so on. Along this same line of thought, it is my assessment that more than 99% of the area in a typical river does not hold resting steelhead. Most of any given river is too shallow, too fast, too slow, too exposed, too warm, too cold for steelhead to linger for long. The astute angler must discover the "Sweet 1%".

For locating my "Sweet 1%", I give thought to the three following considerations:

1. Adequate depth to protect the fish from inordinate exposure to predators and continued disturbance from boaters and anglers. As a fly-fisherman, I focus on water depths of three to seven feet.
2. Reasonable current velocity, best described vaguely as "walking speed".
3. Streamside or river bottom structure, including boulders, ledges, depressions, and channels.

Expanding on Desirable Traits

The initial characteristic of the water I consider prime for prospecting for steelhead with a fly is the correct depth. I seek out flows that are 3-7 feet deep. Can steelhead be found in shallower water? Yes. Will they hold in deeper water? Most definitely. However, I focus on areas where the water is a minimum of 3' because such depths *will* hold steelhead and I can usually approach stealthily to get quite near without alarming them, especially if the water's surface is choppy. If the water does not exceed 7', I have a chance, with polarized glasses, to see specific boulders, slots, ledges, and depressions that give me visual clues as to where exactly a steelhead might be. I may be able to actually see the fish if the light and clarity are right. Additionally, it is in this depth range that I can most effectively present my fly from top to bottom, maintaining excellent line control, and instantly detect a strike.

A steelhead in 7' of water or less is often willing to come all the way to the surface to intercept a dry fly or shallow-running wet fly when water temperatures are warm enough in late spring, summer and fall. If it is sitting on the bottom at 8-15 feet, that's a significantly greater distance to see the fly in riffly water and be willing to swim that far to intercept it. Other anglers may differ here, so know that I am relating my own observations and biases.

I have hooked steelhead in water so shallow it barely covered their backs. Additionally, fish in more than ten feet of water have fallen for my fly and I have landed them. So, of course, there are exceptions to my advice about water depth. But, unless you have no other choices, you will maximize your success by focusing your fishing time on the depths I suggest as optimal.

If I might generalize, I would state that good rainbow trout water in a river is also good steelhead water. For, after all, a steelhead IS a rainbow trout that, because of its genetics, goes to sea for part of its life. That said, I seek out specific locations in the stream where there is perceptible current. I would describe the pace of the current to be, roughly, "walking speed". I understand this is a nebulous term. Not everyone walks at the same speed. On the other hand, steelhead do not always linger in currents of exactly the same velocity. When the water is very cold—let's say 35-42 degrees Fahrenheit—steelhead hold in slower currents than they would typically hold in at warmer water temperatures in the 55- to 62-degree range. So "walking speed" is descriptive of a general range, something between a slow saunter and jogging. Think reasonably here.

I am seeking walking-speed flows where the current is unidirectional. That is, the current flows, generally, in a straight horizontal line. I don't want upwelling or down-welling currents that move my fly, leader and line four different directions at once. The same goes for back eddies where my line does not move evenly in a mostly straight downstream manner. I will be out of touch with my fly. If a fish intercepted it for a moment, I would never know.

If the stream bottom is uneven, instead of smooth and featureless, the river's surface is typically choppy, or "broken". I am not talking about rolling waves here, but riffles a few inches high at most. Submerged boulders, pockets, and ledges, and submerged debris contribute to this riffling effect. The surface can mirror the contours of the bottom. If there is little gradient (downhill grade) and the water is deep, the surface may be smooth, even though the river bottom is uneven. A choppy surface is desirable, but not mandatory. A broken, riffled surface obscures the fish's vision of things outside the water. You can more closely approach a steelhead in broken water, than a location where the surface is flat and smooth. The closer a fly-angler can approach a holding fish without alarming it, the better he is able to make an accurate cast, get an effective presentation of the fly, and detect the strike.

So, let me expand and fine-tune this second characteristic of prime steelhead holding water. "Ideal" locations have a walking-speed current where the current flows in a straight line, and the water's surface is riffled or ruffled, instead of flat and smooth.

Lastly, my favorite steelhead lies will have some interesting structure or physical features the fish finds appealing: boulders, ledges, scoured depressions, deeper slots or channels. These have the possibility of offering the steelhead comfort from the swift current or bright sun and some degree of protection from predators, including anglers. If you find fish lying in an exposed position, such as a shallow tailout preceding a rapid, they may not linger long as the sun gets high or something or someone disturbs them. Sheltered locations are quickly sought.

Exposed structure, primarily boulders, can prompt the inexperienced angler to waste his time. Rocks that are only partially submerged create an eddy on their downstream edge. The water actually flows around the sides of the stone, then curls back upstream to the rear side of it. Practically every novice angler I have coached is under the impression that

fishing immediately behind (downstream) a rock is a good strategy. Depending on the shape of the boulder and the velocity and depth of the water, start fishing on the downstream side of the rock where the current starts to move downstream in a straight line. Depending on the situation, this could be three feet; it could be twenty feet, or more. Watch the drift of your fly, leader, and fly line as your confirmation you have found fishable water.

I much prefer fishing areas with deeply submerged structure. The current flow is much more dependable, so I get a truer drift of the fly, even as it drifts directly over a boulder.

When fishing around exposed rocks, steelhead will commonly hold near either side, especially if the current speed is in the desirable range, and the depth falls within the prime parameters.

Exceptions, Of Course

So, steelhead may be found in water that is shallower and deeper than my specified depth range. They can be caught where the water is faster or slower than my "walking speed" pace. And, certainly, steelhead can be taken from water that has little or no structure. However, I am always looking to maximize my fishing efforts. This means focusing my fishing time, and that of my clients, where we have the BEST chance of closely approaching resting steelhead in maximum numbers. Making an accurate cast, getting a very controlled and effective drift of the fly, and having the ability to instantly detect and react to the strike of the fish are best accommodated by staying within my recommended guidelines.

Visual Aids for Locating Steelhead

An exciting confirmation that you are learning to locate good steelhead holding water, is actually seeing them. Conditions

*A high bank overlooking holding water
is an excellent vantage point. Stealth required.*

A resting steelhead pauses before continuing its upstream journey. The spots on the back and rainbow coloration usually indicate a steelhead has been in freshwater for several months or more. Its dark back and silvery sides have reverted to those of a trout.

have to be just right—clear, low water, with the sun at your back are ideal—but with practice and *polarized* glasses, you can eventually spot fish. The polarization cuts the reflected glare on the water. Virtually any pair of new polarized glasses has a tag or sticker on it stating that they are polarized. If you are not sure, ask the clerk before you buy them. To double check, you can superimpose your selected lenses over a lens that is known for sure to be polarized. As you rotate the lenses relative to each other as you look through them you will see them "go black", blocking out all light attempting to pass through them.

A variety of polarized lens tints are available: yellow, for very dim light; dark gray, for extremely bright settings; and, brown or copper for "medium" light and all-around general use. If you ask, polarized prescription glasses are readily available.

From an eye safety standpoint, glasses of any type are necessary to protect your eyes from an errant hook. Your sloppy cast or that from a beginner in your proximity can cause serious ocular harm. It is troubling to count the number of times I have had clients bounce a weighted nymph off my lenses. Wear those glasses, even on a rainy morning or evening.

Scout. Then, Scout Some More

Time is required to discover excellent steelhead holding water. Sometimes such locations are obvious. The smaller, overlooked gems are not. Small Sweet Spots are harder to find, but persistence and experimentation will reveal them. One simple shortcut is to watch other anglers, especially if you see them

hook a steelhead. Make a precise mental note of where they are casting.

If you carefully observe the river bottom, using polarized glasses, at low water times, you can discern little pockets where fish will hold when the water is higher. I make mental notes so that on subsequent trips I will remember these small holding lies. In addition, there may be portions of a proven run that I overestimate or underestimate at higher water. Observation at low water may enable me to fine-tune my approach in fishing this spot when high water returns. Logs and clumps of wood debris in a hole are fly grabbers. Low water allows me to chart and memorize their exact position. Wood snags cost you money and fishing time, the latter being a particularly precious commodity.

When I mine little gems—small, not-so-obvious locations—I may very well forgo fishing them if another boat or foot angler is in view. Just as I watch others, others watch me. Any fisherman with even a quarter of the normal gray matter between his ears will see where my clients or I have hooked a steelhead. They will find a way to get to that spot. Over time, more and more determined anglers will find their way to this specific spot. Their fishing success will be witnessed by others who will find a path to the location, too. And, so it goes *ad infinitum*.

This segues perfectly into a couple of stories, of course.

A Guide Story: I Spy You Spying

Every now and then someone tries to "go to school" on me. I spy a boat that anchors upstream of me in a location I know is not a fish-producer. Maybe they pretend to fish a little but

Reconnaissance can be a useful steelheading strategy.

mostly they watch. They loiter. I know what they are looking for: my fishing spots. They are playing the game that I have refined. It can be difficult spying on a spy. One eye is always in my rearview mirror.

There is any number of thwarting strategies, but I used a new one at one of my favorite steelhead fishing spots.

Late morning I watched a drift boat lingering above us more than a hundred yards upriver. He did not strike me as a man on a fishing mission. Too much time on the oars; not enough time fishing. I pushed down the river to see if he would follow us. My suspicions were aroused when the man in question bypassed a lot of water at which any other angler would be tempted to stop to make a few casts. He had not seen us earlier to know where we had and had not fished, so it is only logical the angler should have fished, if even briefly.

When we rounded a sharp bend in the river, he lost sight of us. He had several hundred yards of slow water to traverse so it would be five minutes or more before he reached the same bend. I pushed the oars very forcefully so that we would be around the *next* bend and out of sight before he reached the first. The thought here is that Spy Boy may halt the chase so as not bypass some very good steelhead water that I had left un-touched, and he would not know for sure how far downriver we would drift before anchoring to resume fishing.

As it turns out, my strategy bought us about twenty minutes of privacy. Shortly after one of my clients landed, photographed, and released a magnificent steelhead, the lone boatman came into view. He snugged into the upper end of the run we were fishing, anchoring on the other side of the river in some frog water. He began to cast, making it obvious our spy either did not know he was fishing unproductive water, or he was merely positioning himself to watch us fish. I assumed the latter.

To disappoint him we did not go back out into the main river to resume fishing, but instead watched *him* from the shal-lows near the shore where we landed the fish. After a few min-utes and no indication he was going to move on in the near future, I rowed my boat to the very top of the run so that we were directly across the river from the onlooker. I suggested to my crew that they not even pick up their fishing rods. It was close enough to the mid day hour that I advised we use our waiting time productively, so we ate lunch. While he watched us eat, we watched him make more futile casts. I wanted to fish this particular run more thoroughly before we departed so we were in the midst of a standoff. I would let time wear on our uninvited guest.

If this guy were a typical, undisciplined spy I knew it would not take long before his urge to fish better water, if he thought he could recognize it, would far outweigh the necessary patience to out-wait us. We were only half way through a leisurely lunch before Spy Boy pulled his anchor and drifted downriver; we did not see him again the rest of the day. To this end, I lingered to thoroughly cover every location we fished the rest of the day, wanting to ensure we did not catch up with the spy who, then, might be prompted to study our activities again.

Another simple ploy, most easily used when I anchor in the middle of the river, is to have my guests cast to the "wrong" side of the boat. If we spend a significant amount of time "kill-ing time", I assure my guests I will extend our fishing day a comparable amount so they get are not shorted fishing time.

Sometimes I may stop the boat slightly above or drop a short distance below the actual position from which I want to fish. The exact position from which an angler casts can be extremely important. Upstream too far, or downstream too far, can make a significant difference in the effective drift of the fly to the fish. Discovering the exact coordinates of where to anchor or stand to fish a particular piece of water may be the difference between hooking a fish and not getting a strike. So if another "spying" angler approaches my guests and me, we are not positioned, often, in the sweet spot. In addition, we may purposely fish 180 degrees from our true target to disguise our actual intent. A strategic defensive move. If an "intruder" lingers, I may choose to push down the river rather than reveal a Sweet Spot. What I don't want to do is have one of my anglers (or me) hook a steelhead to confirm quality steelhead holding water. It would only serve to encourage the observer to return to this spot in the future…and bring his friends…who will bring *their* friends. If I choose to leave, my boat—having a mind of its own—may maneuver to drift directly over the heart of the prime water with noisy oar strokes encouraging any steelhead to run for cover elsewhere. One might be inclined to feel a bit like Paul Revere.

Whether anchored or moving, my neck muscles are always stretched and loose from constantly looking over my shoulder. I will be looking for *you*. If you catch me, it *may* be because I wanted it.

If you are wondering…Yes, I do carry binoculars. And, yes, I use them often. I am even contemplating rearview mirrors.

A Zero Sum Game

I do not have very many "almost guaranteed" steelhead holes, but I have one on the Rogue that is very close to this designation. It is ideally located, too. I can see for hundreds of yards upriver to watch for approaching boats. I can see the same downriver if a boat has dropped below me. Should someone be able to observe me if I fish my little nook, I will, instead, drift by as if it wasn't there. Or, if I am already in position, and discover someone within view of me, I will pull anchor and leave. This spot is w-a-a-a-a-y too sweet to give up. The Nook is surrounded by fast, shallow water, while the flow in the heart of this fish magnet is a perfect walking speed. The depth is at least one foot more than its turbulent surroundings. Ten well-placed casts will cover this precious real estate to reveal the presence of a biting fish. So, another big plus of this location is that it can be quickly covered. If a steelhead is hooked, I usually lift the anchor to play the fish downstream, away from our original location. It is just like a hit-and-run covert operation, save for the camouflage face paint: get in; complete the mission; get out, all without being discovered.

Right or wrong, most of the time I view steelhead fishing as a Zero Sum game, as I said earlier. This means there are winners and losers. In an ideal world, there would be lots and lots of biting steelhead for all worthy anglers on the river. Sure… My cats will do housework before that happens! If competent anglers fish my little sweet spots before I get there, I have very little chance of hooking a steelhead. Another fish will eventually take up residence, but maybe not until tomorrow, or two days from now. The redundant lesson here, again, is if little nooks you discover turn out to be more precious than gold, consider not giving away the map to your "silver" mine. Every other angler is a potential claim jumper.

A Zero Sum Maneuver

A father and son team in my boat had just about finished covering the deep slot that held some biting steelhead for us that morning, including the first steelhead the boy had ever landed. God was in his heaven, and all was right with the world. And, things were just about to get even better. As a boat dropped through the rapid above us, it was just about time for us to

Mark Severson floating toward his next steelhead encounter in a small pontoon boat. Think safety if you try this.

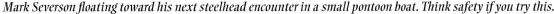

Dale Penn II with Dad Dale Sr. on a memorable fall day on the Rogue River. When my clients pose with a steelhead, I prefer they kneel in shallow water so the fish does not need to be lifted very high. If the fish is dropped or wiggles free, it does not have far to fall into the water.

move. But, oops! Dad hooked another fish. So, I had a decision to make. Stay, or run.

Rather than stay to fight the fish to exhaustion and net it, I pulled the anchor. My guy fighting the fish was good. He knew how much pressure he could put on a steelhead to bend it to his will without breaking the line.

This skill would be a requirement for what we were to do. A spunky steelhead can easily take ten to fifteen minutes to bring to net. We had about ninety seconds before the boat above us passed below our position to stop at the next run *I* wanted to fish. It was time to "walk the dog". I pushed us into the main current to do some multi-tasking. As my guest played his steelhead, I moved the boat toward our next destination, comfortably ahead of the charging boat in our pursuit.

A few minutes later, I dropped anchor at the periphery of the water we wanted to fish next. Everything went according to plan. (It doesn't always.) As we stopped at the next coveted fishing spot, I slipped out of the boat, landing net in hand. Just as the foreign boat passed, I gently cradled the bright buck before its release.

The gamble was worth it. A few casts later Dad hooked another steelhead in the new water. This was a fish, I believe, an angler in the other boat would have hooked if we had not taken a calculated chance to scoot down the river with the hooked steelhead in tow.

This all prompts me to wax on a bit about river etiquette. Everyone has their set of rules on steelhead rivers, a code of

behavior and "good" manners. If you are going to race someone to the next fishing hole, you have to do it with a comfortable cushion, and a certain degree of nonchalance. It's a rare occasion that I would pull out in front of another boat, making it too obvious that I was pushing hard to beat them to the next piece of water. That would be like cutting off someone in highway traffic. You must pull out with plenty of room to spare. Be casual, yet purposeful. I even try to be cordial to other anglers as they drift by us…especially as we net a fish as they pass.

If all this sounds a bit too aggressive, too greedy, then know that I am dedicated to do whatever it takes—within what I consider to be competitive decency—to give my clients and guests the very best opportunities to hook as many steelhead as possible in an eight-hour fishing day. It is what I would want if I were the client: maximum opportunities. Any good guide wants the same. However, a few of us play harder. I am willing to run a short slant pass pattern across the middle of the football field and take a crushing hit from the linebacker as I gather in the ball, even if it means getting knocked silly. My clients are appreciative fans.

You Can Never Have Too Many

Part of being consistently successful at steelheading is intimately knowing *numerous* good fish-holding locations. One or two are not enough. Anglers may be positioned in the heart of the water you want to fish when you arrive. Or, the river flow has raised or dropped and the fish have no interest in resting there. You had better have backup plans.

Prospecting for good fishing holes is time-consuming. Typically, anglers are too busy fishing old reliable haunts to discover new ones. Many times, I pray that an angler in a very well-known spot *will* catch a fish. They are trained, then, to stay there, and to return to that same spot with a hundred other anglers who would be in my way fishing other spots that I want to see vacant when I arrive. The occasional biting fish keeps them fishing, not exploring. Right on! "Hooked another one? Good for you!"

The search for quality Sweet Spots is work. The steelhead treasure may not be in a very obvious location. Many of the best are not. Any given riverine "silver mine" must be approached from a variety of angles (literally), with a variety of methods, under a variety of conditions, including water temperature, light intensity, and water level. I may fish a single steelhead run a dozen fruitless times until I unravel its mystery. It is very much like cracking a safe.

Sometimes I let someone else crack the safe for me. If I watch an angler playing a fish, I make a mental note of his exact position. I watch where they cast as they resume fishing the same spot. *How* they present their lure, bait, or fly is also valuable information.

The eye angled down confirms a live fish.

Some silver mines never produce. Some river runs look perfect to me: an excellent combination of current speed, depth and structure. Nevertheless, try as I might, diligent and repeated prospecting turns up nothing. Either the fish will not hold in these locations as I think they should, or the holding fish will not bite in these spots.

An author whom I cannot remember wrote in a book I cannot find about certain fish-holding runs on the North Umpqua River where steelhead would not bite. He knew they held in these runs because he could see them. As these same (apparently) fish moved upstream into other holding locations they *would* strike his fly. The biting and non-biting locales appeared

very similar as to their depth, current and structure. What accounted for the difference is open to speculation. My own experiences support this author's observations. For reasons not discernable to me, some runs that appear to be prime will never give up a steelhead to my strategies. After multiple worthy attempts to "strike silver", I will forgo spending any more fishing time here. I will only resume digging if I should chance upon another angling "miner" who shows me that silver can indeed be found at this location. And, occasionally,

Big fish can be found in small water.

it does happen. Until then, I am moving on in search of the Mother Lode elsewhere.

On the other hand, there are dependable fishing holes that do not appear to be anything special. In fact, these can be downright unlikely fish-holding areas. The water depth is too shallow or too deep for my liking, the current appears too fast or too slow, and no good submerged structure is obvious, even upon intense inspection. However, biting steelhead prefer it here. These particular places remind me that the steelhead, ultimately, make the rules, and can break the rules. It is with some degree of humility (but not too much) that I pause often to enable my clients to add to their store of steelhead-catching memories.

Old Dogs and Improved Tricks

I am thinking about a particular once-unlikely, big steelhead hole that I have grown fond of after many years of avoiding it. The water is too deep, the current too swirly. My boat is constantly being thrown out of position by an untamable, multi-directional current. It is maddening to fish here. Maddening, that is, until a client hooks a steelhead. Then, I'm liking it. As an added bonus, we are adjacent to a wonderful quiet-water expanse to fight, net and photograph fish. Though hooking steelhead here usually demands persistence, many anglers fished it. Occasionally I would see a fish landed, but rarely by a *fly*-fisherman. The successful anglers were using spinning rods in the deep swirling flows. Their thin fishing line allowed them to keep their bait or lures near the bottom, get a reasonable deep drift of their offering, and stay in tight line contact in order to set the hook in short order.

In addition, I had heard reliable stories of some skilled fly-fishers who could coax fish out of this obnoxious water. Spurred on by, and envious of, the success of others in this spot, I resigned/assigned myself to figure out the hydraulics of this water.

I learned to accept that at times my boat would be out of position, too close or too far from the fish. There would be times that a perfect drift of the fly would be unexpectedly swept from its intended path. Accept it. Often my anglers would miss a subtle strike in the turbulent water. I was forced to be even more precise than usual about my leader and flies setup, using a finer tippet and heavier flies. In short, the steelhead taught me the rules necessary to intrigue them to the point of taking the fly. An old dog with a little patience can always learn one more new trick. I will: work harder on the oars; alter the leader; change the flies; keep the faith; remember The Rules.

Now, roll over, Michael. Good boy!

The Search Never Ends

Sometimes, when I am able to overcome my Steelhead Fever for a while, I look for and fish spots I have not fished before, or I will fish unproven areas I *have* fished before but approach them from a different position in the stream. For instance, I may discover I get a better presentation and drift of the fly if I position myself on the left side of the suspected lie instead of the right side. Alternatively, I may position myself farther upstream or farther downstream than I normally would.

As the water, flows decrease in mid to late summer, the sweet spots change. An old reliable spot may no longer hold fish, or steelhead may prefer a different portion of the run. Areas where the water had been too deep or too swift may become prime holding locations at lower water. The same holds true when the water rises in the fall, winter or spring. Areas that were too shallow and slow in low water become prime as the river rises. If you realize these changes are natural courses of events you will make appropriate changes about where you fish at any given water level.

I much prefer spots where the water's surface is choppy or riffled, rather than glassy and flat. An angler can get closer to the fish for a more accurate and controlled presentation of his fly. Fish cannot easily see out through riffled water, so, within reason, an angler does not have to rely so heavily on stealth. Do be conscious of the color of the jacket or shirt you wear. While wearing bright red, white and yellow shirts or jackets, I *have* caught steelhead, but I now avoid these colors. I do not

Small tributary streams of major steelhead rivers may or may not be open to fishing. Where the stream flows into the river can be an excellent location to catch steelhead resting there to continue upriver or enter the tributary.

A narrow bottleneck on a small stream can be an excellent location for an angling ambush.

want to look back on my fishing day and wonder if we could have caught a steelhead, or more steelhead, if a guest had not insisted on wearing that bright yellow rain jacket. This potential "problem" is easily remedied before it becomes an issue.

If there is a long expanse of shallow, exposed water that the steelhead have to traverse as they migrate upstream, look for an oasis in the desert. Seek an area, often just a small pocket, of slightly deeper water where a fish will rest, feeling less exposed and threatened. Remember, the fish that have survived predators for their entire lives have done so because they are wary. They naturally seek safety. If they have had to swim through a substantial stretch of water that is two feet deep from bank to bank, a wary steelhead will often linger in that little depression that is four feet deep.

I am thinking of such a place on the North Santiam River. For almost 100 yards the steelhead have to migrate through water that varies from six inches to two feet deep. The flow is gin clear and the surface is glassy. Maximum exposure. On the right bank is a scoured depression near a ledge. Here is the oasis, a "deep-water" haven where the fish feel a bit more secure. When I position my boat just right—not too

far, not too close—I can stand on my rower's seat and see a resting fish without being seen. Because the pocket is small, I may quickly scan the spot to locate a holding steelhead. An adequate fly-caster can reach this pocket. You can imagine how exciting it is to watch a big fish move to strike the fly! Beware of Buck Fever—pulling the fly away from the fish as it approaches, or breaking it off with an overly enthusiastic setting of the hook.

I am thinking of another desert oasis on the South Santiam River where the lower reaches of the desert extend, again, at least the length of a football field. Flat, shallow water offers no hiding opportunities...until the steelhead approach The Rock. A very prominent midstream rock has a 3'-4' scour (depending on the water level) downstream and to each side of the big nugget. Above the rock, the desert continues to stretch upstream. So, The Rock acts as a fish magnet, prompting wary steelhead to rest and hide out for a while. Astute anglers stay far enough away to remain unseen, but close enough to cast into the deeper water.

Walking-speed current, 3-7 feet deep, and structure. Focus, find 'em, fish smart.

CHAPTER 5
Thoughts on Steelhead Flies

As I write this chapter,

I am wondering how many readers have skipped
most of what precedes, and come directly to this section of the book.
I myself might be tempted to do the same. It is no coincidence
that this is the longest chapter in the book.

Flies are fun. Flies are fascinating. Once an experienced angler has settled into his preferred equipment and methods, the one variable left that can be continually changed is the fly on the end of the line.

When "knowledgeable" steelheaders tell me the fly pattern is not of paramount importance, insisting that as long as the fly is convincingly presented, a willing steelhead will

A steelhead that ate a Hot Bead Assassin, a particularly effective fly in murky water.

eat it, they are partially correct. The single most important element in such cases are *suicidal* steelhead in the mood to attack anything. I pray for these fish but they do not seem very abundant in our heavily fished steelhead rivers. If these happen to be hatchery fish, they are quickly extracted from the population by the angling hordes. Those native fish that are released unharmed are educated not to bite too readily. What steelhead remain are wary by nature or training, and not so easily duped.

As a steelhead addict and fishing guide who spends more than 100 days in a calendar year in pursuit of steelhead, I gather much empirical data about these fish and their willingness to bite particular flies. I am motivated on two fronts: I personally want to catch fish when I put in my time, and my clients must have an excellent chance to hook a steelhead or two (or ten) if they will happily pony up my guide fee again and again. Simple math. No steelhead caught = No guiding business.

So, if a steelhead fly-rodder insists to me that the fly doesn't matter much, then I would only ask them to let *me* select the fly pattern for them to use, and invite them to a little contest. I would select something silly for them, like a Foam Ant. In fact, they can tie on a classic Green Butt Skunk or the fashionable Egg Sucking Leech, and we will go head to head for a day's fishing. Let the games begin!

Two anglers enter the arena. One angler leaves.

Useful Fish Groupings

As stated before, steelhead do not have to eat during their spawning migration, able to live comfortably utilizing the fat reserves created by the ocean's bounty. But, as the glutton at the buffet will testify, if a culinary temptation is placed in its path a steelhead will sometimes eat it. Some are more easily enticed than others. This leads me to classify steelhead into three arbitrary groups: *Suicidals, No Way/ No Hows* and *Fence Riders*.

Suicidals will eat anything, including that "Yellow & Purple Thing" tied on a rusty hook that has been hanging around in your fly box for years waiting for you to throw it in the trash. *Suicidals* are determined to make someone catch them, no matter what. Unfortunately, for most anglers, these individuals are in the extreme minority. Maybe one in fifty. Maybe one in a hundred. This rare breed does not swim for long in its spawning stream. Someone soon invites these fish home to be the "guest of honor" at a backyard BBQ.

While I crave suicidal steelhead, especially for my clients, these fish can mislead an angler. For a beginner or unthinking veteran, catching a few suicidal steelhead can tempt the angler (or guide) to believe that fly pattern and precise presentation are not so important. This prompts me to remember my guide friend Glenn who referred to steelhead as "stupid". (Yikes! I am concerned about the classification of my intellect when I fail to catch a steelhead when I know they are obstinately resting in the water I am fishing.) Suicidal fish can reinforce mediocre fishing behavior as the angler underestimates the attention to detail that is necessary to catch steelhead *consistently*. Be aware of this trap.

The *No Way/No Hows* are very common. With no imperative to eat, they don't. These fish are experts in discouragement. This group of fussy steelhead discourages many fly-fishers, returning them to angling exclusively for gullible trout for the remainder of their natural lives.

Fence Riders are the intriguing lot, and have much to teach the attentive and persistent. These are a much larger minority than the *Suicidals*. *Fence Riders* may grab a fly, but only after being coaxed and cajoled, courted and convinced. Stealth is important, as is presentation. The third key element is the fly pattern.

Because the migrating steelhead does not need to eat, you must appeal to or arouse something else in the fish. Without trying to ascribe human characteristics to the fish, it is helpful, I think, to speak of curiosity, territoriality, and defensive aggression. A steelhead *may* (just an educated guess) have these traits. These might explain why a *Fence Rider* may be enticed to take a fly.

In those situations where I am fishing to a reluctant *Fence Rider* I can actually see, and the only variable I have changed is my fly pattern, it tells me much about the appeal of that fly when the fish finally bites it. Or, if I fish through a proven stretch of productive steelhead water, getting no strikes, then go through again with a different fly and hook a fish, I have been granted an important clue. If you gather enough such clues over a span of more than twenty years, you cannot help but formulate about what *Fence Riders* might want, and what they do not. It is with this broad experience and experimentation that an astute steelhead angler can develop a stable of fly patterns that have proven themselves capable of knocking some reluctant steelhead off the fence.

In my experience, there are three significant characteristics of a properly presented fly that prompt a moody steelhead to bite: size, color, and intriguing (to the fish) materials. Let's take each one at a time.

Sorry, fellas, size *is* important. And, when in doubt, smaller is better. Steelhead have tremendous eyesight, having little trouble spying your tiny fly in clear water when it is five or six feet from them. They might not eat it, but they see it. Where a big fly may startle or alarm a fish, a small fly can often intrigue it. This is one of the reasons I suspect egg patterns are so effective. Not so much that they imitate edible fish eggs, but because they are small. Size can have inhibition-overriding appeal.

Strange Steelhead Eye Candy

Fish can distinguish color. They might not see green exactly as we see green but they can perceive color differences. Steelhead can definitely show preferences for a certain color or colors in fly patterns. I have caught steelhead on flies that are predominantly black, brown, pink, red, orange, green, purple, chartreuse, tan, straw, and colors I have forgotten. A *Fence Rider* may show a willingness to strike at one, several, or none of these colors.

James Phillips, age 10. My youngest guest to ever hook, play, and land a steelhead without help.

The Veiled Assassin can be fished dead-drift or swung like a wet fly.

The Greenback Hare's Ear is both buggy and flashy.

The Gorman Bead Egg is an exceptional steelhead producer throughout the year, and also accounts for many fish hooked as the fly swings across the current. Go figure.

At this point, let me say that I know well that an angler tends to catch more steelhead with fly colors he favors. If you never fish a purple pattern you may assume that purple is not a worthy color. If you only fish pink, then pink is the best fish-catching color in your universe. This is one of the reasons I usually fish two flies of different colors simultaneously when steelheading. One of the colors is a proven favorite in which I have high confidence, while the other may be an unproven or unlikely color that I am granting another trial to prove its worth.

For me the strangest color for appeal to my eye that ever caught a steelhead is tan/straw. Jim Teeny of Gresham, Oregon, and originator of the Teeny Nymph, invited me to fish the Sandy River, east of Portland. Though he has a garage full of flies which he wholesales to retail stores, Jim had not a single fly in his vest when we arrived at our fishing destination. Not having ever caught a steelhead on a Teeny Nymph I was hoping to do so. I had plenty of my own ties but it would not quite be the same.

Lady Luck smiled. Jim ran into one of his fishing friends on the river who gladly shared some of the Teeny Nymphs he had personally created. Teeny picked through some sizes and colors he surmised might work, and we were on our way.

Of all the colors he had to select from, Jim handed me a size 4 straw-colored nymph to tie on my leader. His first choice would have been my last choice, but he was the "guide" and I was the obliging guest.

Besides knowing the Sandy River intimately, Jim also has excellent eyesight. He has a knack for spotting fish. As we got into position at the chosen spot, Jim climbed onto a huge rock to peer into the river's depths. Soon he spied three holding fish near the far side of the river. Joining him atop his stony perch, I was unable to make out the quarry, even as he pointed to the precise area with his rod tip. No matter. I jumped from the rock, waded into the river, and positioned myself where Jim directed.

After a couple of false casts, I slung the heavy sink-tip fly line upstream of the intended target, allowing the fly to sink near the bottom as it approached the area where the steelhead lay. After less than a dozen casts, my line stopped in the current. Setting the hook, I was fast into a sprinting steelhead that had eaten the straw-colored Teeny Nymph. I was pleasantly surprised.

After a photo session with the native buck, I released it from frozen hands. Though I would have loved to cast for a second fish, I invited my host to step into the run and try his luck. As I recall Jim had tied on a black fly. Repeatedly he put it out into the same current line where I had found my fish. Shortly he hooked a fish. He played it skillfully, put it on the beach, and we had a second photo session.

My turn again. Sparing you any more dramatic descriptive prose…I hooked and landed another steelhead on the straw Teeny Nymph. Incredible. Unless my two fish were both *Suicidals* willing to hit anything, I learned that whether or not a fly color has eye appeal for me is totally irrelevant to the appeal found in a steelhead's eye. Be willing to experiment.

As for intriguing fly-tying materials, steelhead like rubber legs, colored wire, marabou, rabbit fur, metallic beads, and all sorts of pearlescent strands, to name some. There are endless mix-and-match possibilities in creating flies with these effective materials, and creative fly-tiers discover new materials constantly. Subtle changes in materials can be significant. Out

One of the downside risks of fishing two flies.

of a myriad of possibilities, I will relate a couple of stories from the summer and fall of 2009.

My nephew Mark is an enthusiastic and skilled steelhead nympher. We fished together several times each year. Mark ties many of his own flies. Because he did not have the peacock feathers needed for the tail of one of our steelhead nymphs, Mark substituted strands of green tinsel. Everything else about the fly was exactly the same. Over the course of four days fishing together, Mark's version of the nymph was the clear winner. Though four days is not a long time frame, we hooked more than twenty steelhead, the majority of which took the fly with the green tinsel tail.

When spawning salmon are in steelhead rivers, the eggs that are set adrift during egg-laying activities are tasty tidbits. Subsequently, egg imitations are effective for catching steelhead. During weeks of guided fall fishing in 2009, my Bead Egg flies—tied with pink chenille and strands of pearlescent mylar incorporated into them—were distinctively more effective than those flies tied with standard chenille. Most of my guided trips involve two anglers in my boat. I would rig one angler with the standard Bead Egg, the other with the mylar in the body of the fly. Both patterns caught fish, but the mylar variation definitely hooked more steelhead.

Now, let me issue a little caveat. This year's most effective flies may not be next year's All Stars. How steelhead preferences in the same river can change year to year is a mystery to me. However, I have seen this phenomenon numerous times over three decades.

Just as it is with people, preferences can vary among individual steelhead. Different individual fish may bite one fly, while ignoring ten others. Experimenting with new flies, or creating them if you are a fly-tier, adds greatly to the enjoyment of our sport.

A Guide Story: Steelhead Sudden Suicidal Syndrome, or SSSS

Clients Ken and Dave were fishing with me on the Santiam River. This was a trout-fishing trip for two old school chums who had not seen each other since the elementary grades decades ago. Fishing was good and the weather perfect, the reunion pleasant and memorable.

In early afternoon, the sun was high in a cloudless sky. Our short shadows were directly downstream of us as my anchor found purchase on the river bottom, holding us securely in place to fish a section of water replete with boulders and fish-holding scours. After only a few casts from our new fishing position, I watched in amazement as a bright steelhead of about 28" darted to and tracked Dave's swinging soft-hackle trout fly. As the fly swept a large arc, from 45 degrees across to straight downstream, this incredible fish kept its nose within a few inches of the fly. Though obviously intrigued, the steelhead refused to bite the fly. When it lost interest the fish settled into a resting position about two rod lengths directly downstream of the boat, nestled among some large boulders.

Though the fish was quite near the boat, we were in direct line with the sun as the fish looked in our direction. The sun's glare, I surmise, masked our presence to some degree. The fish acted as if it could not see us. All of us could watch the fish and its every move.

After repeated futile casts with the soft hackle, the finning steelhead showed only faint interest. I suggested to Dave that he put down the soft-hackle rod, and pick up another with a Prince Nymph tied on it. As he started to strip line into the current with the nymph rod, I was busy giving him a few simple instructions to present the Prince to the steelhead. Foremost among these was to set the hook gently, since the size-14 nymph was secured to a 5X (!) tippet. If the fish is hooked, Dave needed to let it run with a minimum of tension, lest the leader be parted. I was concerned that if I took the necessary time to change the leader or tippet the fish would eventually see us and move on. Time, I assumed, was of the essence.

Swinging the Prince on a tight line above the steelhead's face garnered only a slight change in the steelhead's activity. Several times, it turned its head slightly to study the nymph's journey as it swam overhead. Interest soon waned.

New strategy. With a couple of removable split shot a foot above the Prince to sink it more deeply, I suggested to Dave that he flip the fly into the current beside the boat, pull it slightly as it sank to get it to drift almost underneath the boat, in a direct current line with the fish's position. This is a clumsy maneuver even for a skilled nymph fisher, but Dave managed the feat as well as needed. Because it was impossible to watch the drift of the small fly in its journey, I stayed focused on the steelhead, watching its movements.

During one drift, I watched the large fish open its mouth as it turned its head slightly to one side. Certain that the steelhead had taken the nymph I yelled politely for Dave to set the hook. There is always a reaction delay when one angler screams to elicit a response from another. Dave was too late. As he lifted the rod tip smartly to the vertical, I could see the fly lifted from the water right at the fish's location. There was no doubt that the fish had taken the fly. Unbelievably, the steelhead held its position in spite of all the commotion in the boat. This foolish individual was determined to be hooked!

After all the adrenalin-high parties settled down, including the guide, I gave Dave one more instruction. "Be prepared to set the hook," if the guide yells softly "Set the hook!" Another dozen casts or so I watched the steelhead open its mouth twice in very quick succession, revealing its very visible white interior. The order went out and Dave responded perfectly. The rod came up solidly and stayed bent. We all watched as the steelhead began to swing its head left and right, left and right, trying to shake the tiny hook from its jaw.

I am sure the sentiment in the boat was unanimous at this time: Dave was not going to land this large steelhead on a 5X tippet secured on a 5-weight trout rod. The odds were long, but this *was* a suicidal steelhead.

We anchored at the boundary of very fast shallow water and slower deep water on our left and directly below us. The game would quickly end if the steelhead would zoom out a short distance into midstream and turn down the river with current, headed for swift rapids that would carry the fish to certain freedom. The fish bolted to midstream, just as anyone would suppose the fish would instinctively do. However, instead of turning downstream with the flow, the determined-to-be-caught steelhead turned to run *upstream*. I could not have scripted the events better. The fish would expend much of its precious energy by swimming against the strong current. As long as the fish did not strip off more than the entire length of the fly line plus 50 yards of braided Dacron backing, Dave merely needed to keep a little tension on the line and let the steelhead go where it willed to go.

The longer the fish persisted in fighting the current the more tired, and manageable, it would become. Each passing minute would decrease the odds a bit that the fish would escape. When the fish made its eventual downstream move, Dave was ready. The plan was to increase the tension in the line if the fish came back downstream, leading it gently in our direction into quieter water. If the fish could be coaxed to us without breaking the line, I would lift the anchor, then row the boat to the left bank and down into the backwater "lake" below our position, well inside the rapids on the right side of the river.

The script played out just as I would have written it. The exhausted fish finally turned down river, Dave steered it toward the boat, and I moved the boat to quiet water. Liking walking a dog on a leash.

Dave masterfully led the steelhead into the quiet water. If we were going to have a chance to net the fish, Dave and I would need to get out of the boat. We managed to do so without the fish parting company. Several tense times the steelhead ran away to the very edge of the swift water, but the angler was up to the task. Taking the rod tip low and applying good tension Dave was able to bring the fish back from the brink twice. He exhibited great patience and a willingness to take directions. These paid great dividends as I slid the 28" 9-pound steelhead into the net!

What a great memory. None of us will ever forget the tremendous, foolish steelhead that was determined to be caught. Dave flew that hatchery fish from Oregon to his home in New Mexico, where it was the "honored guest" at a BBQ party. No doubt, the Great Battle was recounted several times for the dining guests.

Wet Flies

A wet fly is a pattern fished subsurface, at a depth ranging from a couple of inches beneath the surface all the way down to the river's bottom. Generally, cast the fly slightly upstream, or slightly downstream, from straight across the current flow. Mend the fly line to slow the drift of the fly. Inevitably, the fly swings on a tight line across the current. I prefer to let it swing to a point directly below me, letting the fly hold stationary

A snowy backdrop for this photo, January on the Siletz River.

in the current for a count of ten. I, then, lengthen my line, or move my position downstream slightly, to cast again.

Depending on the light intensity, water temperature, and mood of the steelhead, I make a determination of the size, color and design of the wet fly. In dim light, summer temperatures, I gravitate toward black and purple wet flies. In summer and fall's mid-day light, I like various combinations of red, orange and white. In the cold water of winter and spring, I prefer brighter colors, especially pink and chartreuse green. Any time the water is murky, I want a larger hook—one or two sizes—and often add a bit more flash and, perhaps, an orange bead at the head.

Wet-Fly Designs

There has been an evolution in steelhead fly design over my thirty-plus years of pursuing these fish. Virtually all the fly-anglers I knew or read about used what I will refer to as a West Coast Standard wet-fly design. The prototypical, West Coast wet fly has a tail of feather fibers, a rather slim body of one or two colors, ribbing spiraled over the body, a hair wing, and a soft feather hackle. There are literally thousands of mix-and-match combinations of colors and materials used in tying the modern "standard" steelhead fly. Well-known examples of this design include the Skunk, Purple Peril, Green Butt Skunk, and Thor.

The use of feather tips as wet-fly wings instead of calf tail, arctic fox, bucktail or elk hair makes for an effective pattern. The Silver Hilton is probably the best-known example. This barred gray wing, hackle and tail, with a predominantly black body looks drab compared to many of the glitzy, colorful designs. However, this plain sister without makeup is a steelhead killer.

When in doubt, select a wet fly, especially the classic standards, that is thinner rather than fatter. I cannot always separate aesthetics from effectiveness, but I, also, prefer natural or synthetic furs for the body instead of yarn or chenille. However, I do like the mylar highlights and multicolor mixes of glitter chenille and New Age chenille. The halo and sparkle of

furs seem to hold greater appeal for the steelhead. And, new fly designs crop up periodically, employing old materials in new ways.

Another wet-fly design that has served me well is the Spey. Spey flies grew in popularity in the 1970's and 1980's. Long, soft feathers from geese, pheasants, ducks and guinea fowl are added to favorite standard wet flies to produce a lively underwater movement and enticing silhouette. These flowing fibers often extend way beyond (behind) the bend of the hook. Popular steelhead Spey flies are usually tied on larger 1/0-3/0 hooks, much larger than 2, 4, 6, and 8 hook sizes of the

The Green Butt Skunk Spey fly with its long marabou hackle is a pattern that has fish-attracting colors and maximum lifelike movement in the water.

standard steelhead wet fly. Steelhead like them, and they look really cool in my fly box.

Though I am sure they were tied and used before the 1980's, it was in this decade that more and more steelhead anglers started using simple marabou designs. If you are a fly tier, the materials—primarily marabou feathers—are relatively inexpensive, and flies are quick to tie. And, they catch fish. There is no material quite like soft marabou feathers for conveying lifelike movement as they slowly drift in the current. Like the Spey designs, these, too, were usually tied on oversized hooks. Steelhead will either run from these big flies or viciously attack them.

Popular leech flies tied with strips of rabbit fur used for fishing trout, found their way into steelheader fly boxes. Today, the typical steelhead leech design has a heavy cone head at the hook eye, a long rabbit-fur body accented with a few strands of mylar, and a trailing stinger hook at the rear. Like the steelhead marabou patterns, these large flies are inexpensive and quick to tie, ideal for the fly tier. Rabbit fur, like marabou, has lots of movement as it swims in the current towards a waiting, willing fish.

Currently the Intruder is the rage among wet-fly anglers. This is a very large fly, tied sparsely with lively materials that swim seductively in the current. Long ostrich and rhea feathers give the Intruder life and an intriguing silhouette. At first glance, the fly's construction seems simple. However, to produce effective movement and the desired silhouette, meticulous care must be taken to achieve the right "look" during the tying process. However, tying them is worth the effort. They catch lots of steelhead throughout the entire year.

Part of the thinking behind employing a large fly is that it will evoke a very aggressive strike by a steelhead drawn to this type of artificial—big fly, big strike. And, there may be something to this thinking, especially since a steelhead knows it might have to utilize maximum strength and speed to drive off such a large "intruder" invading its personal space or trying to harm the fish. If you get seriously involved with fishing wet flies for steelhead, especially when using a two-handed rod, you will encounter Intruder patterns because of their popularity.

These large steelhead flies can be both heavy and air-resistant when cast, and are very difficult and tiring to present on a single-hand rod. More and more steelhead fly-fishers are discovering the superiority of casting such flies on a two-handed rod. Besides greater casting distance and line control, longer rods more easily propel leech and Intruder flies to their intended targets. If you insist on casting a five-inch waterlogged, cone-head Rabbit Leech with a nine-foot rod, a hockey goalie mask is an excellent choice for headgear.

For the most part, commonly used wet flies seem to fall into one of the above designs, or a hybrid combining features and materials from several types. As examples, you may find a Silver Hilton Spey fly, or a Skunk with feather-tip wings. Ostrich, marabou, and rabbit strips can be combined on the same hook, producing all sorts of exotic steelhead leeches. Colorful mylar strands to complement the fly have been popular additions to many, many patterns since the 1980's. Glitzy strands are usually added to the tail, wing, or along the body, as the fly is tied. When mylar strands are used in my fly ting, my preference is to use it sparingly. More is not necessarily better.

I Do Not Mean to Intrude, But…

Jason Mariner is a twenty-something steelhead junkie. He has all the desirable characteristics of a fishing Young Gun: high energy, athleticism, an open schedule, determination, discipline, creativity, resourcefulness, excellent fly-fishing skills, experience, all the right gear, passion, and a willingness to pay the price to seek out steelhead anywhere at any time. He is a tremendously strong wader who will cross a river where it cannot be crossed. I know him well. He is one of my all-star former OSU students. Jason guides for me, and we fish together often. In January 2010, he landed more than 100 steelhead. This is more steelhead than most anglers land in ten seasons; he did it in a month. Moreover, he is not a one-trick pony fishing just one river he knows well. He is all over the map on the Oregon coast.

Because of cool, sometimes frigid, winter water temperatures, Jason naturally gravitates to the nymph fishing method for catching steelhead, fishing a dead-drifted egg imitation near the river bottom. It is this fly-fishing method that allows him to rack up such outrageous numbers. However, as you might imagine, from time to time Jason looks for a more challenging way—outside of skating dry flies—to entice winter steelhead. He is looking for the Big Tug moment when a big steelhead slams his fly on a tight line. For his wet fly of choice, he usually fishes Intruder flies, cast on his two-hand rod. To ensure he is able to resist resorting to his effective nymph-fishing methods during a slow day, he leaves that gear at home, to focus solely on the wet fly.

A huge part of steelheading success is knowing where the fish are. A second piece of the success formula is choosing the right river with the best conditions for the fly-fishing method you choose. Through study and experience, Jason is the master of being on the right river at the right water level. My point here is that when Jason takes up the two-hand rod to fish wet flies he is casting over fish, during very good fishing conditions. He is fishing proven steelhead-holding areas with which he is intimately familiar.

Even during ideal conditions, skillfully casting over steelhead, Jason can get skunked fishing wet flies, winter or summer. However, any time he resorts to fishing his hook under an indicator with a floating fly line, he is going to catch fish. Most of the time it's multiple fish; sometimes his tally for the day can be double digits!

While it may cause many steelhead to flee for cover, the Intruder flies were designed to elicit arm-wrenching strikes from the most aggressive fish.

Wet fly-fishing for winter steelhead can be done successfully. However, even skilled, experienced anglers can be shut out, even under excellent fishing conditions on quality rivers. If you choose the wet-fly route in the winter, even with effective patterns like the Ed Ward's Intruder, be prepared for the possibility of few or no strikes in a long fishing day. Even The Magic Fly—whatever you think it to be—is sometimes not enough, even in skilled, experienced hands. Beginners or inexperienced steelhead wet-fly anglers need to know this, to be psychologically prepared for skunk days, days without a strike, especially in the cold months of late fall, winter and early spring. If even 100-steelhead-landed-in-January Jason Mariner cannot coax them to the wet fly, I truly believe few other anglers—if any—could do better on that day on that river.

Many times, fly pattern matters, being the thin-line difference that separates success from a skunk day. An Intruder design can be the difference. Other days, the key is an aggressive fish willing to smash anything invading its Personal Space. Therefore, an Intruder, leech, Veiled Assassin, or an orange gob of fur on a hook will work equally well when swung in front of that suicidal steelhead. Here comes the hard yank on the end of the line!

If you live for the hard strike, wet flies fished on a tight line are the way to go. The rhythm of the casting stroke and the satisfaction of shooting a smooth, long line can add to the fishing enjoyment. The warm-water months will find you with active fish often willing to pursue a wet fly. This method is crazy effective on the summer and fall steelhead of Oregon's Deschutes or North Umpqua rivers. If you have the patience and special psyche, you can be successful in the colder seasons, too.

Dry Flies

I continue to be baffled. Every time I see an adult steelhead, a fish that does not need to eat during its spawning migration, surface to inhale a skating dry fly, I watch in disbelief. What is this fish thinking? Why would it rise from the bottom in six feet of water to intercept a waking tidbit the fish may not have an appetite for, and certainly does not need to consume for its survival?

Though I cannot understand the reasons why it entices steelhead to act foolish, I relish raising them on dry flies. Many other fly-anglers do too. I know a few who dedicate themselves almost exclusively to surface flies for steelhead, putting aside, or even disdaining, the use of wet flies or nymphs.

There are exceptions to every rule, but I have found that surface-striking steelhead can be best enticed when the sun is not directly on their water. This means early or late in the day, areas shaded by trees or high banks, or overcast sky conditions.

Purple Bomber dry fly. This is a dangerous fly for those with weak hearts.

Water temperatures that range from 50 to 65 degrees Fahrenheit produce the biggest numbers of fish willing to come to the top. Holding locations where the water's moving surface is smooth, unriffled—like tailouts—allow for a steady, even presentation of the fly without sinking it. The point here is to be selective about the where and when you fish dry flies.

It is not unheard of to hook steelhead with a dead-drifted dry fly. I know of a former guide on Oregon's North Umpqua River who made this method his specialty. In this, he took great pleasure. So, it was this dark art in which he schooled his fishing clients. I had the pleasure of fishing with this man for part of a day in mid-summer years ago. At that time, he had quit guiding for hire.

Experienced steelhead anglers and guides know that these fish do not always strike. In fact, it is amazing that steelhead bite as often as they do. Every guide knows there will be days where he will do his best but his clients will not land a fish. The paying customers may not even hook a fish. These tend to be long, emotionally draining days for a guide. Too often, a good steelhead guide will get all the blame on a fishless day, even when he has done his best and fished overtime. So it goes.

A worse scenario for the guide is being blamed when the fault of a no-fish-landed day lies squarely on the client. The guide enables his guest to make contact with a striking steelhead only to have the angler miss the strike, pull the fly away from the fish, set the hook too late, or break the line during the battle. A guided client through inexperience, impatience, or bad luck may lose one or several steelhead, and, at day's end, blame the guide! For me this will be a one-time client… one way or another.

Nick the Guide in this story told me about his last day as a guide. He worked hard all day with a client of mediocre skills and unappreciative attitude. Nick put the guy in position twice during their outing in which a steelhead engulfed a dead-drifting Humpy dry fly. From my perspective as a steelhead guide and angler, this is an amazing feat. *Dead-drift* dry fly! The client biffed both opportunities—his fault, not the guide's. However, at the end of the fishing day the client let it be known he was not pleased, having not landed a single fish. The rare opportunity to watch two steelhead in the same day rise to a dry fly was totally lost on him. Not only was he unappreciative, he was unhappy. Nick was already on the brink of quitting guiding. This day pushed him over the edge.

Most steelhead dry-fly specialists skate their flies. Common sense says that a fly that creates a surface-disturbing wake will draw the attention of more steelhead than a natural-drifting floating fly. The number one problem the angler will encounter is keeping the fly from sinking, especially if the water's surface is choppy. The fly-tying materials and design are critical to keep the artificial afloat.

As an artificial fly is skated on the river's current, it is *usually* the tail and hackle, or beard, of the fly that support it.

In the more "classic" style of modern steelhead dry flies, the Humpy is a good example. The tail is moose hair. The body is mostly deer or elk. Elk or calf tail make up the wing. The hackle is composed of very stiff, high-quality dry-fly rooster feathers. Two or three hackle feathers are used to maximize floatability.

In fly patterns like the Bomber, the hackle feathers are palmered over the length of the body, rather than being spiraled tightly in a grouping at the front of the fly. This design relies heavily on having the body of the fly support it on the water. Deer or caribou hair, which is spun and trimmed, are employed. Because this design tends to ride lower in the water, a single, forward-leaning "wing" assists in floating the fly, and enhances the wake created by the fly as it tracks across the current on a tight line.

For steelhead dry flies in general, the body and wing should be tied with water-resistant materials. The construction of the tail and hackle (or beard) is critical to sustained floatability and "skateability". Moose body hair has proven to be the best material for these. In addition to being water resistant, it is stiff. This stiffness allows the fly to plane on the surface as it is pulled tight against the current.

I got my introduction to effective dry-fly fishing on British Columbia's Babine River. There the guides my friends and I employed for our week's fishing showed us simple, almost crude skaters constructed solely of moose hair fashioned on a hook. There is no hackle or beard. The fly had a tail, body, wing, and stiff, semicircular "face". The face is created from the trimmed forward ends of the hair used to form the wings. Fashion the face into a semicircle by applying fly-tying head cement or rubber-based adhesive. The stiffened face creates a magnified wake that steelhead seemed to love. The single, forward-leaning wing on patterns like the Bomber may serve the same purpose.

The effectiveness of the B.C. Stiff Upper Lip, a name I find more flattering than that used by the guides there, indicated to me that color, shape and precision fly-tying methods were, apparently, not the most important features of a dry fly that steelhead find most attractive. Rather, a fly that maintains its skating mode and creates a great wake on the surface are most important.

Nymphs and Egg Patterns

Fishing a sunken fly slowly along the stream bottom for steelhead is growing in popularity as anglers discover its effectiveness. The exploding plethora of steelhead nymphs and egg patterns confirms this. When the water temperature is less than 50 degrees, a well-presented nymph or egg will seriously outfish dries and wets.

Unlike the statement I made about how nonspecific and imprecise, *in general*, my dry flies are, my nymph patterns must be much more precise. The design, color, glitter (or lack thereof), and size can all be extremely important.

While I prefer to use a large hook to hold and land a big fish, I am amazed at how small flies, at times, are most

Stonefly nymphs are a staple in any summer steelhead nympher's fly box.

attractive to steelhead. Sometimes these small hooks are bent straight as a fish escapes, but at least the steelhead was enticed to strike after refusing larger fare. When you finally land an eight-pound fish on a size-14 hook, it's a proud feat. Though I've seen it hundreds (yes, it's true) of times, I always find it incredible that a big fish, which does not need to eat during its spawning run, finds fascination in such small flies that drift into their visual zone.

As for materials, "buggy" dubbing furs, such as hare's ear Angora goat, and "lively" feathers such as peacock, partridge and mottled hen back, have proven themselves as attractive to steelhead. Thin rubber legs, metallic beads, wire, and various pearlescent and metallic mylar strands can enhance the attractiveness of a fly pattern. My preference is to use glitter and flash sparingly, not overdressing with these materials. I definitely use them, but not to the extremes I see employed in many current patterns. When I tie flies, less is better.

As with my wet flies and Victoria's Secret models, "thin is in". I don't care for fat, blocky flies. Part of this is due to my personal sense of aesthetics, while the balance results from my observations that this seems to be the preference of many nymph-caught steelhead. Given the exact same steelhead nymph tied on the exact same hook model and size, I will always choose, within reason, skinny over adipose. Though the dirigible-esque fly may catch steelhead, I believe I can entice a greater number with the anorexic rendition. One man's opinion…

In presenting nymphs and egg patterns, I want the flies near the bottom. Incorporating weight into or onto the fly is important. Lead wire wound on the hook underneath the body as the fly is tied adds weight. Lead dumbbell eyes or metal beads placed on the hook at or near the hook eye serve to sink the fly.

Because it is not possible to tie enough weight onto or into small (sizes 10, 12, 14) nymphs, these are best fished with a larger, heavy pattern. When fishing a small fly and large fly in tandem—like a G. G. Stonefly Nymph and Flashback Hare's Ear—the larger, heavily weighted fly serves to sink the smaller, lightly weighted pattern.

Though it may sound counterintuitive, I use a floating fly line for nymph fishing. A standard sinking fly line or sinking-tip may get my fly to the bottom, but I do not have good contact with the fly as it drifts deep with the current. When a steelhead intercepts a fly, it holds it a very brief time, perhaps less than a second. Any time the line hesitates, set the hook immediately. The submerged curves and coils naturally created in a drifting sunken fly line delay an indication the fish has taken the fly. In fact, I am sure many strikes would go completely undetected. This hesitation in the line when the nymph is intercepted by the steelhead is best revealed with a floating, brightly colored fly line. When the fly line deviates from its normal drift in the current the hook must be immediately set. A strike indicator on the leader also serves as an excellent visual clue that a fish has grabbed the fly.

Barbed vs. De-barbed Hooks

The simple argument for using a hook with a barb on it is that an angler has a greater chance of landing a fish because, once penetrated, the "holding power" of the barb makes the chance of escape less likely. At face value, this sounds reasonable. But, as the Devil's Advocate, let me pose a question in the form of a gruesome analogy: If a competent professional was to give you an injection with a hypodermic needle, which would slide into your arm easier and deeper with less effort—a standard, sleek, deadly-sharp needle, or the same needle with a pronounced barb on it? This question has nothing to do with the *removal* of the needle, only its entry. Instinctively we know the barbless option makes for easier, deeper penetration with the same force applied. Some extra force would be required to get the same penetration with the barbed needle. My point is that you can get a deeper, easier penetration of a de-barbed hook than a barbed one when the same force is applied. My contention is that the potential for deeply hooking *more* fish lies with the barbless or de-barbed hook. More fish hooked deeply with less force required trumps the holding ability of the barbed hook.

Additionally, since many of us are concerned about the safe release of native fish, or those hatchery ones we choose not to keep, a de-barbed hook is MUCH easier to dislodge from the steelhead. To drive this point home (no intended pun) I pose another question to my unconvinced students and clients: As you try to subdue a thrashing fish, struggling to dislodge a stubborn barbed hook from the fish's mouth, what is your natural, though perhaps unconscious, tendency as you attempt to control the panicked steelhead in your hands? Answer: You squeeze it; you naturally tighten your grip. Even though the fish may swim away when you let it go after a wrestling match, serious damage to its internal organs may soon kill it. That little croaking or gurgling sound emitted by

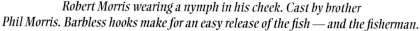

Robert Morris wearing a nymph in his cheek. Cast by brother Phil Morris. Barbless hooks make for an easy release of the fish — and the fisherman.

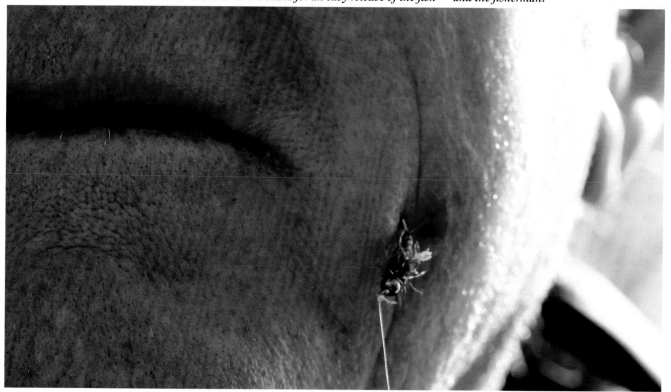

the fish as you held it too tightly could have signaled a serious injury. In addition, there is always the possibility of external injury. Rough handling, or the abrasion from a hard nylon net bag, can remove a significant amount of the slime covering the fish's body. The slime serves as a protective barrier against water-borne diseases. One of the natural defenses of the steelhead is temporarily removed.

More Terrifying Than a Visit to the Dentist

Every fisherman has stories about himself or a companion being stuck in some interesting location by a hook. It is statistically fascinating how many of these tales involve an ear. In fact one of the best photos I ever had escape me involved a client's ear.

Every fall the Cooper brothers—Andrew and Matt—fish the Rogue with me. They are both excellent anglers, and always entertaining as they banter and chide each other, as brothers are prone to do. Most of the time, the verbal exchanges are good-natured, even supportive or complimentary. But every now and then one sibling will express a little irritation with the other, especially where the heart of the matter involves a lost fish, tangled lines, or one brother being struck or hooked by the other's fly. The incident I am specifically recalling had Matt in the front of my boat, and Andrew in the rear on a warm fall morning. After dropping my anchor very near some likely water I sat back in my rower's seat to watch and coach.

We were only a few casts into this particular spot when Matt let out a loud "Aaaaaahh!" Matt would insist I tell you it was a *manly* startled yell, not the high-pitched scream of a little girl. That being said, when the cause of the excitement was examined we discovered Matt's right ear lobe pierced almost dead center with a size-12 nymph. The hook point easily and cleanly penetrated the lobe in such a manner that the fly hung perfectly, like an earring. Blood instantly appeared, slowly dripping down the lobe.

In a heartbeat, I recognized a great photo opportunity. My challenge, however, would be to get Matt's consent. As I closely examined the intrusion, Matt made it very clear he wanted the fly removed NOW! He was agitated and insistent—in a manly way, of course—to the degree I dared not ask him to wait while I messed with my camera settings. I sensed that such a request might have been like throwing gasoline on a fire, so I refrained. The fact that I was laughing—just a little—would not have aided my case. Bypassing one of the most interesting hooked-man photos of my career, I promptly locked my forceps on the barbless fly, and slid it without resistance from Matt's ear. Fortunately, a fistfight did not ensue, in part due to the fact that I was seated between a smiling—but apologetic—Andrew and his injured brother. In such cases, to insist that you are smiling or laughing *with* the injured, not *at* them, is not only quite unfitting, but the explanation has a snowball's chance in hell of being accepted as sincere. However, for the unhooked to restrain their amusement is much like trying hard not to laugh in church when your friend loudly passes gas. It can't be done.

On another occasion, I actually had to abort early a guided father-and-son fishing trip on the North Santiam River. Among other things, what this means is the guide cannot expect to be paid for a full fishing day; the right thing to do is prorate the fee. Because the hooked client insisted on going to seek immediate medical care instead of letting me tear the barbed hook out of his finger with my forceps, we lost about half of our fishing day, and me about half of my day's pay.

The mishap occurred when the son insisted he tie on a pattern from his fly box that the son had tied. What I failed to do was ensure that the barb was crimped; it was not. I should have checked, but didn't. Subsequently, when Dad was hooked the fly was not easily budged, so the trip ended. Though many people (and anglers) fear a trip to the dentist or doctor more than anything, I truly believe the fear of someone yanking a small barbed hook from their flesh trumps dentist drills and doctor needles.

I Thought *You* Did!

I have one story about being personally hooked I make sure to always tell students in my OSU classes. Most of my guided clients have endured this one, too. It was another incident on a summer day on southern Oregon's Rogue River with clients Paul Botts and Chuck Frank.

Events began to unfold when Chuck, fishing in the rear of my boat, hooked a steelhead. The hot fish escaped when it broke the tippet, taking the fly with it. I asked Chuck if he had another of the same fly that was lost to the fish. He did not, so I hurriedly handed him the same size-12 nymph from my personal fly box. Just as I did, Paul, standing in the bow of the boat, hooked a steelhead. He excitedly asked for his friend Chuck to come to the front of the boat to assist him, so Chuck hastily tied on his new fly and began to move forward.

In his haste, Chuck attempted to lay his fly rod horizontall along the left gunnel (side) of my boat. The commotion-caused movement in the boat resulted in the rod and the expensive reel on it to begin their fall toward the bottom of the boat. Not wanting to see the reel scratched or seriously dinged upon impact, I reached for the falling rod. As I grabbed the rod, the new fly dangling on the line was also enclosed in my hand. The hook point stung me seriously so I instinctively released my grip, only to find that the hook buried itself in my middle finger pulled in deeply by the falling weight of the rod and reel. Chuck *inadvertently* made sure the hook had penetrated my finger all the way to the body of the fly when he reached out to grab the rod when he saw my trouble. There is no doubt his intentions were good, but the result was "disconcertingly exciting" to me.

Once we put some slack in the line to take the tension off the fly in my finger, I literally chewed the leader to cut the fly free from the system. Then I gave a serious tug on the fly with the fingers of my uninjured hand. There was no hint of dislodging the fly. A second harder pull had the same result. So, I asked Chuck "Did you crimp the barb on this fly?" His reply: "No." I thought you did!" Hmmmmmm. Paul continued excitedly seeking assistance, trying to control the jumping steelhead.

I dropped the anchor to stop the drifting boat so I could fully appreciate the chaos. As Chuck and Paul focused on the fish, I laid out a quick plan of action. I knew exactly what needed to be done. In light of the fact I was not going to prematurely end our fishing day, my plan was simple. I reached for the forceps dangling from my vest pocket.

I will digress for a moment before the climax of my story to tell you that if you take too long to carry out a potentially painful plan of action there is the possibility you will lose your resolve. As you continue to ponder, your courage may wander. Act quickly *and decisively*. Do what needs to be done.

With the forceps in my right hand, I locked it onto the fly buried in the tip of my middle finger of the left. Knowing with certainty I did not want to attempt this twice, this hook was absolutely going to come out on my first attempt. Like a baseball batter allotted only one swing of the bat to hit the ball over the homerun wall for $10, 000 or the Girl of His Dreams, I swung the bat hard. I tore that barbed hook out of my finger. Before I could reach overboard to soothe my digit in

the cold river, blood flowed onto my waders, my white cooler lid and the bottom of the boat. The relief overwhelmed any pain I might have felt. I am sure it was nothing compared to the removal of a bullet with a red-hot knife blade wielded by your cowboy companion as you try to ward off the pain with a drink of whiskey and biting down on a worn leather belt during the surgery.

To conclude…Paul landed his steelhead, and we landed several more by day's end. I was paid for a full day's work on the river. As for my throbbing finger, the pain abated in a week. Just kidding! It was only five days.

The king of hooked stoics is my client friend Chuck Beck. I watched him as a size-6 stonefly hook penetrated the underside of his thumb while he released a steelhead. As the entangled fish vigorously swam away, it drew the leader through his fingers, lodging the hook. The point of the hook went completely through his thumb, with the point protruding out his thumbnail! Chuck never made a sound, not a word. Using only the fingers on his wounded hand, he nimbly reversed the path of the *barbless* hook and pulled it clear. Very manly. After seeing this feat, I am sure waterboarding interrogation would never work on this guy! I know with confidence the secret fishing holes I have shared with Chuck are safe.

Barbless hooks. Believe.

CHAPTER 6
Wet-Fly Strategies and Methods

A CONSISTENTLY EFFECTIVE
steelhead fly-angler must have an array of fly-fishing techniques,
able to fish the water column from the surface to the bottom. These would
include skilled presentations of a dry fly, wet fly, and nymphs.

It seems that most fly-anglers I've observed, including steelhead fishing guides, are one dimensional, skilled in only one fly-fishing method.

The most popularly employed fly-fishing method for steelhead is the standard wet-fly presentation. The fly is cast across the current, or slightly downstream. As the drift of the fly proceeds, the fly line is *mended* (repositioning the line, usually upstream) to slow and sink the fly. Generally, the line is tight throughout the drift. The strike will be felt when the steelhead intercepts the fly.

A proper mend prevents the fly from drifting or swinging too fast.

If you were to examine a cross section of "typical" stream flow, you would observe that the highest water flow velocities are, essentially, at the surface. With depth, the water's velocity slows due to friction of the uneven stream bottom. Near the bottom, especially sections replete with boulders and scours, the current speed may be virtually zero. Therefore, what all this means for the fly-angler is that as the fly sinks, it slows

down relative to the fly line and leader that are above the fly in faster water. If nothing is done after the cast and the drift begins, the leader and line will, shortly, drag the fly down and across the current unnaturally fast; much faster than a sinking fly dropped into the water and allowed to sink unattached, uninhibited by leader and line.

A steelhead is aware of its surroundings. Those without this awareness have not survived to adulthood. Inert things drifting in the current past a resting steelhead—leaf bits, fir needles, tiny shards of wood, vegetation, and debris—all travel near the same velocity. It is understandable how a fish might go into "alert mode" when an object in its immediate environment moves unnaturally faster than everything else. A sinking wet fly pulled by line and leader swept in swifter surface currents can be alarming to steelhead. Except for the aggressively suicidal steelhead, the fly needs to be slowed to entice a strike.

A *mend* is a manipulation of the fly line and leader whereby they are lifted and repositioned *upstream* of the relatively slower-moving wet fly. To accomplish a successful mend lift the rod tip approximately 45 degrees above horizontal, then smartly move the tip upstream in a semi-circular arc. My clients and students seem to grasp this movement when I describe it as turning a jump rope. This is a slow, high, grandiose movement of the rod tip, which, ideally, repositions the entire fly line and most of the leader upstream of the fly. As the drift progresses, a downstream curve in the line may develop. At this point, a second mend is made to, again, reposition the line. Turn the jump rope!

I will say it again: assuming your fly has landed in a current line through which you wish to drift your fly, a good mend would affect the line and most of the leader, but move the fly slightly, if at all. On a down-and-across cast, not affecting

Two Michael Gorman originals—the Brown & Gold and Midnight Steely Trout wet flies. My Steelie Trout wet flies were designed to attract both steelhead and trout. My guests have entertaining trout fishing while waiting for the Big Grab.

STEELHEAD WET FLIES
PHOTOGRAPHED BY JIM SCHOLLMEYER

Brad's Brat

Egg Sucking Leech, Black

Tiger's Paw, Variation

Gorman Caballero

Gorman Chartreuse Caballero

Gorman Purple Ibis

Gorman SteelyTrout, Brown and Gold

Gorman Midnight SteelyTrout wet fly

the line of drift of the fly is virtually impossible, so throw the fly beyond the current line you want to drift, knowing that when the mend is made it will pull the fly back towards you. An ineffective, but very common, mend is attempted with the rod tip much too close to horizontal. Repeat after me: "For a good drift of the fly, I will be mending high." Effective mends resulting in the slowing of the fly can be the difference between success and failure to entice a steelhead to strike. A story is in order…

Those In-The-Know Make the Fly Go Slow

After more than forty years of fishing it, Jack Decius knew the North Umpqua and its steelhead well. One summer he invited me to join him for a couple of days on this fabled stream.

Being paralleled by high banks along much of its course, the North Umpqua lends itself to sight-fishing for steelhead. From an elevated position, the observant angler using polarized glasses and binoculars can visually locate steelhead before casting to them. When the water flows remain at a constant level, migrating steelhead often linger in very specific holding locations. As one fish moves upstream, another will move in to sit in the same preferred position. There is something peculiar and desirable to the fish about the hydraulics, light, depth, and/or sense of protection in these sweet spots.

At midsummer flows on the North Umpqua, Jack knew of one of these specific holding lies just barely upstream of the Wright Creek Bridge. Generous host that he was, Jack pointed out a resting steelhead exactly where he knew it would be. With a little study, viewing the area through polarized glasses, I, too, soon located the fish.

Jack formulated our game plan. He would stand on the bridge to watch the fish as I cast to it. So, I waded as deeply as I was able into the river from the right river bank. The steelhead was located left of center-stream, nestled in a cut in the stream's bedrock bottom, and about 60 compass degrees down from straight across the current flow from me. The distance from me to the fish was approximately sixty feet. From my very low vantage point, having waded almost to my chest, I could not see the fish. Jack would be my eyes.

As I cast a size-6 Green Butt Skunk—probably the most popular pattern on the North Umpqua—Jack would orchestrate my actions. He dictated the angle of my cast, when to mend, and when to lengthen my line on successive casts.

On a long cast where the fly was thrown at a few degrees downstream of straight across the current, and mended mightily, Jack excitedly relayed that the steelhead had followed my swinging fly a short distance, then returned to its favored holding location. "Slow the fly" was his simple suggestion.

In my mind, I had a slight problem. Considering the monster mend I had performed on the previous cast, I did not know if I could slow the fly any more than I just had. The mend was as perfect as I could make it. However, if I angled the cast a little more upstream and mended an additional time maybe I could slow the fly just a little more.

The difference that seemed quite subtle to me made a major difference to the steelhead. As Jack watched and simultaneously commented on the fish's behavior, I heard him say, "Here he comes!" As he finished the phrase, I felt the yank at the end of my line. Run, jump. Run some more, jump. Oh, no! The fish shortly won its freedom. That's steelheading.

The lesson I learned that day was one of the invaluable nuances of enticing a steelhead on a wet fly: slow is good. I thought I had made the best presentation to the fish that I possibly could. I assumed that my presentation of the wet fly, including my mending of the line and leader, were as good as I was capable. However, because Jack was able to watch the fly presentation and the reaction of the fish, he prompted me to make another cast with specific encouragement to

Lively rabbit-strip leeches account for lots of steelhead on the standard wet-fly presentation.

slow the drift of the fly. A fish I assumed was not interested in striking my fly *was* willing to do so *if* I would only make a subtle change in the presentation. It made me wonder how many steelhead I could have hooked in past years if only I had slowed my wet fly just ever so slightly more.

There is a hackneyed phrase that says, "Even a blind pig finds a truffle now and then." Even the unsophisticated, relatively unskilled steelhead fly-fisherman catches an aggressive steelhead on a swinging wet fly sometimes. Because they catch the occasional fish, they may assume that their presentation of the fly is adequate. If they do not hook a fish it is only because the steelhead is not interested, when, in fact, the fish *would* be interested if the presentation was refined a bit, including subtleties like slowing the fly with effective line mending. Another case of the Devil dwelling in the details.

What Fly Line Is Right?

Fly lines of all types are used to present the wet fly: floating, full-sinking, and all lengths of sink-tips. A broad spectrum of sink rates—from 3/4" up to 10" per second—is available for the sinking lines. Every successful angler develops his or her own favorites.

STEELHEAD WET FLIES

PHOTOGRAPHED BY JIM SCHOLLMEYER

Gorman Summer Favorite

Gorman Veiled Assassin

Green Butt Spey

Green Butt Skunk

Howell Signature Purple Intruder

Lady Caroline Spey

Lead-Eye Caballero Bugger (Dubbed)

Lead-Eye Caballero Bugger

Wet flies with lead eyes can be fished deep on a floating fly line, which makes for better mending control than a sinking fly line.

Floating lines are most popular in the summertime when water temperatures are in the upper 40's, 50's, and 60's. These are easiest to cast, mend, and pick up to re-cast. Sinking lines are most popular in winter and spring when water temperatures are in the upper 30's and 40's. In cold water, flies are more effectively fished near the bottom where steelhead are holding. They may be unwilling to move very far to intercept the fly, so the idea is to put it down in front of them.

Another situation in which to seriously consider using a sinking fly line to swing the fly deeply is when the holding water is in direct sunlight. Steelhead, like most other fish, have no eyelids. I doubt they even have the ability to squint. With the sun on the water, they are usually reluctant to ascend very far to strike a fly. Many summer wet-fly anglers who are determined to fish wet flies only on a floating fly line confine their fishing time strictly to very early in the morning and evening when the water is in shade or the sun is below the horizon. The typical wet-fly steelheader forgoes most of the fishing day from mid morning through late afternoon. By limiting themselves to one technique with one fly line, such fishermen may be missing some of the best fishing times. The willingness of steelhead to take a fly may be greatly increased as the water temperature warms a few degrees during the day. This is particularly true in the spring and fall. So, for the seriously determined wet-fly guy or gal, add a fast-sinking fly line to your arsenal. Overcome the natural inertia involved in learning to cast, mend and lifting to re-cast this type of line. It can pay fish-catching dividends for you to persist after most other fishermen have deserted the river when the sun arrives.

Simplicity, I think, explains the popularity of the wet-fly presentation. Starting at the top of a likely steelhead run, the effective angler begins with a short cast across the current. The angle of the cast can vary from 45 degrees upstream to 45 degrees downstream. An upstream cast accompanied by one or more mends of the fly line allows the fly to gain depth, and to slow as it descends in the water column.

An important little change in the mending of a cast made at an angle upstream is to wait for a count of two or three before repositioning line and leader. Waiting a couple of seconds between cast and mend allows slack line to form as the system drifts back downstream toward the angler. The slack line and leader are lifted and repositioned, and this can be accomplished—with practice—without pulling the fly much. To pull the fly retards or interrupts its ability to sink quickly to the bottom when that is where you want it to be.

Allow the Steelhead to See Your Fly

Let us consider the basics of effectively and methodically covering a stretch of river that has the potential to hold resting steelhead.

First, a quick review of the type of water I seek out to locate steelhead. Only a small, even minute, portion of a river's expanse will hold steelhead. These fish are discriminating. You must be, too. For best use of your angling time seek out water that has a depth of 3 to 7 feet. (Yes, I know steelhead can hold in much deeper water.) Choose a "walking-speed", straight-line current flow, not swirly, and no vertical upwelling. Definitely avoid the dead or swirly currents behind exposed rocks. For whatever reason, inexperienced steelheaders have it in their heads that dead or chaotic eddies behind exposed boulders are excellent locations for a steelhead to linger. Don't waste your fishing time. However, depending on the shape of the rock and the angle of the current, steelhead may find a comfortable resting lie in front of or beside the stone that creates an eddy.

Lastly, focus on water that has a plethora of structure around which steelhead may feel comfortable and protected. Boulders, ledges, scours, wood debris, and locations where shallow water areas transition into deeper water are all components of desirable steelhead holding lies.

Now, let us assume you have located a very likely stretch of river such as I have just described, and you are going to use a wet-fly presentation to cover it. Start by positioning yourself at the upstream terminus of the likely water. Your first cast should have the fly drift and swing through the nearest water that may hold a fish. Do not charge out into the river as you begin, and end up standing in water you should be fishing. Some careful study is required for your approach. The steelhead can actually be holding along the nearside river bank. Plan and approach accordingly.

Once establishing your initial position, cast short, slightly downstream from straight across; cast upstream if you are concerned about getting your wet fly deep in the water column. Mend the line immediately. Make successive mends as needed to slow the drift of the fly and straighten the line and leader. Prevent, as best you can, a downstream "belly" in the line that will drag the fly too quickly across the current. Allow the fly to drift until it comes straight downstream, no longer tracking across the current. Count to five before picking up to re-cast. I have had many steelhead wait to take

STEELHEAD WET FLIES

PHOTOGRAPHED BY JIM SCHOLLMEYER

Lead-Eye Skunk Bugger

Pick Yer Pocket, Orange

Pick Yer Pocket, Pink

Purple Angel

Red Wing Blackbird Variation

a wet fly until it was hanging directly below me. Be patient. Most anglers—maybe you—will not do this. But, remember. In steelhead fishing, one strike can make or break your day. Allowing your fly to hang briefly before casting again may be the difference on any given day. Do you have the discipline?

If I am fishing summertime water temperatures in the 50's and 60's, I will make only one cast—assuming I get a good mend and proper presentation of the fly—of the same length from the same position. In my experience, an interested steelhead will come to the fly the first time the fish sees it. Unless

I can visually locate a steelhead to know without doubt that I have a fish in my zone, I give an *unseen* steelhead only one chance to grab my offering. It is like my former dating philosophy. Ask her out once. If there is no interest, move on. There are other fish in the sea (steelhead in the river).

For several years, I made the exact same wet-fly cast twice—same line length, same swing of the fly. My thinking was that a semi-interested steelhead would decide to strike the *second* time it saw the fly. However, if the fly was properly presented the first time I never—repeat *never*—got a strike on the

The Strip & Cast Method for Systematically Covering Holding Water

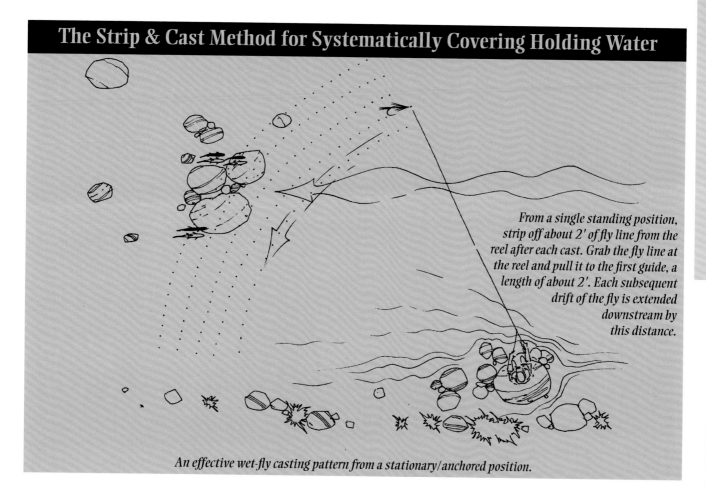

From a single standing position, strip off about 2' of fly line from the reel after each cast. Grab the fly line at the reel and pull it to the first guide, a length of about 2'. Each subsequent drift of the fly is extended downstream by this distance.

An effective wet-fly casting pattern from a stationary/anchored position.

same second cast. For the years that I repeated the same cast twice I, in essence, cut my productive fishing time in half. For every one thousand casts I made, five hundred were a waste of my fishing time. Good lessons come at a price.

Let's go back to our piece of prime steelhead water…

After your initial short cast, which may involve only one rod length of fly line, lengthen your line by two feet for your next cast. Cast the line at the same angle. Mend as necessary. Let the fly swing slowly (and play the fife lowly). And, let it hang.

Another digression. Many of my clients and students do not have a good grasp of 24 inches. When I suggest they lengthen their lines two feet for successive casts, some pull six inches from the reel, while others pull six feet. To make it easier, and create a standard, I suggest they—and you—grasp the fly line at the reel and pull the line until you touch the nearest guide on your rod with the thumb and fingers that are pulling the line. This distance will stand as an easy constant. Grab the line at the reel. Pull it to the first guide. Make the cast. Be consistent. Be methodical. Catch more fish. *(See illustration above.)*

From the initial standing position at the head of the likely steelhead run, lengthen successive casts by two feet. Repeat the same cast only if you do not get a good drift of the fly, or if you get what you figure was a missed steelhead strike. Sometimes a willing steelhead will strike a fly half-heartedly. It is interested, but not committed. This fish deserves a second and third chance. Maybe more.

I start by making the exact same presentation of the fly, which means the same length of line and the same angle on the cast, making sure to mend well. Slowing the fly ever so slightly more may prompt the steelhead to grab with authority. Sometimes I get the fish on the next cast. Many times I don't, so I alter my tactics a bit.

A steelhead that has pursued and struck my fly, but missed, may very well return to the very same position near the stream bottom it was holding when it first saw the fly. Or, it may not. There is a chance that it settled into a new position after the failed attempt. The fish may have repositioned itself closer to me, or farther away. I must accommodate all possibilities. It makes sense to me to cover the nearer position first.

After a couple of the same casts that initially intrigued the fish fail to elicit a second response, I methodically shorten my line by two "standard" two-foot strips. Do this by reversing the procedure for lengthening the line. Grab the fly line at the first guide and draw it back to the fly reel. Wind this slack back onto the reel. Do this a second time. You will have wound approximately four feet of fly line back on the reel.

Cast the shortened line once. Lengthen the line, cast again. Lengthening a third time puts the fly into the same drift that enticed the fish the first time. Continue to lengthen and cast another five or six times.

I count how many casts I have made since I shortened up; of course, there is a good reason. If I cannot get the fish to strike a second time, I am going to eventually change flies and

The Step & Cast Method for Systematically Covering Holding Water

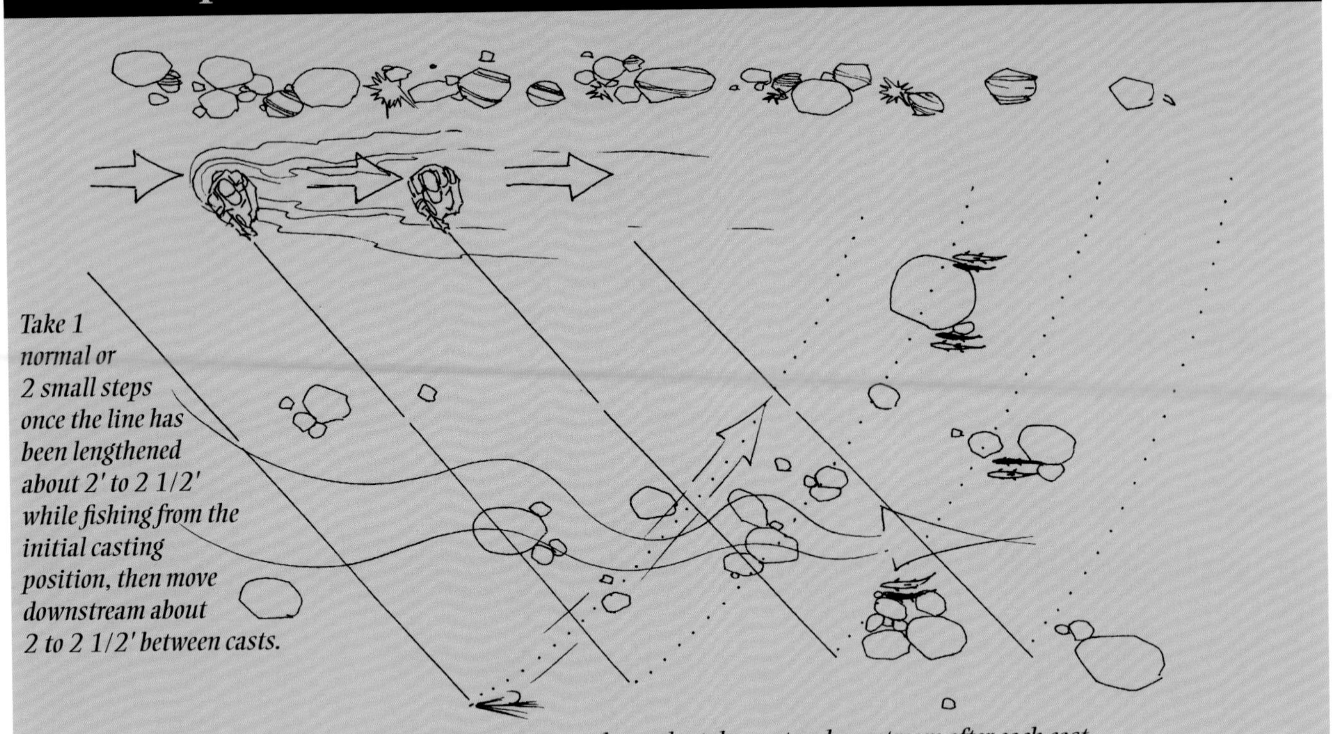

Take 1 normal or 2 small steps once the line has been lengthened about 2' to 2 1/2' while fishing from the initial casting position, then move downstream about 2 to 2 1/2' between casts.

Effective wet-fly casting pattern as the angler takes a step downstream after each cast.

cover the same water from the same position. I want to know what length of line I had beyond my rod tip when the fish showed itself. If I have counted the number of times, I have lengthened my fly line since I shortened it after the strike, I can precisely spool the line back onto the reel, returning the line length to the same shortened position.

If I was using a dark wet fly, I usually change to a bright fly. If my first fly was a large size 2 or 4, I may switch to a smaller size 8 or 10. Show the fish something different and it may elicit a favorable response. How many times should an angler change flies and repeat the process? It depends on your patience. If there is much good water yet to be covered, my preference is to change flies once and call it good.

Change Can Be Good

Once upon a time on a river far far away—British Columbia's famous Kispiox—I was casting a size-4 Skykomish Sunrise wet fly near a tasty submerged boulder on an early October afternoon. As this bright red/yellow/white pattern hung near the boulder's right side, I felt a steelhead softly pluck my hook. Without altering my line length or position, I cast again several times without getting a response. So, I shortened my line to cover water nearer me if the fish had changed position. Nothing. I lengthened my line on successive casts another six or eight times. Nothing.

Having counted the number of two-foot strips I had pulled from my reel, I retrieved my line back to the same shortened length that I was using after the strike. Clipping off the Sunrise, I tied on a smaller, sparsely-tied Black Prince wet fly.

Apparently, this steelhead had returned to its initial position next to the big boulder. As my new fly swung into the same location that had triggered the first take the steelhead struck hard, hooking itself solidly as it ran across the river. The bright 7-pound hen made a good showing, but I eventually wore her down. As I gently slid her onto the beach before the release, I could see the little fly lodged in the corner of the jaw. If you ever have the choice (you don't), this is the spot you want the hook point buried. However, it took little effort to remove the barbless hook and send the fish on her way.

Cast and Step, Cast and Step

From your initial, uppermost standing position in a steelhead run, after you have finally reached the far side of the fishable water, or you have cast as far as your skill allows, leave the line length the same for successive casts. What you will change, if circumstances allow, is your standing/wading position. Rather than changing the line length by two feet, step downstream about two feet. Step and cast. Step and cast. Don't rush. Too often—and I have done this myself—there is a tendency to step as the cast is being made or the fly is in the midst of its drift. When the strike comes, you are not ready, perhaps off balance. Step, stop, and then cast. Let the fly hang below you for a count of five. Continue to let the fly hang as you step and stop. Do not be surprised if a steelhead strikes the hanging fly as you step downriver for the next cast.(*See illustration above.*)

If the step-and-cast method is interrupted by obstructions or undesirable water, merely move down to the next logical position and begin your routine again with a short cast. Lengthen successive casts by two feet from this same position until you have again reached the far side of the fishable water or your casting limit. Then, it's step, stop, and cast. Step, stop, and cast.

To better visualize methodically and thoroughly covering a piece of steelhead water with the wet-fly method, sketch the run on a piece of paper. Put an "X" at your initial standing position. Draw a line from the "X" to represent the angle and length of your first cast. Draw an arc that represents the path of your fly, as it swings back to a position straight downstream from you. Now draw the lines and the swinging arcs of successive casts. The result should be a concise, overlapping grid of lines and arcs. If there were, indeed, steelhead in the piece of water that you fished with this system, know with confidence that, at least, the fish saw your fly. Attention to details = More steelhead hooked.

Just Hangin' Out

I love it when the sun shines in a blue cloudless sky in November. While it sometimes happens in the Willamette Valley of western Oregon where I live, blue sky and sunshine are common this time of year on southern Oregon's Rogue River.

Fishing with client/friend Chuck Wagner and his guest Harry, I parked the drift boat for lunch on the periphery of a good steelhead run. While setting up for lunch I spied a drift boat with three anglers in it headed our general direction. Because I wanted Chuck and Harry to have the opportunity to fish the prime water near our boat once they had finished dining I needed to act, as best I could, to indicate to the oncoming boat of our intentions.

To many anglers, common courtesy is definitely an attitude of the past. In this overcrowded, rude steelhead fishing era in which we live, too many boaters (and foot anglers) will not hesitate to invade your personal space, willing to cast their bait, lure or fly into the water you are fishing or intending to fish. To inhibit the possibility of invasion while my clients dined, I picked up one of the rods and began to cast a long line into the water my guys were going to fish at the conclusion of lunch. My casts were not intended to present the fly to a waiting steelhead, only to prevent the oncoming anglers from throwing their lines into "our" water.

The terminal fly on the leader was a Caballero Egg. Along the stream bottom is where this fly is effectively fished, drifting slowly, naturally with the current.

Clever wet-fly design? Sometimes the Gorman Bead Egg is an effective swinging wet fly. Go figure.

The other boat was at least a hundred feet above us, near the opposite bank, when one of the fishermen hooked a steelhead. Of course, we watched the action as the oarsman dropped the anchor to fight the fish from a stationary position and, perhaps, land the fish. While the scene played out I reeled in most of the fly line I'd been casting, letting the flies hang high in the swift current no more than six feet off the bow of my boat. The egg pattern could not be more than a few inches from the surface.

A few minutes into watching the battle in the other boat, my dangling egg was grabbed hard by a steelhead! What was this fish thinking? As I apologized to my clients for hooking "their" fish, I handed the rod off to Chuck. After the other boat netted their steelhead, Chuck eventually slid a beautiful seven-pound hen into my net.

A loop of line can be released when a steelhead intercepts the wet fly.

Chuck and Harry landed other Rogue steelhead that day, but the suicidal maniac that grabbed an egg fished in the wrong manner, in the wrong water, hanging near the bow of the boat, turned out to be the largest fish of the day, too.

Logic-defying moments like these keep me humble as I try to understand steelhead.

Hold This Thought: Don't Hold the Line

Think you are quick? As quick as a gunfighter on the dusty streets of Laredo circa 1880? I used to think I was.

While in the act of fishing, fly-anglers love to hold a little slack loop of fly line in their off-hand, or press the line against the cork grip with one of the fingers of their rod hand. It's comfortably natural and everybody does it. The idea is to offer a striking fish severe resistance as the hook is set. Sometimes this works, culminating in putting the fish in the net. Too often, a hard strike combined with too much resistance from the ham-handed fisherman, results in an immediate break off. Mr. Quick Draw cannot always get his hand or finger off the line soon enough to prevent a sudden

impact parting of the leader. Opportunity lost; Maybe the only opportunity of the day.

My simple solution is keeping your hands and fingers off the line. Assuming you have a reliable disc drag (or comparable, dependable design) fly reel, adjust the drag tension so that when the hook is set against a fish, the hook point is buried deeply in the jaw while at the same time some fly line is naturally pulled from the reel. The line coming off the reel serves to "cushion" the impact of the hook-set; there is some "give" to prevent line breakage.

For this all-holds-barred technique to work correctly, the correct amount of drag tension is paramount. You need enough resistance to bury the hook point on the set, but not so tightly that line cannot be pulled from the reel at the same time. If the tension is too light, the hook will not penetrate and you may get overrun and a tangle of your fly line on the reel can occur. A little common-sense experimentation will help you find the correct tension.

Yes, I know there are skilled steelhead fly-rodders who prefer to hold a loose loop of fly line in their rod hand fingers as they fish. When the strike comes, release the loop. The idea is that the fly will drop back to the fish, and once the steelhead turns, the hook will be secured in the corner of the jaw.

As usual, the experienced, veteran fly-anglers present the biggest challenge for me. They ALL want to hold onto the fly line while fishing. First, I suggest they put their off hands behind their backs or in their pockets. When that does not work, I threaten to duct tape the incorrigible arm to the upper thigh. Yes, I would cut them free for bathroom breaks and lunch. Though I do not own one yet, I am contemplating the use of a shock collar, like the ones used to train disobedient dogs. "If I have to tell you one more time… And, it's for your own good I must do this."

This rule holds true, not only for wet-fly fishing, but for dry-fly and nymph methods, too. If your hooks are sharp, your knots true, tippet strength appropriate, and your drag tension set correctly, you will not break off a steelhead on the strike ever again.

To Have and to Hold

Many good wet-fly anglers lightly pin a loose loop of fly line against the cork grip with a finger or two during the drift and swing of the fly. As the steelhead strikes the fly, the line loop is pulled tight by the steelhead. Because the angler gently holds it, the line offers very little resistance to the steelhead until the loop is eventually pulled tight by the fish. The hope with this technique is that the hook is more likely to be secured in the *corner* of the fish's mouth. Most anglers will agree a hook penetrating tough tissue in the corner of the

Big fish can be found in small water.

jaw is less likely to come out during the fight than any other location a steelhead can be legally hooked.

Here is the thought process. At the moment a steelhead intercepts a wet fly it is directly facing it. Logically, the fish does not hold its head steady for long once the fly is grabbed. It will turn left or right. But, it *will* turn, even if only slightly. The slack line (loop) gently released by the fisherman drifts with the fish as it turns its head, and is drawn into the corner of the mouth as the line finally comes tight.

I have caught steelhead on wet flies while holding the loose coil of line. This technique looks very cool, and adds drama to the telling of steelhead stories. So, I will leave it to you, dear reader, to decide whether this is truly more effective than making the appropriate drag adjustment, keeping your fingers off the fly line, and let a striking steelhead pull line directly from the fly reel as it strikes and turns. I contend that steelhead are most often lost on the strike or soon in the battle when an angler over-reacts to the fish's take, setting the hook too soon or too hard against tight line. This is especially true if the fisherman insists on tightly pinning the fly line against the rod grip while fishing. Therefore, there is no cushioning "give" when the steelhead strikes; the fly is pulled or torn from the fish's mouth.

To further my musings on the necessity of the loose line coil while swinging wet flies, I will draw from my many years of steelhead nymphing experiences. As I will elaborate in another chapter, the nymph-fishing method is the one I employ

most when fishing or guiding for steelhead. Simply, the flies are cast upstream, allowed to sink on a slack line, and drifted naturally with the current. At the end of the drift, as the line naturally comes tight, swing and ascend towards the surface. It is not unusual during a full day's fishing to have a steelhead aggressively intercept the nymph or egg pattern when the line is tight, the same sort of strike you come to expect when fishing a wet fly. Since I ask my nymph anglers to refrain at all times from holding or pinning the fly line, the striking impact is cushioned a little. More often than not, by a wide margin, these fish are solidly hooked and landed. It is not unusual to hook and land two or three steelhead in a day that have taken a swinging, tight-line nymph. Because I have witnessed this hundreds, if not a thousand, times in more than thirty years, I am led to wonder about the need for the line loop. It is debating issues such as this that add some spicy fun to our sport.

Wet Flies on a Longer Rod

As I wrote earlier, a Spey or switch rod offers significant advantages in most fishing situations where long distance and/or dealing with tricky currents are issues. Long-distance casts with less effort and little back-cast room are handled nicely with rods of 11 to 14 feet. The longer the fishing stick, the easier the mending. Additionally, anglers even slightly proficient with two-handed casting have less arm fatigue through a long fishing day. Spey casting is very proactive and fun, too. 'Nuff said.

CHAPTER 7
Dry-Fly Fishing

THERE ARE SOME THINGS ABOUT STEELHEAD
I will never understand. For example, why a large fish that has
minimal appetite on its spawning run up its home river will rise from the
bottom through six feet of flowing water to intercept
a floating fly baffles me.

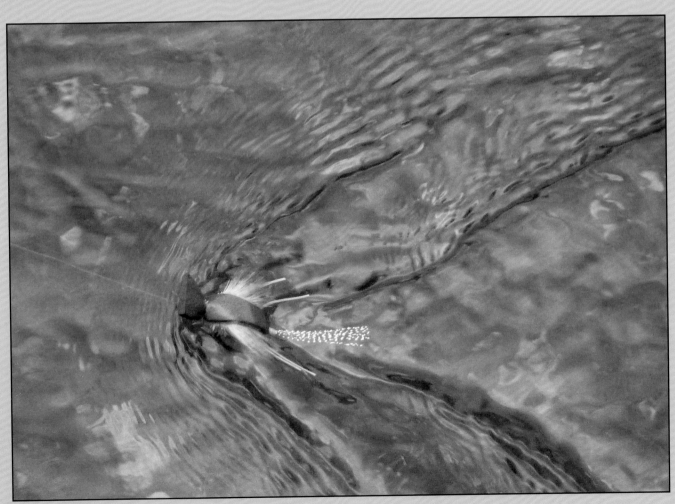

And, this is not a rare occurrence. I know a few anglers who use this method exclusively to entice steelhead.

The traditional presentation of a floating fly in streams when fishing for trout is to quarter the cast upstream, letting the fly drift naturally with the current. Most of the time, little or no movement is imparted to the artificial. Though a steelhead angler may dead-drift the dry fly to his quarry, the vast majority cast down and across stream, skating the dry on a

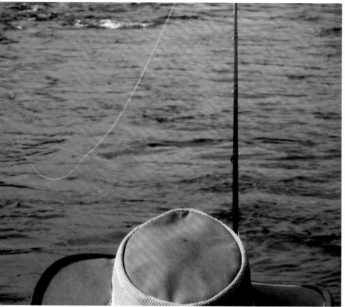

Skating a dry fly in quieter water above a riffle or rapids can prompt an aggressive steelhead to attempt to eat it.

tight line. The wake created by tension on the line serves as a visual (and audible?) trigger for the fish.

I was first introduced to the dry fly as a viable steelheading tactic on British Columbia's Babine River. After talk around the lodge at which I was staying by the guides and other angling guests I decided to dedicate some precious, limited fishing time skating a floating fly.

Having already beached some good fish using reliable wet flies delivered on the standard down-and-across presentation, I tied on an improvised skater I had fashioned at the vise the night before at the lodge. It had a body of peacock herl, brown rooster hackle, and a stiff tail and wing of moose mane. To enhance its waking "skatability", I flattened and glued a prominent head from the cut ends of the moose mane wing. This stiff, flat head over the eye of the fly causes it to plane nicely, with the fly held against the current on a tight line.

I fancied that my creation was much more refined than the crude, though effective, Moose Turd, tied by the guides. Theirs was created in its simple entirety with a single large clump of moose mane. You had a stiff, long gray tail, a body formed by spiraling the clump around the hook shank, and flat, planed head from the cut ends of the body. Fly head cement or rubber-based glue is used to maintain the shape and rigidity of the head.

In front of me for my first dry-fly venture was excellent steelhead holding water: depths ranging from 3'-6'; medium

current speed; and, a plethora of submerged structure to break the current a bit and provide protection for the fish, if needed. The surface currents were fairly flat and unriffled. Bouncy water tends to sink a skating fly.

A little trial and error revealed to me the downstream-and-across casting angle I needed to quickly get the fly into skating mode. Lifting and lowering the rod tip during the drift of the fly allowed me to adjust the amount of line tension. Too much tension caused the fly to sink. Too little tension, the fly did not skate; and may lead to a sinking of the artificial.

I was less than ten minutes into my inaugural attempt with a dry fly when the water underneath my fly erupted. Though I knew better, having been warned by the guides, I lifted my rod tip quickly, attempting to set the hook. I felt nothing. A clean swing and a miss.

After some derisive self-talk, I cast again. No adjustments were made in my presentation. The line length and casting angle were identical to the last. I held little hope the fish would return for a second attempt. This lack of preparedness led me to, again, pull the fly away from the steelhead when it made a second attempt to eat it.

More self-talk. More derision. Cast Number 3: same scenario, and the same result. Unbelievable! This fish was not deterred, no matter how inept I continued to be.

The desired response on the part of the angler who has a take from a rising steelhead is to do nothing, at least

When larger adult aquatic insects, like the October Caddis, are active on the surface during hatching or egg-laying, steelhead may show an interest in dry flies.

immediately. Keeping his wits about him, the angler waits after the rise, holding the rod tip steady. Once the fly line is pulled tight by the descending fish, and the line is actually being pulled from the reel, the strike is made. What happens—if the angler is controlled and patient until striking—is that the striking fish will descend and turn either left or right, drawing the fly to the left or right in its mouth. With a little luck, the hook will be drawn into the corner of the fish's jaw, where it will be securely hooked. Though,

STEELHEAD DRY FLIES

PHOTOGRAPHED BY JIM SCHOLLMEYER

Buggenhagen NFL

Caddis Muddler, Dark

Caddis Muddler, Light

Howell Caddis Stone Skater

Howell Ska Opper

Red Mint Muddler, Variation

Mint Muddler, Variation

Muddler Minnow

as we know, things do not always go according to the game plan, this is our hope.

When my fourth opportunity came from this steelhead, I had further proof that miracles *do* happen. And, just as miraculous was the fact that I actually did the correct things to hook the steelhead. I waited for line to be pulled from my reel before I reacted to the rise. Once that sweet sound was heard, I lifted the rod tip to tighten against the running fish. What a rush!

I continued to make the right moves as the fish ran and jumped. Eventually, I slid the bright hen onto the gravel beach for some admiration and a smooth release.

It's always special to hook, play, and land a steelhead, no matter the fly-fishing method. However, to watch a big fish swirl or explode underneath a skating dry fly definitely turns up the excitement level. I can understand why some anglers will fish this method to the exclusion of all others. I hope the DEA isn't reading here, but I suspect that this may be the closest thing to fly-fishing heroin I've encountered. The possibility of addiction is definitely present. I will illustrate with an aside about an angler I met at the lodge I stayed at on the Babine.

Even With the Water High, I'm Fishing Dry

On another fall trip to the Babine, the river was high, cold, and murky. Even fishing a deeply sunk wet fly produced only the occasional fish. The steelhead were definitely in the river, but they were moody. Too often I wondered if the fish could even see my large 1/0 wet fly swimming in their holding zone.

To prove to myself that my first skating-fly encounter wasn't a total fluke, I committed to try it again the same day; and the next, if conditions allowed. They did.

My guide motored me up the river to a gravel bar. To his professional credit, he approached the fishing area with as much stealth as is possible in a boat powered by an outboard motor.

He departed and I surveyed the shallow tailout below me where the guide had indicated a fish might be stationed. The water was smooth, had a uniform current velocity, and was easy to approach. As I prepared to cast, another guide in a powerboat steamed up the river at high speed. Though he did not pass directly over my water, he did pass irritatingly near. Briefly, I considered not even fishing. It was hard for me to believe that any steelhead in the vicinity would not be disturbed to the point they would have no interest in biting a fly, let alone a skating dry fly. At the very least, I figured, practicing the presentation of the dry fly would add to my store of experience and expertise.

As I surmised, the hydrology of this tailout made for easy presentations of the fly to the fish, if any steelhead should care. To my astonishment, one did. Early in a drift that looked similar to the dozens I'd already made, a fish swirled at my fly. Having learned my lesson—repeatedly—earlier in the day, I did nothing except let fly continue doing what it was doing when the steelhead showed. The fish did not grab the fly, perhaps not convinced of a good result if it did. Strangely, this

steelhead did not descend and disappear. Instead this determined specimen swam a few feet downstream of the fly, then, did a broad U-turn. The barely-subsurface wake created by this maneuver was reminiscent of a cruising shark as it moves to intercept a swimmer. Just as a Great White would pull an unsuspecting surfer from his board as he waited to catch the next wave, this fish engulfed my fly. Through the persistent mumbling to myself not to set the hook too quickly, I let the steelhead turn down. Line started to pull from the reel. A solid hook-set followed, and the fight was on. The streaking steelhead made some great moves attempting to escape, but I won the battle. I captured another magnificent hen, admired her briefly, and then, released the fish. Lightning had struck me twice on the same day.

I hooked and landed two more steelhead that rose to a waking dry fly before my week on the Babine ended.

Presenting the Skated Dry Fly

For the most part, skating a dry fly is a short-line game in which most of the *fly* line, sometimes all of it, is held above the water. A longer rod is of great assistance to accomplish this. If too much line is allowed on the water, tension and hydraulics will cause the fly to sink.

A longer fly rod makes it easier to control the drift of the fly. A tool of significant length (9 1/2'-15') also enables longer, extended drifts. It seems a growing number of fly-anglers are discovering the advantage of two-handed Spey rods. (See the chapter on fly-fishing equipment.)

Tailouts are excellent ambush points when casting dry flies for steelhead.

STEELHEAD DRY FLIES
PHOTOGRAPHED BY JIM SCHOLLMEYER

Peacock Skater

Purple Mint Muddler, Variation

Purple Bomber

Reynolds Red Head Skater

Reynolds Steelhead Caddis

Steelhead Skater

Kaufmann Stimulator

The fly is presented by casting it across the current and downstream at about 45 degrees. Depending on the direction and velocity of the current, the angler will lift and lower the rod to control the tension on the line during the drift of the fly. The goal is to get a slow, waking presentation over likely holding water.

My ideal skating dry-fly water has a medium to fast current velocity; a flat, unriffled surface flow, with a depth of 2-4 feet; and, finally, excellent structure in the form of submerged boulders, ledges, or defined channels. I want the holding water to be shaded, not in direct sunlight. And, if I could be granted one final wish, let me be the very first angler to fish the run.

Because the artificial is cast down-and-across the current, the steelhead fly-angler, typically, positions himself at the head (upstream) of a likely looking piece of holding water, just as a wet-fly angler would. The first cast should be to the nearest water that could hold a fish. Because the steelhead are facing upstream into the current, the fisherman needs to stand back a reasonable distance so as not to be seen, and that includes the waving of a visible rod tip, especially if the water surface is flat, un-riffled.

On shorter casts—those that may be less than 25'—the entire fly line and leader can be held above the water with a high rod tip. Only the fly has contact with the river. Longer casts will result in the leader and a short length of the line on the surface. Make sure your floating fly line is in excellent floating condition. Clean it regularly. If the coating is cracked because of age or accident, water will penetrate the core, causing it to sink. Either refurbish or replace the line.

As the dry fly first lands on the water, slowly lift the rod tip to tighten the entire fly line, leader, fly system. The fly should start to wake across the current. As the fly proceeds down and across the current I turn and follow it with my rod tip. I prefer not to hold, or even touch, the fly line. The reel drag is adjusted so that a striking fish can pull line from the spool, but at the same time there is, also, adequate tension so that when I set the hook the resistance is sufficient to bury the hook point.

Systematically cover all the likely water. From a single stationary position, lengthen your fly line about two feet on successive casts until you can no longer get a good presentation of the fly. Then, move your standing (or boat) position downstream a short ways (I suggest a rod length), and begin the casting routine again. Start short, and then lengthen your line slightly on successive casts. Do this until all the viable water has been covered.

To maximize my chances of hooking a fish in a given piece of water, I may fish it with a dry fly, then fish through it again with a wet fly. If I deem that re-fishing the run or pool is not worth trying from its head to the downstream terminus a second time because the steelhead will have seen me the first time I progress through the area, I carry two fly rods with me. From my initial position, I cover the water with a dry fly, systematically covering all the water I can effectively cover from this

one position. I reel up the dry fly, and pick up the wet-fly rod. From the very same position, I ply the water from near to far. A potentially willing steelhead has been offered two different flies at two different depths. Showing no interest in a skater, an individual may be willing to intercept a sunken wet fly.

Sometimes, I encounter a steelhead that will slash or roll at a dry, but refuse to eat it. When I, then, swim a wet fly over its head, the fish may grab with authority.

The converse can be true. Steelhead having no interest in a wet fly swimming a few feet in front of, or just over their head, may refuse it, or lightly pluck it. My first ploy, then, is to change wet flies. I may use a different color or size. Sometimes it is a smaller fly of a different color. If no response is forthcoming, I'll skate a dry fly.

Mine Is Not To Reason Why. When In Doubt, Fish It Dry.

A midsummer's eve found me on southern Oregon's North Umpqua River. Before the afternoon sun had left the water, I positioned myself at the top of a very dependable steelhead run. Many fish in this pool had succumbed to my flies in the past. I staked claim to this little piece of real estate before the hordes of other angling vampires came out from hiding once the river fell into shadow. My early arrival broke a few hearts of late arrivals. And, they had good reason for disappointment.

The After Dinner Mint Muddler (variation) is an excellent pattern to wake above an aggressive steelhead.

Though I often fish a floating fly line with my wet fly, this particular evening I opted for a slow-sinking, 10' sink-tip. With a few feet of depth, the fly progresses across the current just a little more slowly than it would just a few inches beneath the faster surface currents. For many steelhead, I have discovered that slower is better. It allows the fish to see the fly better and longer, and they do not have to swim so aggressively to bite it. I have a suspicion that some individuals may be irritated to attack an upstart fly that lingers a little too long in its Personal Space.

Though I can never be certain about its motives, a chrome hen of, perhaps, 7 pounds, impaled itself on my #6 Red & Purple Thang. A high rod tip and patient reel hand allowed me to beach this pretty girl before I sent her back to the depths.

Who knows? I may have a chance to catch her again in the morning.

Just as I had the night before, I headed off any claim jumpers who might have considered trespassing on "my property" in the first glimmer of dawn. I was in the same wading position I had visited less than ten hours before. Though steelhead can be very moody and unpredictable, I liked my odds for hooking a fish—maybe two—from the water in front of me.

Progressing through the pool, from top to the bottom, I anticipated a jarring strike on every cast. Though it is my habit to make only a single cast before moving the fly a little farther downstream on the next one, I lapsed into fishing two identical casts before lengthening my line a little to probe new water. I did this because I could not believe I had not enticed a fish in the first dozen casts. My disappointment and impatience were clouding clear thinking.

Fishing (actually, over-fishing) the entire run produced not a single strike. Incredulous! Perfect time of day. First one on the water. Proven, killer fly. Perfect presentations. And, I sensed—I knew—there were steelhead in this pool.

Though I love fishing the dry fly, and have had some encouraging success, I had always believed that a biting steelhead would virtually always prefer a wet fly to a dry fly. And, why wouldn't it? They rarely have to swim as far or expend as much energy to intercept a wet fly. It's so logical!

Ah, there I'd done it again: used "logical" and "steelhead" in the same train of thought. How many times has that proven me silly?

Though the sun was advancing toward the tops of the Douglas firs, I had time to pick up my second rod, the one with the Purple Bomber tied to the tippet. What the heck…

Riffle Hitch: Fishing the Dry Fly

The Riffle Hitch can add enticing movement to a skating dry fly or a waking wet fly.

Near the top of this pool, near the grassy bank on the far side, lives a huge round boulder. Just to the side of this rock, and slightly downstream, multiple hooked steelhead over the years have proven they like something about this watery nook. Think of this stone as a fish magnet. I was barely six casts into my second pass through the run when there was a small explosion underneath my Bomber. As had become my routine when angling the dry fly, I was quietly talking to myself. I was uttering reminders not to set the hook if a fish should rise. Only when the fish started pulling line from my reel did I smoothly lift the rod tip to drive the hook point into the jaw.

This spectacular buck did everything a steelhead should do: sprint up and down the pool, jump, charge the angler, and the dreaded underwater "spin". But, because the hook was in the corner of the jaw, it held fast. Without touching the buck, I slid him part way into some grass at the water's edge. With my rod laid beside my beautiful prize, I photographed him multiple times to ensure at least one picture would be in focus. My favorite was a close-up showing the dry fly in perfect fish-hooking position.

Besides joy, I felt lucky and, somehow, redeemed.

Riffling Hitch Presentation

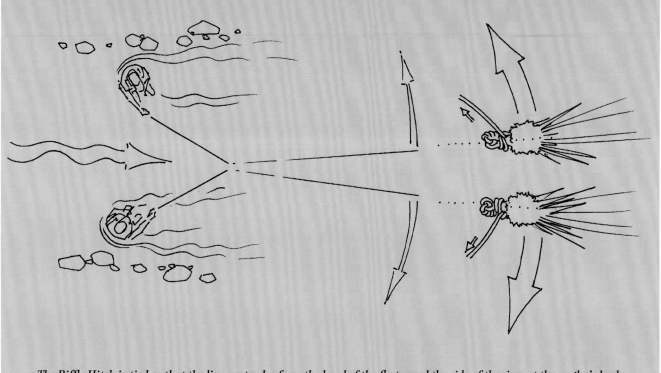

The Riffle Hitch is tied so that the line protrudes from the head of the fly toward the side of the river at the angler's back.

After I settled down, I realized a little time yet remained before the sun caught me. So, I resumed from whence I had left off, plying the water with more casts of the dry fly.

Near the end of the run, a location I had worked thoroughly with my wet fly, a second steelhead swirled at my dry fly. I did all the right things…nothing…but the fish had not securely grabbed the fly. Repeated casts proved fruitless, but I was thrilled that a second steelhead that had seen my wet fly, and ignored it, was actually willing to come to the surface for a skater.

What were these fish thinking? I am thinking they were determined to teach me another steelhead fishing lesson: do not assume you know everything. In fact, do not assume to know very much at all about these fabulous, unpredictable creatures.

Chance Discovery

To extend the life of a fly, 19th century Newfoundland Atlantic salmon fishermen looped and secured the tippet behind the eye of the fly. The hook eye was made of a loop of silkworm gut that disintegrated or wore thin with use. By securing the tippet behind the eye with a couple of half-hitch knots, there was less wear and stress on the fly eye. At the same time, the disposition of the fly in the current was altered. Because the leader no longer came straight off the hook eye, the fly tended to wake, skitter, or wobble, depending on the final angle of the tippet as it came off the fly. This unusual action of the fly secured behind the head was often quite intriguing to the fish. The *riffle hitch* was born and its popularity spread.

Just like the Atlantic salmon, steelhead will often strike at a riffle-hitched fly. There are times that the riffle hitch can coax a shy steelhead that needs just a little more action in the waking dry fly to strike it. Some flies, like the Muddler Minnow, which are usually fished as wet or shallow-running "damp" patterns, can be prompted to skate like dry flies when correctly tied with a riffle hitch.

When the two half-hitch knots are snugged up behind the hook eye, the tippet will protrude off the hook to side of the fly nearest the fisherman as the fly swings in the current. Once the knot is pulled tight on the fly, you can pull and muscle the knot in order to orient the protruding tippet as you want it. For a little different action of the fly, try positioning the knot so that the tippet comes straight off the bottom of the hook rather than from the side. Such a move might cause the fly to swim on its side. Some crazy steelhead just might find this particularly appealing.

Downstream Mend

Another little maneuver that may enhance the attractiveness of a skating dry fly in certain situations is a *downstream* mend. In slower current flows, when it may be necessary to speed up skating your dry fly to prevent its sinking or enhance its wake, mending the fly line downstream can help. While mending upstream is what an angler normally does to slow the drift of a fly, reversing the direction of the mend has the opposite effect. Again, this little detail can be the difference that makes for another memorable steelhead moment.

CHAPTER 8
Nymph Fishing for Steelhead

THE DEADLIEST OF ALL FLY-FISHING METHODS
is *nymphing*. Most fly-anglers employ this technique for trout.
However, this is the only fly-fishing strategy enabling the
angler to *consistently* catch steelhead year-round.

Even in the toughest of fly-fishing conditions, when the sun is high overhead on a hot July day or the water is frigid in January, nymph fishing for steelhead will catch fish.

To a fly-fisherman a *nymph* is a reference to an immature aquatic insect that lives the majority of its life among the rocks, wood debris or vegetation along the river bottom. There are dozens of insect families giving rise to hundreds of various species. As with resident trout, young stream-reared

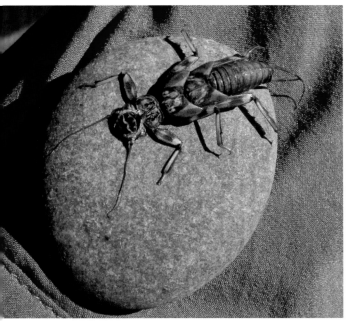

Large stonefly nymphs are abundant and available to steelhead in many western rivers.

steelhead eat aquatic insects for the year or two they live in fresh water before swimming to sea where they dine on the ocean's bounty of small fish and crustaceans.

Nymph fishing for steelhead is a reference, therefore, to a technique rather than a specific type of fly. Though some effective steelhead nymph patterns specifically imitate actual immature stoneflies or mayflies that populate many steelhead streams, others may replicate salmon eggs or flashy psychedelic morsels that look nothing like an insect from this planet. These latter patterns are referred to as attractors. Such flies are not meant to imitate anything specifically, but, instead, arouse the steelhead's interest to the point that it will strike it or attempt to eat it.

Every steelhead nympher has her or his favorite fly patterns. These can change constantly. New effective steelhead flies are created constantly. As I alluded to earlier, last year's all-star may be relegated to third team this year. Flies in favor can change as quickly as women's fashion.

As for my personal fly patterns, I let the steelhead decide. I have fallen in love with some beautiful, intriguing steelhead flies that have proven to have little or no fish appeal. As much as I *want* the fly to prompt the fish to bite it, they show no interest. Therefore, I have learned if "this dog don't hunt", it's of no use to me. Such a pattern no longer has residence in my fly box.

Having fished and guided steelhead for more than thirty years, typically more than a hundred days in a calendar year, I have a few observations about steelhead and their fly preferences. For some of them I have no logical explanation. I just try to follow the rules and preferences that the fish lay before me.

The good steelhead anglers I know experiment constantly with nymph fly patterns. I do the same. Fishing with multiple flies facilitates trying new flies paired with an "old reliable". Steelhead fly preference can change constantly, often week to week. Occasionally preferences can change on a day-to-day basis. This can be driven by such things as changes in water temperature, light intensity, water level, water clarity, weather, insect activity, and the presence of spawning salmon. I cannot understand the impetus for change in most cases. Except for spawning salmon, I am unable to predict what the exact fly preferences will be. A bit of trial-and-error experimentation is often called for.

Something I am at a complete loss to explain is how preferred fly patterns can change from year to year. All environmental conditions—as far as I can perceive—can be identical to the corresponding conditions for the same period of the previous year, but the steelhead as a group will show a distinct preference for a different "old reliable" fly that was a mediocre producer the year before. As an example, I have seen years when a Bead Head Prince produced only fair results, then, next

When using trout nymphs for steelhead, it pays to check the hook closely after landing a big fish.

year—same time, same water flow—it's the "go to" pattern. The steelhead cannot get enough of it. What has changed? I am at a loss.

Another example is a change in preference for a different color of the exact same fly. I fish a rubber-leg stonefly almost constantly as one of my steelhead nymphs. I used to have a bias (because the fish did) for a golden brown color. Then, it

STEELHEAD NYMPH FLIES

PHOTOGRAPHED BY JIM SCHOLLMEYER

Bead Head Prince

Flashback Hare's Ear

Gorman Bead Egg, New Age Pink

Gorman Bead Egg, Orange Cream

Gorman Bead Egg, Orange

Gorman Bead Egg, Pink

Gorman Bead Thorax Hare's Ear

Gorman Egg Sucking Stonefly

Proper mending for a slow the drift of the fly is absolutely critical in most nymphing situations.

In light of our objective—a slow, deep drift of the fly—let's start at the beginning by considering the best choices for fly line and leader. Though it seems counterintuitive, a floating fly line is used for effective nymphing. To this a 9'-10' leader is attached. I prefer fluorocarbon because of its enhanced "invisibility" to the fish. The tippet will typically range in diameter from 3X to 0X (0.009"-0.011"), depending on the sizes of the flies to be used. In terms of breaking strength, we are talking 8-15 pounds.

In virtually all situations, lead wire or lead shot is employed in the system to get the flies to the depths in moving, sometimes swift, water. The weight may be incorporated into or onto the fly as it is tied. Lead wire wrapped on the hook before the fly is tied is one possibility. Lead dumbbell eyes, or a heavy bead, placed at the head of the hook as the fly is tied is an additional weight-adding procedure.

If the angling regulations allow, lead shot can be pinched onto the leader. I use the removable type in sizes BB and 3/0. It is important to match the amount of weight to the combination of current velocity and depth being fished. Too much

fell out of favor, replaced by black. Then black lost out in favor to chocolate brown. Each year I give all colors a chance to prove themselves, but one will tend to dominate year to year. This is a head scratcher. Mysteries like these keep The Game interesting.

Because steelhead have great vision, big flies are not necessary to intrigue them. My clients and I have landed scores of steelhead on small fare, sizes 12 and 14.

The individual steelhead, that has survived migration in and out of their home river, in addition to a year or two in the dangerous open ocean, has acute senses. Seeing danger in time to avoid it is imperative. A size-14 fly, or smaller, does not go unseen in relatively clear water by a steelhead six to ten feet away. The fish may not be interested in the artificial bug at this moment, but the fly is on its visual radar screen.

As I indicated earlier, I am a proponent of small flies. Whereas larger flies may put off a willing fish, he or she might be induced to take a non-threatening smaller one. Size can be critical. Experiment.

When the sun is bright, I lean toward bright reflective or metallic-bodied flies. Nymphs and wet flies that contain mylar tinsel, Flashabou, Krystal Flash, shiny bead head, or metallic wire can prove especially effective. In less intense lighting, I prefer darker patterns that offer contrast with the stream bottom. Egg flies, which I fish just like nymphs, are a color exception. Soft pink, hot pink, orange, and tangerine eggs are good in any light condition when spawning fish are in the river.

There are many nuances to nymph fishing, but the prime directive is to present the fly in such a manner that it drifts slowly, naturally near the stream bottom. A willing steelhead, holding near the bottom, merely has to move slightly left or right to intercept the artificial. Minimal effort is required of the fish, and most are reluctant to move very far, especially when the water is cold.

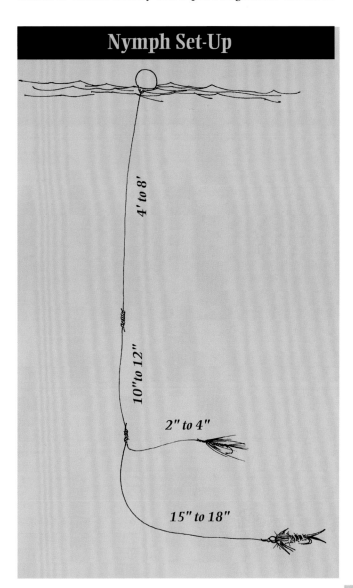

Nymph Set-Up

4' to 8'

10" to 12"

2" to 4"

15" to 18"

STEELHEAD NYMPH FLIES

PHOTOGRAPHED BY JIM SCHOLLMEYER

Gorman Flashback Hare's Ear

Gorman GG Rubber Leg Stonefly Nymph

Gorman GG Stonefly Nymph

Gorman Hot Bead Assassin, Chartreuse

Gorman Hot Bead Assassin, Orange

Gorman Hot Bead Assassin, Pink

Gorman Hot Bead GG Stonefly Nymph

Gorman Lead Eye Bead Egg

Drifting a Nymph with No Mend

Because the current velocity near the stream bottom is usually much slower than at the surface, the sinking flies will be dragged unnaturally fast by the floating fly line and indicator.

weight, the flies are always dragging or stuck on the stream bottom. Too little weight, the flies drift over the heads of the fish.

To present the fly to the steelhead, the line is cast upstream, generally at an angle of 45 to 60 degrees. The flies should be allowed to sink on a slack line as they drift back toward you. Most, but not all, of the slack is removed as the fly proceeds downstream. If none of the slack is removed, you will not be able to quickly and effectively set the hook. Conversely, if the line is tightened because all slack is removed, the flies

Drifting a Nymph With a Mend

A proper mend repositions the fly line and indicator upstream of the flies to prevent dragging the nymphs. Multiple mends may be necessary during one complete drift of the flies.

STEELHEAD NYMPH FLIES

PHOTOGRAPHED BY JIM SCHOLLMEYER

Gorman Scorpion Stonefly, Black Tan (top view)

Gorman Scorpion Stonefly, Brown Black (top view)

Gorman Scorpion Stonefly, Brown Gold (top view)

Gorman Scorpion Stonefly, Midnight and Red (top view)

Gorman Scorpion Stonefly, Hot Bead (top view)

Gorman Steelhead, Brown Yellow

Barr's Jumbo John, Orange

Kaufmann's Bead Head Rubber Leg Stonefly Nymph

Watch the drift of your fly line and indicator for any hint they are dragging the flies too quickly downstream.
Combed-out synthetic yarn makes an excellent strike indicator.

will drift too high in the water column, not staying down in the steelhead's zone. Additionally, lack of *any* slack my cause the flies to drift unnaturally fast in the current, which can be a deterrent for the fish, too.

A *mend* is a manipulation of the fly line by the fisherman to slow the drift of the fly, minimizing drag, preventing the fly from coursing too fast in the current. The angler lifts his rod tip high and flips (repositions) the slack in the fly line upstream of the nymph. Think of the movement you would make to turn a jump rope, with the far end tied to a doorknob. Multiple mends may be necessary during a single drift.

Underwater observations and sight-fishing to visible steelhead have shown me that steelhead may hold a fly for a mere second or less before they expel it. An artificial fly does not have the texture, taste and smell of a real food item, so a fish tends to spit it quickly. For the fisherman to detect the strike immediately, and then react quickly to set the hook, is imperative.

A nymph angler cannot depend on feeling the strike as the steelhead takes the fly on a slack line. By the time the line would be tightened to that degree, the fish has made its exit.

However, there may be a *visual* indication of the strike to alert the angler to set the hook. Some will watch the tip of the floating fly line. If the line, which has some degree of slack in it to keep the flies drifting near the bottom, hesitates, stops, or is pulled under the surface, the rod tip is immediately raised to drive the hook point home. A brightly colored line is a great aid. All my floating lines are yellow, orange, fluorescent red or pale green.

Now, let's circle back to answer the question "Why not use a sinking fly line, or sink-tip, to present the fly along the stream bottom?" Keeping in mind that our prime directive is to present the fly in a manner whereby it drifts slowly and naturally with the current, know that the subsurface portion of a sinking fly line must remain slack just as the leader must remain slack to keep the flies drifting naturally. Instead of merely having to pull the leader tight to indicate a strike, the slack in the sinking fly line must also be tightened by the biting fish so the angler knows to set the hook. The delay is usually too late. Additionally, sinking fly lines, or the sinking tip, is invariably a dark color, and very difficult to see. A visual indication by the fly line that a steelhead has intercepted the fly is improbable.

STEELHEAD NYMPH FLIES

PHOTOGRAPHED BY JIM SCHOLLMEYER

Gorman Flashback Hot Bead Prince

Barr's Rubber Leg Copper John, Chartreuse

Barr's Rubber Leg Copper John, Copper & Gold

Barr's Rubber Leg Copper John, Green

Barr's Rubber Leg Copper John, Red

The majority of nymph fishers utilize a floating strike indicator. Attach this on the upper portion of the leader, anywhere from two inches to two feet from the fly line. Synthetic yarn, cork, and adhesive Styrofoam are examples of materials commonly used as strike indicators. While riding the current, if the indicator deviates in any way from its natural drift, the hook should be set.

With rare exception, I always fish two flies on the leader. As individuals, fish may prefer one fly to another, so I give them a choice. Additionally, since many steelhead will strike a fly only if it comes a few inches of them I like my increased odds with the second. If one fly does not pass close enough to the steelhead to interest it, the other fly may.

Indicator position on the leader is important. Ideally, I prefer to locate my indicator so that distance between it and my uppermost (dropper) fly is 1 1/2 to 2 feet greater than the water depth. Since the water depth varies from one fishing location to the next I will change the distance often. Too much distance between flies and indicator, and the delay between the interception of the fly by a fish and the hesitation or sinking of the indicator is increased. Too short a distance, the flies may float over the head of a fish that may strike a fly if it was at eye level or drifting along the stream bottom.

The upper fly is referred to as the "dropper fly", often secured to the leader by means of a short "dropper line". The dropper line can be created in a variety of ways. My preference is to cut the leader at the desired point then rejoin the line with a surgeon knot. The surgeon knot (see illustration, page 42) is simple, fast to tie, and retains 95% of the original line strength. Once the knot is tied, instead of trimming both tag ends, trim only one; leave the tag which points away from the rod tip. This is important because the mechanics of the knot are such that if you choose the wrong tag to trim, and secure the dropper fly to it, the knot will break with a strong strike.

I know some very good nymph anglers who secure the uppermost fly of a two-fly setup by tying directly to the leader with a clinch or turle knot. Then, secure a 15"-18" section of tippet (lower portion of the leader) to the bend of the hook by means of a clinch knot, with the second (terminal) artificial tied on to complete the system. Having experimented with securing the lower fly by tying the tippet to the bend of the upper hook, I am not a believer. Though it makes changing flies and tippet length fast and easy, I believe there is the possibility that a striking steelhead may not be fully or securely hooked on the upper fly. The fish may bump the line at the hook bend

The Scorpion Stonefly Nymph has a combination of color, flash and movement that steelhead like.

with its snout, pushing the fly away as it tries to bite it. Or, the hook point may not fully penetrate the mouth, being partially blocked or deflected by the line secured at the hook bend.

Now, if an angler has two dozen steelhead strikes in a day, it may be no big deal to lose a few fish. However, if an angler gets only three, two, or one strike in a fishing day, he may wish to assure, as best he can, that the steelhead stays hooked. I, of course, would invite every fly-angler to experiment with a variety of dropper-creation methods. But, the next time you lose a precious steelhead opportunity as the fish throws the fly or you miss a solid strike…Doh!…you may wonder if the line secured to the hook bend of the upper fly was the problem.

Let's review the water type in which to successfully locate a holding steelhead that might bite the fly. Be very particular since you cannot catch fish where they are not. Look for flows that approximate a "walking pace". I know this is not a very precise description of the desirable current velocity, but you are looking for a unidirectional flow of a leisurely to average walking speed. There may be exceptions, but start your search with a common-sense estimation. If the surface waters are slightly choppy or riffly, so much the better.

For effective presentation of the nymph, find water you estimate to be three to seven feet deep. Even though steelhead may hold in shallower or deeper water than my suggested range, three to seven feet maximizes your chances when we factor in stealth, line control and detection of a subtle strike.

The third consideration to enhance locating a likely hot target is underwater structure. Boulders, ledges, scooped depressions, and transitions from shallow water to deep are all appealing resting areas for steelhead. Swirling eddies immediately behind *exposed* midstream boulders intrigue the inexperienced angler. Remember; look for unidirectional, not swirling, multidirectional currents. Depending on its shape and surrounding depth, exposed boulders may have steelhead holding in front or on either side of them. Fully submerged boulders do not present this eddying problem to the same degree.

An experienced steelheader also learns that preferred steelhead lies change as the river flow increases or decreases. Yesterday's hotspot may no longer hold fish as the water drops or rises. At any water level, seek out those locations that fit the three general parameters I have suggested.

It's time to fish. Let us take it from the top. If on foot, I prefer to position myself at the downstream end of the run I have chosen to fish. Since fish face into the current, I am approaching them from behind. With quiet wading, I can get relatively close to a steelhead's position without alarming it. When fishing from a boat, I start at the upstream end of the run and fish it downstream. Because the fish are facing me, and I have a much higher profile standing in the boat I cannot get as close to the fish as I can while wading.

Since most of the time I am unable to locate the fish visually, I must methodically cover the likely holding water. Assuming I can wade close to the water I am fishing, my first cast may land the flies no more than 20 feet away. The cast is angled upstream at 45 to 60 degrees from straight across the current. As the flies drift back with the current toward me, they should quickly sink. To that end, I gather some of the slack by merely raising my rod tip on a short cast, but not all of the slack. Leave about two feet of the floating fly line on the water. In so doing I have an excellent balance between too much slack and too little. A few seconds after the flies hit the water I mend the fly line. Once the line and flies have passed my position on their journey downstream I begin to lower my rod tip slowly to give back line, maintaining a little slack until the current finally pulls the whole system tight at the end of the drift.

Sometimes the angler can get a startling surprise as the leader tightens in the current and the nymphs rise off the stream bottom, lifted toward the surface by tension against a swift current. Just as some steelhead are willing to attack a swinging wet fly, some will intercept a rising nymph.

Sometimes a steelhead inhales a simple, sparse-bodied size-12 nymph just as if it was a meticulously tied, elaborate wet fly. This forces me to ponder how important, at times, the fly pattern is compared to the determined aggression of a particular individual steelhead. This fish may be willing to attack *anything* that invades its personal space. Often, it seems, the chief determining factor in eliciting a striking response from a certain steelhead is the attitude of that fish. The moral here:

do not be too quick to lift the nymphs from the water for the next cast until they have had a couple seconds to swing up and hold in the current. Often I have had a client hesitate before making their next cast, as I give them instructions or reminders. Sometimes lightning strikes as the nymphs hang high in the current. Fish on!

Short and Accurate

Effective nymphing is a short-line game, usually played out within thirty-five feet of the angler. From your initial position make a dozen good casts of varying lengths, then move up- or downstream by about a rod length and start your casting routine again. A typical first cast is no more than a rod-length of fly line. Repeat the cast but change the angle slightly. For the next two casts lengthen the line a couple feet. Make two casts, and then lengthen until you have reached your maximum effective fishing distance, or you've covered the good fishing water. Be thorough, and do not ignore the short casts. Sometimes a steelhead will hold in the water underneath your rod tip. I have seen it happen many times, and if you ignore the water closest to you, you may pass up a willing biter. Which leads me to a story…

When Is Close Not Close Enough?

I had a rare Busman's Holiday on the Rogue late one fall day when a client (whom I immediately promoted to the rank "former client") called to make a last-minute cancellation for

Egg patterns are effectively fished using the steelhead nymphing system. They are especially effective during salmon spawning in the fall, and steelhead spawning time winter and spring.

our scheduled fishing trip. So, I had the chance to fish with my friends Jeff and Rick. Jeff is a long-time friend and client, and Rick was the same, in addition to being a very, very good Montana fishing guide.

I'm on the oars. My buds are fishing. They were landing the occasional trout but the biting steelhead were hiding from us during the first hour of the trip. Having stayed on the move, drifting with the current and casting as we went, I headed to the specific location where we would anchor for the first time. In a deep slot that preceded small rapid, I wanted my guys to spend some time covering the water very thoroughly. This particular spot always held steelhead. I was convinced that the right drift of the fly would entice at least one to bite.

Even though my friends are good anglers, I could not refrain from dispensing the occasional technique reminders about the angle of the cast, the distance, the timing of the mend, the extension of the fly's drift, blah, blah, blah.

In the right piece of water, a steelhead may lay undisturbed quite close to the boat. An angler who does not make a short cast to discover such fish will never catch them. Among many of my reflexive instructions to Jeff and Rick was to make sure a few short casts were made, so as to drift the fly near the boat. As they cast I watched. They made many good presentations in likely water without results. When they had convinced themselves that no fish were to be had, I politely inquired if I could make a few casts before pulling anchor.

I grabbed my nymph rod and stood to cast. Eight to ten feet of fly line hung below my rod tip. I angled the cast upstream in such a way that my line and fly would, essentially, drift directly beneath my rod tip. Yes, on my very first cast the strike indicator hesitated. The hook was set, the battle commenced. A six-pound hen was soon in the boat. My point was illustrated. No need for a second cast. I pulled anchor to drift on. I do not remember whether my friends laughed or cried.

Egg Patterns

Egg patterns are fished in exactly the same manner as nymphs: dead-drifted near the stream bottom, usually underneath a strike indicator. Year-round, steelhead will show an interest in eating fish eggs. A convincing imitation—like my Bead Egg—in shades of pink and orange are "must" patterns in any fly box.

When rivers are low and clear in fall and winter, my clients and I usually fish two eggs, sizes 6 or 8, in lieu of all other patterns. Small, non-threatening morsels fool steelhead. These are my best chance of catching fish on crowded rivers. With daily fishing pressure on accessible rivers, aggressive hatchery fish are quickly removed from the system. The native steelhead that are caught and released are taught to be more discriminating. Your best chance to cajole and coax more discriminating, wary fish is with a "harmless" little artificial.

Let 'Em Hang

Be aware of the first few seconds as the nymphs or egg flies swim up off the bottom as your line straightens in the current at the end of your drift. Once or twice in a typical fishing day, an aggressive steelhead will grab a nymph as it swings tight. Don't be too anxious about immediately picking up your flies to re-cast because the nymphs have completed their deep, slow drift along the stream bottom. I have witnessed many situations where one angler is letting their nymphs hang in the current, waiting for their fishing partner to complete his cast. During the wait, it is not uncommon to have a steelhead attack one of the nymphs.

Deviate from the Ordinary Now and Then

Though I have said it before, it bears repeating—steelhead fishing, like the Devil, is in the details. "Nuance" is an appealing term to me because it implies subtlety in the details. Subtle adjustments. Exacting finesse.

Unicorns frequent steelhead rivers.

In a broad expanse of river, steelhead can hold in very specific locations. These are spots where they find the river-flow hydraulics, light, perceived proximity to cover, and general comfort to their liking. This eliminates 99% of the water into which you could cast. Exact holding locations are money IF the angler can locate them. If such an area allows the fisherman to observe steelhead holding in a specific location time after time—assuming the river flow levels are generally the same each time—a pot of steelhead gold has been found. Most of the time preferred holding locations are discovered when the angler consistently hooks steelhead in the same spot as the water is fished "blind", where holding fish cannot be seen because of the depth, light, or a rippled or "broken" nature of the water's surface. Some locations are obvious with a little experience. Others are subtle and difficult, remaining hidden even from many with much experience.

Some reliable steelhead-holding locations may be undiscovered by the majority because they fish a likely spot from a vantage point that does not allow them to present the fly, lure or bait in a way that will interest the steelhead enough to cause it to strike. Their offering drifts too fast, too far left or right, or too high in the current to entice. Where you stand as

Caddisflies are a readily available food source if steelhead are in the mood. Because nymphs are fished near and along the stream bottom, caddis cases may collect on the hook point.

A caddisfly larva removed from its protective case. The larva will transform into a pupa, which will make a mad dash to the surface where it will hatch into an adult. Caddisfly pupal patterns can be effective steelhead-catchers, too.

you cast, or drop your boat anchor if floating the river, can be the difference between fishing success and failure.

An example is in order. I am thinking of a favorite tailout on a favorite river where exact casting position is critical. In midstream is a huge rock that splits the river. The left channel is too fast and shallow to hold a fish comfortably. Steelhead naturally ascend the rapid, and rest in the deeper right channel. This channel is replete with submerged boulders that break the current, offering the fish comfort and protection during its travels.

There is quiet water off the right bank, an easy and obvious place to drop anchor and fish from a stationary boat. I have watched scores of skilled boating anglers park here to fish the channel. On many occasions, I have done exactly the same thing, having my clients fish the run from the obvious and easy vantage point. One of my clients hooked five steelhead fishing the right channel from the *right-hand* side, the obvious and easy position that all boating anglers naturally choose. It can be a very good vantage point to present the fly to the fish. But, as the river flow continues to drop throughout late summer and fall, success is scarce. Some good anglers and fishing guides who often fish this run get discouraged. They begin to bypass fishing the channel and move down river. I love to see this. Warms my cold heart.

Preferably, other anglers are out of sight. I back ferry (row backwards with the oars) to hold my boat without anchoring in the swift water at the lower right side of the right channel, just before it spills into the rapids below. It's work, and it's tricky. The currents will constantly attempt to force the boat out of the position I want to hold it. If I end up too far left, the boat is pulled into the channel, and on top of the fish. If swept too far right, my clients cannot get an accurate and correct drift of the fly. I am riding a fine line and continuously making little rowing adjustments to keep the boat in the perfect fishing position. One of my clients will often hook a steelhead if they are attentive to the strike. I watch each cast while simultaneously tending our position. Experience has told me which casts have a chance to drift correctly to a fish that may be willing to bite. I have the clients re-cast immediately if the fly has little chance of drifting into the Sweet Spot. Even fishing behind other boaters who have fished the channel, I would estimate we hook a steelhead here 50% of the time.

Then I have a move that I have never seen another boater or guide make. I row the boat back upstream, careful to stay out of the main channel, and then slide the boat to the *left* side of the deep channel. I let the boat drift down to the lower end of the channel, to the point where the water is swift, barely above the rapids. Back ferrying here, again, is a tricky chore. The currents tend to move me out of position if I am not careful.

The fish-holding spot I am seeking is very small, very specific. The steelhead tend to hold behind a particular boulder that I can see, though I cannot see the fish in the riffly flow. The right cast will produce a steelhead strike about 80% of the time. If you have any steelheading experience, there is an outrageous degree of reliability for hooking a steelhead. The angler in the *front* of the boat is always the one to hook the fish. The angler in the rear of the boat may be more skilled but cannot get the right vantage point to present the fly. If I dropped the boat farther downstream to accommodate the client in the stern, I would be swept into the rapid.

So, let's recount the nuances. Lower water flows often cause steelhead to hold in a different portion of a dependable fishing hole. It is imperative to pinpoint where the specific,

often small, Sweet Spots are located. Emphasis: *specific* locations. Experimentation is necessary to locate the subtle and difficult spots where a steelhead may rest. Additionally, it may be tedious and tricky to position the angler in the necessary vantage point from which to make an accurate and good drift of the fly to the fish. Whether wading or boating, a position a few feet in one direction or another can make for success or failure. The fly must be near enough, slow enough and deep enough to entice the strike. This is often a game of inches. If the fly drifts a few inches too far right or left, or above the holding fish, it will not take. The strike can be quite subtle. Be alert, and be quick.

In Summary

Successful nymph fishing for steelhead is a network of small, but extremely significant, details. Pay attention, be creatively adaptive, and persist. Because it is the most effective fly-fishing method for catching steelhead, time and practice must be allotted to nymphing in order to master it. And, remember the steelhead make the rules. To catch them on a consistent basis, be open, be experimental, and expect to be surprised from time to time. They lead the dance, the steps may be intricate, and you must learn to follow as best you can.

Karl "BigFish" Brantley and brother David.

CHAPTER 9
Productive Steelhead Water Types and Fly-Presentation Options

EVERY STEELHEAD RIVER
has named fishing "holes". The Powerline Hole; Meat Hole;
Dead Man's Hole; Ace-in-the-Hole Hole. "Hole" is too generic for me,
and is probably not helpful to the inexperienced angler
trying to recognize productive steelhead water.

I arbitrarily classify worthy water into seven general types: tailouts, runs, channels, pockets, seams, transition zones, and pools. My definitions/descriptions of these are my own. I realize that some good fish-holding areas are some sort of hybrid of the seven water types I will be describing.

As for fishing methods and particular flies in various water types, in summer and fall, because the water temperatures are conducive to active steelhead, I will ply most fishable locations with a wet fly if the water is in shade. The method is simple, I can cover the water quickly and efficiently, and I love to feel the hard grab of a steelhead. It's like being struck by lightning, only in a *good* way. If I think I may be the first angler to fish this particular spot for the day, I can choose to skate a dry fly. If the area is in direct sunlight, I can choose to fish it deep with a wet fly on a fast-sinking sink-tip or my Hybrid Line system, or nymph fish with a floating line and indicator. In shade or overcast, in a high-probability piece of water, I may actually employ all three fly-angling methods. Because as individual steelhead exhibit individual preferences, there is actually a chance I could hook steelhead employing all three methods in a single location in summer and fall.

During the cold-water temperatures of winter and early spring, I can swing a wet fly deep. After doing so, I will definitely fish a nymph or egg pattern under an indicator, casting a floating fly line. Then, I may fish through with nymphs and egg patterns presented with my Hybrid Line System to give the steelhead a slightly different drift of the flies. The Hybrid Line is particularly useful to me where I am probing deeper runs where the depths range from six to ten feet. As stated earlier, the Hybrid Line presentation fishes like a cross between a deep-swinging wet fly and a nymph fished under an indicator with a floating fly line. This presentation may hold a special appeal to a steelhead not interested in the flies drifted or swung to it with other methods.

Tailouts

Think of running uphill against the wind. Migrating steelhead coursing their way upstream against the swift currents of a rapid may be inclined to rest a bit once they have reached quiet water. The smooth, tamer water immediately upstream of a rapid is a tailout. Using round numbers, the tailout may extend from ten to fifty feet upstream of a rapid. Though no two are exactly alike, the typical tailout will range from a few inches to a few feet deep across its breadth, from bank to bank. Factoring in the combination of current velocity, depth, and stream-bottom structure, a steelhead may linger just above the rapid for a while if left undisturbed. Because the typical tailout has flat, unriffled surface currents, and is rather shallow, the fish is exposed. Observant predators and anglers will be able to locate a steelhead parked in a tailout. You can bet the steelhead is on high alert for danger. It has not survived to this point in its life by being careless. Therefore, stealth is of extreme importance to the would-be successful fisherman.

The fly-angler has two viable fly-fishing options in the typical tailout: the skated dry fly and the swinging wet fly.

Most steelhead fly-anglers, novice and veteran alike, are probably most familiar with the wet-fly presentation. If the ambient light is dim due to time of day, an overcast sky, or the fish is in water shaded by tall trees or high terrain, a floating fly line is typically used. Unless the current is very swift, the wet fly drifts from a few inches to a few feet below the surface. The strategy is to have the fly swing across the current in a broad arc in front of the fish, close enough to stir its striking interest. The angler should position himself upstream and off to the side of the fish, as opposed to directly upstream of the quarry. Present the fly at an angle slightly downstream from across the current. Successive casts are about two feet longer than the preceding one until the fishable area has been completely covered.

Soon after each wet-fly cast, mend the fly line. A mend is a lifting and repositioning of the fly line upstream of the fly to slow the fly a bit, as it arcs across the river. Multiple mends may be necessary. A slow-moving wet fly has been repeatedly proven most provocative to willing steelhead. Should the fish refuse the fly, consider changing to a smaller pattern, and maybe a different color, too.

For a steelhead holding in direct sunlight, it may be necessary to utilize a full-sinking or sink-tip fly line. In bright light, a fish may need to have the fly presented at its holding level near the stream bottom, unwilling to move upward to a fly drifting overhead. An alternative to the sinking line would be a weighted wet fly that will swim deep as it approaches the steelhead. Lead wire wrapped underneath the body of the fly as it is created, or lead eyes tied near the hook eye will work to this end.

If the light is dim, or the water is in shade, and you are willing to risk a heart attack, consider skating a dry fly over a steelhead holding in a tailout. Using a floating fly line, of course, the fly-fisherman casts the fly down and across the current at the same angle as the wet fly. A mend to the line may

Steelhead will often linger in the quiet water of a tailout after expending energy to push through swift whitewater.

Because runs may be expansive and steelhead spread throughout, they must be methodically covered.

or may not be necessary. The angler must watch the progress of the fly. To be most effective the skating fly should create a wake as it progresses through its arc near the fish. Though this does not work on every fish in a tailout, the wake of the floating fly, for some reason, will excite the right steelhead.

When the strike, slash or sip of the dry comes, do nothing! Wait until the fish has submerged with the hook in its mouth AND begins to pull line off your fly reel. Set the hook too quickly, which is our natural instinct, and the fly will be pulled from the fish's mouth. This is a hard lesson, but necessary. You need nerves of steel for this technique. Welcome and enjoy the challenge.

Runs

I define a steelhead *run* as a wide and long expanse of river where the aggregate of current velocity, depth and structure is abundant throughout. Submerged boulders often abound in such areas. The steelhead are happy to rest just about anywhere in a good run, so an angler must very systematically cover this type of prime water throughout its entire width and length, though there may be a few special boulders or pockets within the run that are especially attractive to traveling steelhead. Think of these as the best "homes" in an excellent neighborhood.

Runs lend themselves to fishing with wet flies for sure, as described previously. For those portions of a run where the surface flows are relatively smooth, not too riffled, the skating

dry fly can be effective. Where the run is three to seven feet deep, nymph fishing can be deadly.

Most nymph flies are imitations of immature aquatic insects. However, egg flies and colorful concoctions, generally referred to as *attractor flies*, are also fished using the nymphing technique. Cast the fly upstream, roughly at an angle of 45-60 degrees from straight across the river's current. Allow the flies to sink on a slack line. Most of the slack, but not all, is gathered by the fly-fisherman as it drifts back toward him with the current. If a steelhead intercepts the fly, the line will hesitate or tighten. The angler should not expect to feel the strike. Since an artificial fly has no agreeable, taste, smell or texture, the steelhead holds it only briefly before expelling it. From interception to expulsion may be a second or less. This is a game of quick draw. The angler must be alert and respond quickly to have any hope of hooking the fish. A strike indicator made of cork, foam or synthetic yarn secured on the leader at a distance above the fly equal to the water depth plus two feet, serves as a great visual aid in detecting a grab.

A fourth fly-fishing method that can be employed in covering a steelhead run involves the use of my Hybrid Line System. Using interchangeable sinking-tips attached to a running line, the angler casts upstream at approximately a 45-degree angle. Let the fly sink on a slack line, just as in nymph fishing. The nymphing method is employed during the drift until the system is approximately 45 degrees downstream of your

A good run can produce multiple steelhead hookups, and may take an hour or more to thoroughly fish.

position. Then, after the line is mended upstream of the fly, it arcs across the current on a tight line, fished just as a wet fly would be. Two fly-fishing methods—nymphing and wet fly—are utilized on a single drift of the fly.

Channels

A *channel* is a well-defined narrow band of deep water bounded by shallow water. Often, these are found near the river's edge, close to the bank. In pointing them out to my fishing clients, I refer to them as "dark green highways". Where a run is broad, a channel is narrow. They are literally used as highways for traveling steelhead. Where the fish find depth, cover, and suitable structure in the course of a channel, they are prompted to linger.

Think of channels as steelhead highways, an obvious route where an astute angler will focus his casts

All three fly-fishing methods used for prospecting runs can be used in channels. Your options will be driven by the usual factors: depth, current velocity, choppy or smooth surface conditions, direct sunlight or shade, and overhanging tree limbs if near the riverbank.

Pockets

Pockets are small fish-holding locations usually associated with swift water and structure. In a boulder-strewn rapid, you find areas of quieter (not dead still) water in front of, behind, or beside large rocks. If a boulder is submerged, the pocket immediately downstream of it may be fishable. If the rock is exposed above the river's surface, the pocket behind it may have slack "dead" water or an eddy that does not hold a steelhead, or makes it impossible to present a fly in a convincing manner. So do not maintain the notion that the pocket immediately behind a boulder is always a good fishing-holding spot. Be discriminating. Seek a uni-directional current, not a swirling eddy.

Though most pockets are associated with a rapid, there are solitary steelhead pockets near a solitary boulder or a scour in the stream bottom where the river's currents have carved out an obvious deeper water depression surrounded entirely

Seams provide narrow focal points for an angler's casts, and can usually be quickly and thoroughly fished.

by shallower water. These are like little oases in the desert. A migrating steelhead may have traveled a considerable distance through unsuitable holding water when it finally happens upon a pocket where a pause is in order.

Depending on the specific characteristics of a pocket, dry flies, wet flies or nymphs can be used. Because they are usually small, pockets do not take long to cover. Fish them thoroughly and quickly; then, move on. Pocket steelhead, if interested at all, are usually aggressive as they respond to the fly.

Seams

The boundary between fast water and slow water is a *seam*. It is a transition zone where the water may be to the liking of a resting steelhead, typically a band two to six feet wide. The swift current on one side of the seam is too fast for a fish to

Pocket water provides safe haven as a steelhead traverses its route through swift currents. The choppy nature of the surface currents decreases the ability to see and be seen from above, giving the fish a sense of security.

Transition zones are a natural place for steelhead to linger before the fish commits to exposing itself when moving into shallow water, especially when the sun is high and visibility is good.

hold comfortably. The slower moving, or slack water, on the other side of the seam is too quiet to be attractive or secure for the steelhead, so it travels and holds on the seam.

I prefer to use either the wet-fly method or nymphing to fish seams. I cast the wet fly into the faster water, then, swing it into and across the seam. I start at the upstream end of the target area and systematically work my way downstream until I have covered its entire length. If I choose to probe the water with nymphs—usually my first choice—I can start at either the upstream or downstream terminus of the productive water, working until I have covered the entire length of the seam. Drop the nymph into the seam and allow it to drift naturally with the current through the heart of the prime water.

Transition Zones

There are obvious fish-holding zones where shallow-water areas transition into deeper water. The river bottom slopes downward from being too shallow to hold fish into deeper, prime-fishing water of three to seven feet in depth.

A transition can work the opposite way, too: water that may be too deep to fish effectively with a fly starts to "shallow up" at its downstream end. A pool or run that may be ten to twenty feet deep will eventually transition into the desirable three to seven feet range.

In summer and fall, I will be most inclined to ply transition zones with a wet fly if the water is in shade. If the surface is not too choppy, I can choose to skate a dry fly. In direct sunlight, I may fish it deep with a wet fly on a fast-sinking sink-tip fly line, or just nymph-fish it. In shade or overcast, in a high-probability piece of water, I may actually employ all three fly-angling methods.

In winter and early spring I usually nymph-fish it with egg or shrimp-like flies, using a floating line and indicator. To seek out steelhead that prefer a different presentation of the fly, I go through a second time with the Hybrid Line System, and same flies. For those who wish to swing a large wet fly or leech pattern deep, try a heavy sink-tip line and a standard wet-fly presentation.

As I said earlier, there are steelhead-holding locations that do not easily fall into any one single category as described above. Don't fret about it. Rather than worrying about how to specifically define the water where you are trying to find a willing steelhead, try to discern if the water in front of you has the characteristics that would encourage a fish to hold there: current velocity, depth and structure. Match the fly-fishing methods to the light and river conditions, the structural nature of your chosen piece of water, your skills, and the fishing methods you enjoy.

Pools

Pools are obvious steelhead-holding locations. Pools can be large or small; wide or narrow; have fast currents, or slow; be monstrously deep, or only moderately so. But, they all have three portions in common: a transition zone at the head, a deep 'heart', and a tailout. Since identifying and fishing *tailouts* and *transition zones* has already been addressed, let's focus on fishing the heart of the pool.

As I assess the potential of hooking a steelhead in a pool, I take into consideration the current velocity, depth and structure of the piece of water. The very first thing I study is the direction and evenness of the current. Swirling, multi-directional currents are difficult to fish effectively. The direction of the fly drift is unpredictable, and not only do you have a goofy horizontal drift of your hook, but you may have an up-and-down component as the fly moves. I want a straight line, uni-directional drift where I am in contact with what is happening. Strikes are often quite subtle, a quiet interception. There is very little time to sense the take and set the hook. Unless I can actually see a fish in swirly water, I bypass it to focus on those portions of the pool with a uniform current.

The depth of any given pool can vary greatly: degrees of shallow along its periphery, and deep to very deep in the heart. I may adjust the fly-fishing method and flies as I fish the edges, then the deep center. Think of breaking the central portion of the pool into smaller parts. Each part is a fishing entity unto itself. If the current is right, I can fish the shallower edges (3'-7') with any fly-angling method, wet, dry, or nymph. Direct sunlight or shade, broken water or smooth surface, and limitations on my fishing position as I make the cast all have bearings on my method and fly choice.

Assuming the center of the pool's heart is deeper than seven feet, my usual choice is nymphing. Adjustments in leader length and indicator location are necessary in deep water. I may have to lengthen my 9'-10' leader to 15'. The easiest way to do so is merely add more tippet with a double surgeon's knot. If the water is more than 10 feet deep, I may remove my indicator and focus on the movement of my floating fly line. Because of the great distance from the water's surface to the river bottom there is usually a large disparity in water velocities from top to bottom. A leader without an indicator, especially if there is a little upwelling and downwelling of the current, seems to get a truer, more natural drift. Since the detection of the strike is usually lessened without an indicator, set the hook more often, at the slightest hint of a hesitation in the line or leader. You will be surprised when you come tight against a fish when you fancied the small hesitation in your drift could not possibly have been a strike. Again, there are no penalty points for setting the hook. Look for any excuse to do so. This type of situation is also tailor-made for my Hybrid Line. This line system excels in deeper water.

There are obvious fish-holding positions in a transition zone with pockets and seams.

PRODUCTIVE STEELHEAD WATER TYPES AND FLY-PRESENTATION OPTIONS

If the current in the heart of the pool is slower than a walking speed, I may scale down the tippet diameter and tie on a smaller fly. A suspicious steelhead has a longer time to study the fly and detect the leader tied to it. Smaller and lighter is less threatening, more apt to result in a hookup. Other anglers may ignore slower currents, or they may fail to scale back their terminal gear. These can offer you—the astute guerilla—with an overlooked opportunity. Take advantage.

Pools are prime candidates for holding resting steelhead, top, middle and bottom. Be particularly patient and willing to change up the method and flies to fish the heart of the pools. When the sun is high, and there is a lot of human activity on the river, the deepest heart of the pool offers maximum protection for wary steelhead. The first requisite for effective steelhead fishing is to focus your angling time where fish are actually holding. Gotta learn to fish pools. They can be tricky; be trickier. Welcome the challenge.

Bull's Eye

I love Robin Hood movies. As a boy, I had a fascination with swordplay and long bows. Every single one of these movies has an archery contest sponsored by the wicked Sheriff of Nottingham. Hood always shows up in some lame peasant's disguise to claim the prize on the very last shot of the tournament. This final shot is always dramatic. The preceding effort by another bowman has struck the bull's eye dead center on the distant, distant target. How can Sir Robin (King Richard the LionHeart, ending his frolics at the Crusades, returns in some movies to bestow knighthood) top this? Of course, he does so by *evenly* splitting the tiny, tiny shaft of the preceding arrow. He wins the day, the hearts of the oppressed, and the beautiful Maid Marion. This reminds of steelhead fishing.

The upper reaches of Oregon's Alsea River are twenty-five minutes from my home. Late December through early February

Pools are likely resting areas where steelhead may linger for a few hours or a few days. Because some pools can be very deep, an angler must be willing to change lines, leaders, and flies to effectively cover a variety of depths.

is prime time for the mix of hatchery and native winter steelhead on their spawning migration. I may spend a few hours two or three days a week here if the flows are fishable.

On any steelhead river, it has been my experience that more water appears fishable and productive than actually is. In virtually every good-looking run that holds fish there is a "Sweet Spot", a small pocket that is just big enough to hold a couple of steelhead, and not much more. One of my goals is to position myself precisely—literally, within a few small steps upstream or downstream—to get the fly to drift perfectly through the small Target Area. If slightly too far upstream, the line pulls tight in the current lifting the fly off the bottom. Two steps too far downstream you discover the fly has not had sufficient time to sink to the fishes' holding level. Casting position, like desirable real estate, can be everything.

On a frozen January morning, I found the river low and clear. These conditions were ideal for fishing what I call The Distant Bedrock Nook. I moved into perfect position to discover if there might be a biting steelhead in this tiny pocket. The cast would be a long one considering I was under a canopy of trees whose limbs reached out from all directions attempting to grab my leader and flies. I have very little back-cast room and must keep the forward cast relatively low to get to the target safely. Once the flies hit the water, I must mend the line to create necessary slack for the flies to sink. A pull on the line to adjust the line of drift is imperative. Only one in ten casts, sometimes one in twenty, is just right. The steelhead holding area here is both narrow and short. I am speculating when I say six feet long by three or four feet wide.

I watch many anglers fish this little spot. Occasionally I see a fish caught that is not on my hook. Most anglers are unsuccessful during my observations. Often, it is because the bait, lure or fly is not fished deep enough, or slow enough. Sometimes it is because their standing position is not right, so a proper drift in the fish's holding zone is not possible. And, I am certain many do not know the exact location of the Sweet Spot.

On the morning of my story, it took me more than two dozen casts to put all the necessary elements of the perfect drift together. Experienced anglers "sense" the Perfect Drift. My strike indicator was coursing as slowly as the current would allow dead center in the line of drift that would allow the flies to drift lazily through the Spot. I *expected* the strike indicator to go down. It did.

The native hen attached to my line sprinted around the river in front of me for four or five minutes before I finally got a good look at her. As her fight slowed, I coaxed the steelhead downstream to a suitable shallow area where I could slide her onto her side for the release. Backing out the size-6 egg pattern, I watched her sprint into the depths.

It both fascinates and teaches me that getting the Perfect Drift requires repeated effort. The first twenty (or so) casts to this steelhead's zone were not good enough to entice it to bite, drifting either too high or low; drifting too far left, too far right; drifting, perhaps, unnaturally fast.

I frequently tell my clients, "Where there can be one fish there may be two." Taking my own adage to heart, I returned to my original position and made subsequent attempts at a second Perfect Drift. This time it took me less than a dozen tries. It was déjà vu all over again.

If you are a believer in reincarnation, and you come back to this world as a fish, remember that one of the best escape moves you can make is to swim immediately and directly at the angler. Instantly, slack line is created. With little tension on the line, the hook can be thrown before it penetrates deeply.

This steelhead knew this evasive maneuver. I frantically swung my rod tip in many different directions while reeling line trying to tighten against the charging fish. It does not always work, but, finally, I was able to make contact with my quarry. I set the hook to, as best I could, bury the point in its jaw. My efforts were successful. I eventually slid this naughty hatchery buck into the shallows I had visited earlier with the hen.

So, there were *two* steelhead in the little pocket of my interest. Both were very discriminating about the presentation of my fly. The bull's eye can be quite small, and a slow, deep drift of the fly through the target is mandatory.

As I mentioned earlier, the Sweet Spot can move or disappear. At higher, yet fishable, river levels, my Bedrock Nook does not hold steelhead. Apparently, the increased hydraulics makes it too uncomfortable for a fish to linger here. The preferred holding area has moved a short cast upstream to the inside corner of a riffled run. An astute, experienced angler will know this.

Hey, Everybody, Fish Here!

There is a very wadeable steelhead run near a large county park. Within this expanse of fishy water are oval pockets of deeper water and channels edged with bedrock. I call this area Last Chance, since it is the last quality fish-holding location before the boat ramp to take off the river at the end of our fishing day. Once upon a time when the world was as it should be, all anglers fished Last Chance, which stretched for more than a hundred yards, from the shallow, park-side of the river. Day after day I would watch them cast toward what I knew to be the productive water on the far side of the current. Delightfully, their success was dismal. Their problem was not reaching the water where steelhead lay. Unknown to them, I suspect, was that they could not get a controlled, deep, strike-inducing drift. The flies moved too fast in the flow, and did not get deep enough to interest the fish. As I drifted my boat through this area, I would float tight against the far bank, away from the anglers on the opposite side. Since we were almost on top of the steelhead, I would have my clients cast short and hold their rods high to get a deep, slow drift. Many times someone in my boat would hook a fish, to the astonishment and, often, the dismay of the onlookers. Sometimes we would hook two fish. This was pride before the inevitable fall.

Jason Mariner with another one! Hiking into small streams eliminates boat traffic and anglers who won't walk very far.

In this ever-present group of park fishermen was a retired senior citizen who spent just about every day on the river. He was astute, and he was determined. For an older man Mr. Astute was also an able wader. Though he had to walk quite a distance up my side of the river, and the currents were faster and the water deeper on my side, he eventually found his way to the sweet spot which I could not resist fishing in spite of an audience. Astute fashioned a wading staff, and doggedly plowed his way into the correct position to present his fly effectively, just as I had been doing for years without competition. To my dismay, others eventually followed him. My observant competitor shared his bounty with his friends who shared it with their friends. Additionally, other observant anglers stationed themselves on my side of the river to catch the steelhead, which I had little opportunity to fish for on subsequent trips. Because of my lack of discipline, in the throes of Steelhead Fever, I educated the fishing public. In turn, they locked me out of this particular fishing sweet spot. Most days on the river, I do not get to fish here because someone is already standing where I want/need to be. Why must the best lessons always be difficult lessons?

Many would take exception to my hard-line view that fishing, especially for steelhead, can be a zero sum game: there is a finite number of fish and too many anglers wanting to catch them. If I could, I would catch every biting fish in the river

knowing very well that it may mean others would catch none. I would feel no remorse. It is with this attitude that I approach the river every day, every minute on the river. My paying clients know this. They can rest assured, without the slightest doubt, that I will do whatever it takes to put them on steelhead before someone else has a chance to hook THEIR fish. I need not be rude, but I will always play hard, and play to win. That means, given the chance, me or my guys (or gals) will be catching YOUR fish. Think of it as a game of chess. I am looking for checkmate on every move. I wave and even smile on the river, but I am looking to knock your king off the board.

Another Lucky Accident

A very productive seam was brought to my attention by a fortuitous accident when one of my clients persisted casting a wet fly through water I had originally perceived as marginal, and not worth my fishing time. My client got two strikes on his wet fly hanging in the current below my drift boat as we slowly drifted downstream to the next spot I wanted to fish. I made a quick mental note of the exact locations of the strikes. This area was now on my radar, and it has turned out to be very productive over the last few years.

Some seams—interfaces between fast water and slow—are relatively broad, maybe spanning six to eight feet in width. Others, like this spot, Maple Leaf, are no more than two feet in width. Casts must be accurate to fall into this very narrow current lane. On one side of this seam, the water is too fast for a fish to hold comfortably; on the other side, the water has very little movement, and cannot be fished effectively. It is along this very narrow, well-defined band that fish hold, and can be tricked into striking a fly.

One advantage of fishing seams is that they can be fished quickly. Unlike a broad expanse of water, like a wide run, fish concentrated along a narrow band can be covered with a fly in a short amount of time. You know precisely where they are located, and can quickly discover if steelhead here are interested in striking a fly. Such locations lend themselves to a hit-and-run approach, like a commando mission: get in, get out… undetected.

In shade or under overcast skies, I fish this seam with a wet fly first, hoping to get a hard yank from a willing steelhead. Then, I fish Maple Leaf with nymphs or egg flies, depending on the time of year. Some days both methods are good for a hook-up.

As with most good fishing zones, Maple Leaf only fishes well at specific river levels. If the water is too high or too low, it's a no-go. When the flow is just right this spot will consistently produce one or two biting steelhead each day I fish it. Unlike the "advertising" I did to draw other anglers to Last Chance, I will pull my anchor and leave Maple Leaf if other anglers approach. If someone is within sight when I arrive, I pass it by.

In Summary

In addition to generally seeking steelhead water with the appropriate current velocity, depth, and structure, focus, also, on specific water types I have discussed in this chapter. In so doing, you may find some steelhead-holding locations you might normally overlook. Upon closer examination of seams, runs, channels, tailouts, and pockets, you may be able to pinpoint little areas where steelhead will linger long enough to be receptive to a well-presented fly. Fish such discoveries several times at various water levels. You may find some gems.

When it comes to specific fly-fishing methods used in any given water type, a variety of methods may be employed, all being effective. The best choices are shaped by conditions: sunlight, water temperature, river levels, fishing pressure, your skills. Personally, depending on my mood and preferences for the day, I may choose one method over another for no other reason than that is what I like today.

Wading is always easy in a boat. An elevated fishing position makes for easier line control.

CHAPTER 10
Getting Your Fly to the Steelhead: A Process

ARMED WITH SOME STEELHEAD KNOWLEDGE
and good equipment, it's time to formulate
a sound plan to finally get your fly
in front of a steelhead.

*At some river levels, certain rapids are too dangerous to boat, so the craft must be lined
or walked around the hazard, not always an easy task.*

This is a four-stage process: Carefully choosing a steelhead river; Getting to the water's edge; Getting into or onto the river; Lastly, casting the fly to the fish's vicinity. Each stage falls within the range from simple in some cases to difficult in others.

The subsequent stages of fishing-day planning leading up to finally hooking a steelhead are moot if the angler does not first pick a river with steelhead in it. Doh! And even if there are fish in the stream of choice, water conditions or fishing pressure can foil your success. It may be possible to circumvent both these problems on a given river if you know *where* to fish it. If you don't, or such a location does not exist on this stream, choose another. Once the decision is made, always have a Plan B, just in case.

Getting to the river's edge can be as easy as driving on a paved roadway, parking next to the water, taking a few easy steps off the road, and make that first cast. At the other extreme, an angler may have to drive many miles on a nasty dirt road that demands 4-wheel drive. After parking, a steep hike down a trail-less, entangled terrain of trees, thorny vines, and bushes is required to finally get to the stream. Add large backpacks laden with camping gear, supplies, and an inflatable raft to the hike and you've really taken the difficulty of the approach to the extreme.

Once to the river, fly-anglers will either wade into the water or climb into a floating craft in order to get close enough to the fish to cast a fly to them. Wading can be easy and sure-footed, or it can be dangerous in swift, deep flows. A boat ride can be easy, gliding along gentle currents with very few obstructions, or it can be a dangerous matter of negotiating obstacles through powerful rapids which have histories of accidents and death.

Fly-casting to steelhead can mean a short flip of the line to let a wet fly drift and swing in the current, with no complicated manipulations of the fly or line by the angler. In other situations, a cast of eighty feet or more is necessary to reach the steelhead's vicinity. Once the fly has hit the water, tremendous mends of the fly line may be necessary to control and slow the drift of the fly through a variety of challenging currents.

There are a variety of reasons a fly-angler may choose an easy or very difficult path to finally present his fly to a steelhead. Chief among these is to get away from other anglers competing for the same fish. I'm sure that for most steelhead fishermen simple is best: drive to the edge of the river, string up the rod, make a 20-foot cast, hook and land a steelhead. But, in the real world, good river choice (along with Plan B), waders, boats, long-distance casting tools, and tricky fly line manipulations are all part of the mix for *consistent* steelhead fishing success.

Plan for Success

Even when I fish or guide a steelhead river every day for weeks, I formulate a plan for the next day. Every fishing day is different: weather, water, river traffic, skills and experience of my companions or guests, section of river to be fished, river hazards, contingencies for the unexpected that may affect fishing success, comfort, enjoyment, and safety. I try to anticipate what adjustments might be needed, and what my reasonable options are.

Football can be reduced to a simple winning goal: run and pass the ball down the field and score more points than your opponent. A steelhead angler can take the same simplistic approach: drive to the river, cast your fly into the water, reel in a big fish or two; plan the BBQ.

Imagine the football team that does not have a strategic game plan, and doesn't practice. Imagine a wannabe steelheader heading to the river with no plan about where, how, and what. No prior consideration for making adjustments when a steelhead isn't caught. To me it is unimaginable until I start reading the fishing experience reports submitted by my OSU students. Many have given themselves the same chance to catch a steelhead as the proverbial snowball has of staying frozen in hell.

Those new to steelhead angling cannot begin to comprehend the time and preparation required to catch fish that are few in number, very wary, very selective about where they hold in a river, and do not need to eat. Add cutthroat competition from experienced anglers who would sell their dog in order to catch the steelhead in *your* water. Complicate this by attempting to catch a steelhead on a new river never seen, let alone fished, and we have the makings of an angling challenge.

I try to challenge my OSU steelhead-class students with this exercise: think through all the details for a *successful* steelhead trip on a river you have not fished before. I solicit ideas for preparing such a trip, and, then, write their suggestions on the chalkboard in an attempt to fuel more class participation and creative thinking. To further prod them and prompt critical thinking, I tell them there is a $10,000 reward for each steelhead they can catch in a week of fishing. This incentive seems to inspire a bit more plan-thinking.

However, if these students are representative of the public in general, veteran anglers have very little to fear from the new competition. They do a poor job. And, this is why I have little to fear from MOST steelhead anglers. They are content to find a single location and start fishing, and stay put, covering the same barren water for an hour. What worked when the river was 2 feet higher a month ago, they hope will work again, even though the river is now low and clear, the fish are ultra spooky, and the steelhead have moved to other locations in the river in search of comfort and safety. They tend to fish the same locations in the same manner, with—apparently—little regard for changing conditions and mobile targets.

Human nature tells me you will not follow my planning suggestions here, but you may eventually reconsider when you decide you want to increase your steelhead fishing success. When the student is ready, this chapter will appear.

Whether you are new to steelhead fishing, or a veteran ready to seek out steelhead in new waters, consider creating a plan; not one that necessarily takes weeks or days, but maybe thirty minutes to a few hours. Stand back and look at a macro view as you formulate a steelheading attack plan. Eventually, the needed details that demand answers will reveal themselves.

Got Fish? Finding a Productive River

Before you jump in your truck, head filled with steelheading exuberance, you need to know a worthy destination that gives you a reasonable chance to fish a river that actually holds steelhead. Where do you begin your search for steelhead rivers that hold fish right now? Though you may be familiar with two or three, you can never have enough alternatives. The right gear, excellent angling techniques, and killer flies are all for not if you do not fish a stream that holds a reasonable number of steelhead so that you have a chance to catch one.

The cornerstone of any good steelhead fishing plan starts with a potentially productive river; a river that holds lots of steelhead right now. Each river has its own timing. For instance, within two hours of my home, I have a dozen good streams and rivers that hold winter steelhead. Some fish best in December; some are prime in January; others are best February and March.

Let's say you are a rank beginner with a destination in mind, when you are confronted with crowding or poor water conditions on your familiars. How do you track down fishing possibilities?

Possible Sources

Steelhead fishing acquaintances. You may have some friends in the know, or *their* fishing friends may know. Friends occasionally like you to assure them that you are not going to share "privileged" information at Ilovecrowdedsteelheadrivers.com.

Local fly shop. If you drop into a shop *in person* — which means there may be a chance for you to lend some financial support to the business — you may be able to glean some valuable fishing information about where to catch a steelhead. Even though I have thousands of flies and too much gear, I always find something to buy at a helpful fly-fishing establishment.

State Department of Fish & Wildlife. Check out the website and look for steelhead rivers that are referenced. Rivers mentioned which you've never thought of or heard about are worth investigating. The annual fishing regulations guidebook will refer to steelhead waters that were not on your radar screen. Once discovered, do some sleuth work.

Books, magazines, TV, and DVD's. These are not generally the best sources because thousands of other readers and viewers already know what you now know. If you are looking to socialize and practice your fly casting these sources are great.

Professional fishing guides. Check out their websites to discover the rivers they fish, and the time of year that they guide them. You might find a gem. If you want to "shortcut the system", consider booking the guide for a fishing trip. If you do book a trip, ponder what you will say to the guide as you float by in your own boat when you fish it on your own in the future. Wearing a good disguise is a cowardly alternative.

Internet chat. Some fishermen need to brag, need to be a guru, need to get attention. The Chatosphere affords such possibilities. For some, it seems, the chat room is their life. I am happy for them. Souls consumed with posting and responding to their fans won't be in my way where there's fish to be caught off the beaten path. There is rarely an internet connection out there.

Be willing to separate yourself from the herd.

You Have Some New Rivers. What Next?

Run timing. Every river has its Prime Time for catching steelhead. Even those streams in the general proximity of each other can show significant differences as to the best time of the season to fish each of them. And, I am amazed at the number of anglers who assume a good *winter* run steelhead river will have an equivalently good *summer* run of steelhead; many winter-run rivers do not have a summer run of fish, and vice versa.

Access problems. Most anglers are on foot, without a boat. Many quality steelhead rivers are bounded by private property. Access may be available only at parks and bridges. If you think you will not be trespassing because you manage to stay in the river, or at least below the mean high water mark, you will eventually discover an irate landowner who will have a heated debate over this issue. If you anticipate this possibility,

I highly recommend you rehearse what you will say.

Some rivers which require serious wading to access the steelhead can be treacherous. Even small rivers can challenge the weak or timid wader as you make your way along them or cross them where necessary. Wading shoe soles with studs and a wading staff may be necessary. The plus to such waters is less competition.

Access roadways can present difficulties. Some streams are difficult to get to because you will need to negotiate a confusing maze of logging roads to find the river. In addition, even if you do find your way in, can you find your way out? Such roads are often in serious disrepair, also. Large puddles of standing water, deep mud, fallen trees, and steep, bouldered gradients make passage dangerous. My 4-wheel drive has saved me many times.

Have alternatives within striking distance. When the fishing isn't right for any of a number of reasons on today's top choice of a steelhead river, it is a good idea to have nearby alternatives available. There are some locations on the Oregon coast where there are no less than six quality steelhead streams within half an hour of each other. I can reasonably sample three of them in a fishing day. Four, if I make a long day of it.

What Can Stop Me?

Weather & water conditions. Hydrograph data is indispensable. Besides showing the river level, a current hydrograph reading shows the trend of the river level. When you check it, the river level may be perfect, but it is on a hard uptrend because of heavy rains. The flow may seem ideal but the water is muddy with intense rain and will be too high to fish in just a few hours. If this is the case, you may not be going fishing with a high probability of success. On the other hand, if the water level is trending down and not too far from a fishable level, you will know the water is clearing and will be fishable when you arrive later today or tomorrow.

As you look at a hydrograph of your river, everything can look good. However, you had better check the weather forecast, especially in the Pacific Northwest in the winter. If a massive rainstorm is coming in very soon, the river could be blown out by the time you arrive, resulting in wasted travel and fruitless fishing possibilities.

Equipment failure. Rod, reel, waders, boat (broken oar), raft or pontoon boat leak. I break one or two rods a year. I suggest always carrying a spare if you have one. When a rod breaks, it never happens at a convenient time. Waders eventually leak… especially during cold weather months, it seems. As for oars, I once broke two oars in one day while boating the North

Not all launch sites are created equal. Do what others will not.

Santiam River. Carry backups of essential gear, or the means to repair them.

Safety and First Aid. Maybe you are healthy, but what about your fishing companion. My dad had a heart condition. When we dropped into the Crooked River canyon occasionally, this was a concern. My worst leg/ankle/toe injuries have been in rivers. Communication: cell phone. Know that some rivers have no cell phone reception.

Vehicle problems. I have had the start of an early morning road trip delayed as I wait an hour or more for a gas station to open. What about that soft tire I forgot to check? As I prepare to leave, the tire is flat.

I Forgot. Fishing license. Fishing regulations. Credit card/cash. Driver's license. Sunglasses/eye protection. Sunscreen. Wading shoes. Fishing vest. Rain jacket. Gloves. Lunch & drinks. Backpack. Cell phone. Phone number for shuttle. Camera. Camera batteries. Maps & directions.

Make a little checklist. Use it just like a pilot before take-off. Plan to catch more steelhead.

Get Me to the River

It only makes sense that the easier the access to a quality steelhead, the greater the fishing pressure. We are naturally lazy; it's our human nature. M. Scott Peck in his book *The Road Less Travelled* pleads a reasonable case that it is the Original

Sin which all mankind inherits. Good steelheaders find a way to overcome laziness, at least temporarily. You must, when it comes to fishing, or you will be relinquished to fishing with the masses.

The tougher the access, the fewer the anglers…but not always. Even though you are willing to suffer by walking a long way from any road, crashing through brush and bramble to reach the river, it may all be for naught if this section is accessible by boat. All bets for solitude are off if boats with anglers have drifted down to your hard-won access on foot. And it may not matter that you have arrived early since boaters will arrive early, too. You may be well below a launch site, but some boaters — I'm one of them — may push well down the river before fishing in order to escape all the other boaters. So, consider avoiding those portions of the river accessible by boat if you are on foot. Don't assume all boaters will be courteous. Sooner or later you will be disappointed.

Even on those portions of steelhead rivers that may not have an improved boat ramp, fishermen and fishing guides looking for an edge will discover places where they can slide a boat into the water. If it is not feasible for a drift boat to be launched at such locations, someone with a raft or a pontoon boat may have little trouble. In light of this, if you contemplate getting a floating craft you'd better know how to handle one in heavy water and tight spots. To become a good and safe boatman requires lots of practice. Negotiating whitewater is dangerous, even for the experienced. How many highway drivers do you know that don't have a story or two about cheating death? I know of very few boaters that don't also have similar stories.

I go into greater detail on accessing streams on foot in the chapters entitled *A Steelhead Fishing Day on Foot* and *Bushwhacking Your Way to Steelhead and Solitude*. For this reason, I am moving on to the element of the process of getting your fly in front of a steelhead.

In the Water, or *On* the Water?

The ultimate steelhead gunfighter can both wade tough and handle a raft or boat in serious whitewater. These skills present him with maximum options and opportunities. They allow him to separate himself from the pack, to get to places where others can't or won't go in pursuit of fish. Wading and boating can be life-threatening, even for those who've been around water all their lives.

I knew a fly-fishing oceanographer at Oregon State University. Jack Dymond was one of my customers when I owned a fly shop. In the mid and late 1980's Jack explored the depths of southern Oregon's Crater Lake in a one-person submarine called "Deep Rover." This lake sits in a collapsed caldera ("crater") of Mt. Mazama. At more than 1900 feet, Crater is the deepest natural lake in the United States, and 7th deepest in the world. In

that late summer of 2003 Jack Dymond — a man who worked in and around water, and respected its power — drowned in a wading accident on the Rogue River fly-fishing for salmon.

Every serious wading angler I know has gone for unplanned swims, me included. I stepped off a ledge in an Alaskan river wearing two cameras around my neck and holding on to two fly rods. It's difficult enough to swim in loose-fitting chest waders, without the encumbrance of fishing and photographic gear, but I refused to jettison them. This is strictly a case of do as I say (Get rid of the baggage!) and not as I do. Unable to swim against the current to scramble back onto the ledge, I looked downstream on my side of the river to assess my possibilities. Not good. The water flowed along a sheer rock face. My best chance was to swim down and all the way across the river. After experimenting with three different swimming strokes, I discovered the breast stroke worked best with what I was carrying. I laughed with my fishing companions after I struggled to the far shore, but it was definitely no laughing matter during the swim.

There was one key piece of equipment that enabled me to complete my swim — a nylon web wading belt. It was secured snuggly on my upper torso, preventing all but a trickle of water into the lower two thirds of my chest waders. Without it, my waders would have filled with water, holding me down like a sea anchor. There's a chance I would have met the same

As oarsman Mark Severson will testify, good boating skills are necessary on many western rivers like southern Oregon's Rogue River.

Heads up! Fallen trees and logjams are common river hazards. Carefully scout new rivers.

sad fate as my Uncle Mike who drowned in waders in the Willamette River. His accident occurred before I was born, but I think of Mike often when the wading is treacherous.

When it comes to serious wading know your limits. Too many of us overestimate our abilities and underestimate the seriousness of fast-flowing water. Three pieces of equipment will add to your safety and/or wading capabilities. The first I have already mentioned: an adjustable belt that is worn just below your sternum. The second is wading shoes with felt soles for surer footing. For even better traction, use footwear with carbide studs in the soles. Lastly, a wading staff will act as a third leg, giving you greater balance and stability. In a pinch, a dead limb found along the stream bank will do.

Besides allowing you to wade out to the proximity of fishing water, chest waders permit the ability to crisscross rivers from on shore to the other in certain locations. Other anglers on foot may be unwilling or unable to do the same, leaving you with a bit of undisturbed fishing water. This is especially helpful on smaller streams where boats can't be launched or safely floated. Chest waders — not hip boots — are an essential fishing tool to get you into position to present your fly to a steelhead. When fishing on foot, I'd estimate I would lose at least 90% of my fishing without the ability to get into the river. In addition to allowing me to get reasonably close to the fish, wading enables me to get away from the trees and brush that would grab my fly on a back cast.

Because of lack of public access, inability to safely wade the river, or because guided fishing clients are paying for maximum opportunities, a boat is a better choice to access the fishing. The downside, of course, is that it is difficult, if not impossible, to put any significant distance between me and other boaters. Launching at morning's first light is rarely a guarantee of solitude. I know of some anglers who are willing to launch their boat in the dark in an attempt to beat others down the river. The problem with this strategy is that you have to eventually slow down or stop to fish. As soon as you do, company will catch you.

Merrily, Merrily . . .

A boat allows you to cover a lot of water and many fishing-holding locations. Some excellent steelhead water is not reasonably approachable by wading, so a boat is the only answer. If you don't have to contend with many other boating anglers you can have some excellent fish-catching days. However, with the proliferation of anglers in boats and internet communication about weather, water, and fishing conditions, boating can be a very crowded scene. You will not be the only one on the water trying to separate yourself from the hordes; most boatmen will be of like mind. Your mindset is important. If you cannot "hang loose", frustration will be yours in spades. You have a better chance of catching fish on crowded rivers when the water is high; the steelhead are spread out and on the move. However, when the river is low the fish are concentrated in very specific, easy-to-read locations. A boat with a couple of good anglers in it will catch the biters in a run where the fish are grouped up, and alarm the rest. If you are the second, third or tenth boat to fish this spot today, good luck. You probably have a better chance of winning the lottery than catching steelhead!

A strategy I like, especially at high water, is to launch mid or late morning. Most of the boats have launched earlier and are well down the river. Disturbed steelhead have had a chance to settle down. Knowing that many anglers tend to fish their "old reliable" fishing holes, no matter the water level, I seek out the locations which can be overlooked because they don't normally hold steelhead at normal or low river levels.

Since both wading and boating taken alone have drawbacks, if you are physically and financially able, learn and utilize both. The two can be life-threatening, so think safety.

Consider wearing a slim-profile, ripcord CO$_2$-inflatable vest while wading, and floatation vest while boating. Live to fish another day.

Plan for the Unexpected

One of the more significant tasks I perform as a guide is anticipating trouble, trying to determine all the things that can possibly go wrong. This comes with having experienced the thousands of things that can go haywire with a fishing endeavor, most especially when fishing an unfamiliar river. If I am lucky, I will pay with only lost time and money. When I am not quite so lucky, I can lose time, money, clients, and *potential* clients. *Former* clients talk to their friends and fishing acquaintances who might have been my future clients. The disgruntled might not always have high praise for problems that arose during their fishing experience with me. I must anticipate problems before they occur, and often I do. However, even when the logistics or fishing details go wrong which are beyond my control, the guide gets the blame. Ahhhhhh, now you see.

I ran a summer guided steelhead trip on a nearby river. My clients were a father and adult son team. Dad was / is a church minister. Nice guys, good humored and willing students. Everything was going swimmingly since we had hooked a couple of steelhead and many trout to keep the day interesting and the anglers engaged.

During the home stretch part of the day, I encountered a narrow whitewater chute that demands my full attention under normal circumstances. Today I was looking at an abnormal, dangerous circumstance: a large fir tree was blocking part of the chute. Fallen trees overhanging the river's edge or laying in the channel which boaters must negotiate to continue downstream are, by far, the main causes of boating accidents, injuries, and river deaths.

In my brand-new, 17' drift boat, I entered the danger zone with the confident intent of skirting the prone tree. However, the swift current kept forcing me closer and closer to danger. As I am struggling to fend off trouble my left brass oarlock in my new drift boat bent under the strain of adrenaline-powered strokes. As a result, my left oar popped out of the lock and was flailing in the air, useless. We were swept into the tree. I swore enthusiastically while struggling to free the boat from our precarious perch. In spite of my foul mouth, God helped me, and I was able to successfully spin the boat away from the hazard, out of harm's way.

In almost 30 years of rowing drift boats, I had never bent a brass oarlock. I now know good from bad. The ones on my new brand-name boat are not "up to code". I bent a second new

Safety is always an issue on steelhead rivers, especially for the young and bold.

Sound fishing strategies are necessary to succeed on crowded steelhead rivers.

oarlock provided me by the boat manufacturer in question on a subsequent trip.

Back to the minister and his son…I apologized for the near-death experience, but I was still made to look like a rookie on the oars thanks to equipment failure. Secondly, I sincerely apologized a couple of times for my excited and foul verbal tirade in front of the minister and his non-swearing son. I suspect too little too late, and will always wonder if I was held up in a future Sunday sermon as confirmation of the deterioration of Western society.

Fallen trees and attached root wads can be lethal. In the summer of 2006 I saw three young men floating in truck inner tubes down the McKenzie River. Each wore shorts and tennis shoes. None had a life vest. Just above our take out destination, all three men were swept by powerful currents into a fallen tree in the river. All three were washed under and through the tree. Scratched and bruised, they all survived, and were visibly shaken by the experience. They all had used up a lifetime of luck in one afternoon.

That winter, a very experienced guide who had floated the North Fork of the Nehalem River on Oregon's north coast, died on waters he had floated for decades when his raft was upset by a tree that had recently fallen into the stream during a storm.

Too often, I see no respect paid to the possible dangers presented by steelhead rivers. It seems many novices automatically assume that their craft will safely find its way down the currents with minimal skill and piloting from them. If you are new to rafting or boating on rivers, know that injury or death claim even the very experienced. It can be extremely dangerous to float a river sight unseen. If you attempt this perilous feat, at least get out and visually scout rapids and obstructions before attempting to negotiate them. If there are dangerous whitewater, falls or logjams, you need to know about them.

This takes time during your fishing outing, but such an investment may insure that you live to fish another day.

One more boating detail. How will you reunite your trailer and boat? Is there someone who provides a shuttle service? How much? Maybe one of your fishing companions for the day must drive their vehicle to help you shuttle. Some boaters throw a bicycle into the boat. On several occasions I have jogged or hitch-hiked. Hitch-hiking is not always dependable for a variety of reasons. If you try this mode of attempted transportation, here is a tip: carry a fishing rod separated into two halves to make it short and obviously transportable in a car. Carrying a fishing rod as you face traffic with your thumb in the air gives you some degree of trustworthiness.

Longer Can Be Better

I touched on fly rod possibilities in a previous chapter — single-hand, two-hand and switch rods. Because distance and line control after the cast can be crucial, a longer rod is better. There has been a tremendous increase in the popularity of Spey casting, or, maybe, more accurately, casting a fly rod with two hands. These longer rods and the casts made with them are fun and functional. When long casts are required to reach holding steelhead, single-hand casting can become frustrating and fatiguing. If there is not adequate room for a long back cast, a distant cast may be impossible. So being able to utilize *both* hands and arms will provide much more power and less fatigue while casting. With most Spey casts, or improvised variations, minimal back cast room is needed.

Two-Hand Fly Rods:
More Water Covered = More Steelhead

As I stated in the Introduction of this book, this writing is not a guide for casting instruction. I've purposely minimized the

chapter or a book very tedious. So I'm suggesting you seek out an excellent source beyond what little I've written here about fly casting. My own preferences are either DVD's or personal instruction. As for DVD's, seek out those that demonstrate casting in slow motion.

A two-hand cast, in simplest terms, is a roll cast, with varying degrees of complexity. It can be as simple as a standard roll cast like the one performed with a single-hand rod; or, the cast can be composed of three or four rather complicated elements of precise movements and timing that take much practice. And, with so many rods and technically-designed fly lines, matching the correct rod with the appropriate line can be a tremendous challenge. Attempting a complicated cast with a rod and line not suited to each other will frustrate you no matter how good the instruction or the practice time.

Too many anglers do not make an effective mend of the line because they rush it. Once the line lands on the water after the cast, wait for a slow count of three or four before mending. Again, mending is the re-positioning of the slack fly line on the water to prevent it from racing ahead of the fly and dragging or pulling it unnaturally fast in the current. Slowing the drift of the fly by mending when necessary can be crucial to enticing a steelhead to intercept the fly. Tricky currents may require multiple mends during a single drift to keep the fly moving slowly. Even for highly accomplished anglers, not every long distance cast into complicated currents will result in an acceptable presentation of the fly to an interested fish. Often, the same cast is repeated again and again until the line and leader are finally manipulated the correct way at the correct time.

topic here for several reasons. One, there are many other books which address casting methods with diagrams and text. Two, like virtually all technical manuals, such diagrams, sketches and accompanying text makes me dizzy as I try to piece together all the information for making the perfect cast, even though I am very familiar with most casting methods. I can't imagine what frustration a beginner must deal with. Three, though good fly casting is a cornerstone of fly-fishing success, I find that *writing* the detail necessary to do an excellent job in a

CHAPTER 11
Typical Winter Steelhead Fishing Days, and Useful Strategies

First, the title of this chapter is a little misleading. I do not have too many "typical" fishing days. There are too many mix and match combinations of variables to have many "typical" days.

Some winter days you must deal with ice in your guides. The silver lining? Many anglers will stay home.

I will consider some of these variables in any given period throughout an entire steelhead fishing year, and how these affect my thought processes and strategies. I will be talking to you in this chapter almost exclusively from my perspective as a fly-fishing guide, boating down a river with my clients or guests. There are definitely parallel strategies if I am fishing on foot by myself. With clients, I am always in a boat when steelhead are the quarry.

For starters, some variables include time of year, water temperature, and river flows. Assume water temperatures less than 45 degrees Fahrenheit in winter, and 45 degrees or greater in the summer season. Further, I will arbitrarily define "summer" (loosely the migration of summer-run steelhead in the Pacific Northwest) as the late spring through early fall period. "Winter" (generally, the migration of our winter-run steelhead) refers to the late fall through early spring seasons when water temperatures, with some exceptions, are colder.

Water temperature is a key element defining the general comfort, "aggression" and activity level of the steelhead. As I talked about previously, the "ideal" temperature range for a steelhead — an oversize rainbow trout — is upper 40's through the lower 60's Fahrenheit.

Here are six water conditions that I encounter with these three variables of season, flows and water temperatures:

Winter, High Water
Winter, "Normal" Water
Winter Low Water
Summer High Water
Summer, "Normal" Water
Summer Low Water

Other variables that can steer my day's fishing strategy are the skill, experience, and emotional constitution of my clients; the presence of bank anglers; and, competition from other boating anglers.

Slings and Arrows

Every day on the river, I am not just a fishing guide, but, also, a counselor, a psychologist, a competitive strategist, a puzzle solver, and a cheerleader.

Besides counseling my anglers, I am counseling and encouraging myself. Clients are giving me trust and money in advance, hopeful of catching a fish or two. It is pressure on several levels. I want them to feel as if they got their money's worth. I want them to know I did my very best as a fishing guide to maximize their fishing opportunities in light of the fact that they have chosen to pursue winter steelhead with the most demanding of all fishing methods. I want them back to fish with me (and help me pay my mortgage) in the future. Lastly, as I reflect on the day's fishing during my drive home, I want to know that no one could have tried harder or fished better with a fly rod today than we did. I need to KNOW that I was as good as I could be whether the steelhead confirmed my efforts or not, whether my clients appreciated my skills and efforts, or not. I need to KNOW I "left it all on the playing field" today.

I counsel myself that there are attitudes, events and circumstances out of my control. This is hard for a control freak, which I tend to be, because of all the little details I must oversee that will result in a steelhead in the net. Even while I am micro managing and orchestrating every fishing moment, I must remind myself to relax, have fun, and not be overbearing. I try, as best I can, to determine how much firm instruction and its repetition my guys can take. When my assessment is off the mark, I need to "make amends" in subtle ways by being more encouraging, and gentler. It is always a fine line I walk. Interestingly, I find beginners and women to be the most attentive and accepting of my instructions. They tend to be pleasers who want to learn and do well. My most difficult clients are men who think they are skilled fly anglers but actually, they are not. In this latter case, my best ally and illustrator is a co-operative fishing partner who hooks fish by following my directions while the obstinate "know-it-all" does his own thing. I cannot help those who refuse to be helped. This is a circumstance beyond my control. Such an angler will still receive my best efforts, but this may include me just keeping my mouth shut so I do not upset him with fishing instructions. I hope that he will pick up the details he wants as he listens to me teach his cooperative fishing partner who continues to hook fish as he follows my suggestions to the smallest detail.

In light of all these, I will take you on six simulated fishing trip days. Three in the winter; three in the summer. The summer situations are discussed in the next chapter.

Common Elements of Every Fishing Day

As the fishing day starts, I assess how many other anglers may be on the river today. If it's a weekend or holiday, I expect many. But, I also know that many good fishing guides try to avoid the weekends, if possible, for this reason. Therefore, the caliber of the fishing competition may not be as great on busy fishing days. A trade off. I do not worry about being the first boat to launch on winter mornings because this is a losing game on popular rivers. And, my ace is that some fish will not be harassed, being spread out from bank to bank. My goal is to be thorough, but quick, in covering likely water as we progress down the river.

To cover good steelhead-holding locations thoroughly and quickly, I must precisely instruct my inexperienced anglers on

how to make the right cast, get the proper drift of the fly, and detect and respond to a strike. Some pick it up faster than others do. Here, I walk a fine line and must be an attentive psychologist and cheerleader. I have to be demanding in a friendly way, and encouraging, reinforcing the casting and fishing techniques I am trying to convey. I constantly emphasize that success is in the details. Blind luck can account for the occasional landed steelhead, but I cannot count on luck. I never know when it's coming our way. I have to assume it will not. We need to depend on getting the details right, so that when the fish strike comes, we can take full advantage.

For our first cast of the day I usually drop down the river a ways, bypassing a few good fishing locations with the hope that boating anglers who follow me will stop and fish the water I have ignored. This takes a little pressure from me as I set up the fishing rods, fine tune leaders and flies, and begin initial casting and fishing instructions. We make a few practice casts to get warmed up and preview our angling routine. Then, it's Show Time! Here we go.

Winter, High Water Fishing

I used to hate high, *but fishable*, water flows. There are usually fewer places well-defined fish-holding locations. The water can

The Hot Bead Assassin is a go-to fly when the water is a bit murky.

be a bit murky. It is harder to hold the boat in perfect position for my clients, or hold on anchor. To see the beneficial opportunities to these conditions I had to overcome my mental barriers to success.

I now actually *like* high water. On rivers that get a lot of anglers, it's helpful for me and my clients that the steelhead are spread out, not confined to obvious holding areas which fishermen can focus on and pound relentlessly. Even good anglers who precede me through a particularly good location cannot find all the fish, hook, or startle all the fish. Additionally, bank anglers have less access to fishable water when the river is high. And, because the water can be off-color — but still very fishable — I can get much closer to the fish without

Robert Thompson with a January Siletz River hatchery steelhead.

When the water has a bit of color to it, I use flies that are a bit larger and heavier than at normal or low flows. My Gorman Bead Egg in a size 6 in orange, pink, or New Age hot pink, and my Hot Bead Veiled Assassin are my top choices.

Where I can, I "back ferry" the drift boat, holding it in place, stationary against the current, I have my guests methodically cover the area where fish may be resting. Short casts first, then a foot or two farther on subsequent casts. If the area is not too broad, I will hold the boat in the same spot. If the area is wide enough to demand long casts, I will opt instead to move my boat over as the water is covered. I study the drift of every cast. If something is not quite right with the location or proper drift of the fly, I have the angler repeat the cast until they get it right, unless they have indicated they cannot or will not deal with my constant instruction. Again, I can always count on women and beginners to give it their best try.

In locations where fish may rest, but near which the currents are too strong for me to keep the boat stationary, I slow the boat as best I can. I have my anglers "stab it in the heart", meaning they cast to what I assess to be the location for the single best opportunity to intercept a fish. The correct drift line gives their flies the highest probability of pay dirt. Then, we're gone, swept downstream by the current to the next fishing spot. I am constantly looking ahead to move the boat left or right, from one bank to the other when necessary, to put the anglers in the proximity of steelhead. This is why I need miles and miles of river. Being pushed along, unable to hold and anchor in many locations, there is a chance we will run out of river before our eight-hour fishing day is completed.

My pace downstream is somewhat dictated by my watch, but also by the river traffic. When swarmed by other boating anglers, I have three choices: I can choose to ignore them; I can lay back to let them pass; or, I can push down the river ahead of them…maybe. Each choice has its own risks. The choice I make here can determine our fish-catching success or failure for the remainder of the day. How do I decide?

Are the anglers and/or guides in our vicinity fishing effectively? Some will be. Some will not. I always prefer those who

sending them fleeing for cover. My clients can make short, accurate casts to likely areas, better control the drift of their flies, and react more quickly when setting the hook.

After making a few practice casts, it's time to roll. At high water, my inclination is to run a long section of river, eight to ten miles. I may anchor at a few select spots, but most often, we stay on the move. I row the boat from bank, to bank depending on where I suspect a steelhead might hold. I position the boat as close as I dare without alarming the steelhead. There is rarely a need for distance casting, thankfully. We are nymphing most of the time. In the right locations, I may have the angler in the front of the boat swing a wet fly where the water is slow and shallow, three to six feet deep with a broad even current.

I prefer to keep my clients in the boat unless they insist on wading. No time wasted constantly getting in and out of the boat. No time wasted when the angler needs coaching, and I am down the river with his partner. No time lost chasing clients taking an unplanned swim. When I started insisting my guests stay in the boat while fishing — one in the bow, one at the stern — safety concerns were minimized. Additionally, I could coach both anglers simultaneously; I could get them in the perfect casting position for most fish-holding lies; and, we hooked many more steelhead because they were able to make more potentially productive casts in a fishing day. As to this final point, let me reiterate that steelhead fishing is a numbers game. Think of it as pulling the handle on a slot machine. The more times you pull the lever (cast your fly to productive locations), the greater the chance you will hit the jackpot.

don't. Do I sense that any of the boaters are determined to be the first boat down the river? If I get involved with trying to beat this character down the river, we may run out of river before we run out of fishing day as he relentlessly pursues me. How has our fishing day gone to this point? If we hook and land a couple of fish, I don't feel the pressure to be the first boat down the river at all costs. I rest assured that my guys have some confidence in me, in themselves, in the fishing techniques we are using, and the flies. Do I sense that the other boats are not concerned about being the first down

An oarsman in winter never forgets his gloves a second time.

the river? If not, then maybe I will push ahead a little ways, bypassing the next spot to create a little more distance. Do I have a particularly good fishing spot where I want to make sure we get an opportunity to fish without being disturbed? If so, I will push downstream to lock up that spot, then let others pass me if they choose to. One of the things, again, that I like about high, off-color conditions is that my choices to run, stay, or fall back are not as critical because the fish are spread out and no angler or anglers can fish them all.

One good thing about a boat downstream ahead of us, particularly with poor or mediocre anglers in it, is that they can "stir up" the fish a little. When the water is cold, some steelhead may be a little "comatose". These individuals are very reluctant to budge from the exact spot at which they have remained stationary for hours. Even if a fly drifts near them, they may refuse to move. However, I think there are instances when a fish is disturbed to the point that it moves around a little and "wakes up". We may actually have a better chance of catching that fish. I think this gambit works best if there is sufficient time — let's say more than thirty minutes — for the fish to calm down, and ease out of the "danger / red alert" mode.

I am constantly monitoring my progress down the river with the time we have remaining in the fishing day. If we are farther down the river than I prefer, I will fish locations that are a little more marginal; areas that could hold fish, but which I might normally bypass. Sometimes we are behind schedule. It usually means fishing is good! When slowed by the time it takes to play, land and photograph steelhead, then I will push down the river, fishing only those locations that present the highest probability of a hookup.

Being behind schedule or being ahead of schedule each has its advantages. If we are behind, I cherry pick. Ahead of schedule, we are fishing every remaining bit of likely water I can find. It is in this situation where I make new discoveries. Spots that I *thought* were marginal or mediocre can turn out to be hidden gems.

A recent story comes to mind. It was a cold January day when I first caught up with a boat holding two anglers about 9 a.m. Because I wanted a particular fishing spot that produced five hooked steelhead the day before, I decided to push by them. The testosterone was flowing in both boats, and I soon discovered the other boat was determined not to let me pass. I got close enough though for a verbal exchange. The passenger in the other boat was holding up a bottle of liquor with half its contents gone. Yes, it's 9 a.m. I don't know if the oarsman is drinking or not. He spoke (shouted!) more coherently, while the passenger bragged about his drinking prowess. I was constantly gaining on the boat in question, and eventually they surrendered and pulled over to fish. We passed and went down to my target spot where one of my passengers immediately caught a steelhead. Because I am determined to fish this particular run very thoroughly in light of the previous day's success, I let the drunken boat pass.

Later in the day, I caught up with my new best friends again. They saw me coming as I determined to pass them for another spot that had recently been kind to my anglers. As we approached a little island, these characters chose the wrong channel. They were momentarily delayed by a big rock that met them head on whereby they lost all their downstream momentum. They saw us laughing as we sped down the other channel easily taking the lead. When we stopped to fish my next sweet spot, I allowed them to pass again. More drunken blather from them; more laughter from us. After fishing a few more locations without catching them — plus a lengthy, but necessary, bathroom stop — my friends in the other boat could be seen hundreds of yards downstream. They watched constantly for our approach. They were 200 yards below us, determined not to let us pass no matter what. I had one more killer spot I wanted to fish. My hope was to push these guys so hard they would blow right past my last chosen sweet spot. It didn't work out that way.

It seems my sweet spot was also theirs. They anchored up in the hole, hooting and hollering about how they were to catch fish here and that they had "won" the race. I laughed but was disappointed. My plans for a glorious finale did not exactly play out as I'd hoped. So, I opted to fish a marginal run just around the corner and out of sight of the other boat. I had always ignored this spot, but today it was our last hope. Nothing to lose.

The angler in the front of my boat hooked a steelhead on her first cast. It jumped immediately for all to see, then threw the hook. I rowed back upstream along the quiet water on the near bank, then, swung the boat back into the current to fish through this innocuous looking run again. The first cast by the angler in the rear of the boat hooked a fish on our second pass. The battle was a lengthy one, but he eventually brought the

Time to cut and run. Artistically created tangle by Joann Severson.

chrome-bright native hen to the boat. Our fishing day finished in fine fashion. A spot I had always bypassed was discovered to be a new sweet spot. I found it because I was forced to. You can safely wager I will never ignore this little gem of a fishing hole in the future.

Trying to be the first boat down the river can be a tedious, frustrating ploy. Too often, I have pushed ahead of everyone else only to be thwarted by a client who throws a cast into streamside tree branches too high to be rescued. It may take me ten to twelve minutes to tie on new tippet, flies and weights. I must pull into quiet water and sit on anchor to re-rig. In the meantime, boaters determined to lead the parade will pass us. If you choose to lead, be psychologically prepared for such possibilities. It is not easy to deal with after reminding your guests constantly to watch for overhanging limbs in a constantly changing environment created by a drifting boat.

The other circumstance that will cost you the lead in The Great Boat Race is when someone has to answer Nature's Call. A streamside bathroom break cannot be postponed for long when someone tells you he has to go. Of course, I must be accommodating. This is a circumstance beyond my control. Those of us with unhealthy competitive drives must temper our emotions to maintain, as best we can, our pleasant demeanor. I find a way to put aside the intense effort and clever strategies I employed to *finally* get (split infinitive) down the river first, only to give it up when someone in the boat has to water the bushes. With cold fingers, waders, and layers of clothing to deal with on cold days, a simple procedure becomes a laborious and lengthy ordeal. I do my best to be cheery as boats pass us by. I may wave and smile as a boat passes, but if they look closely they might see my lips move a little as I mutter softly, "You bastards…"

As for changing flies if we are not catching fish, I will change the fly color, but usually not the size. I am not a BIG fly aficionado for winter fish, though I have caught them on large flies. I know some good fly anglers who only use large flies and are successful. On my heavily fished winter steelhead streams, I think the fish have frequent opportunities to strike big lures and big baits. My philosophy is to give those steelhead that have wisely refused to eat big things — and end up dead in an ice chest — a chance to sample a smaller, non-threatening morsel. It's just a harmless little piece of pretty fluff drifting into their proximity that almost appears friendly. My faith lies with smaller fare. I landed a steelhead on a size 20 hook while fishing for trout on the Deschutes River. Experiences like this reinforce my notions that steelhead will see and eat small things, and that they can be landed on tiny hooks.

If the water is extremely clear, I may go to a smaller egg pattern, most likely size 8, and a standard Veiled Assassin, no bead. Small flies in black, metallic green, or metallic purple can be excellent choices for the second fly. To mix it up further, I may use flies tied on a gold or silver hook. I have a psychological barrier to flies tied on hooks anodized "gunmetal blue". No faith, because I have had poor results, especially on egg patterns. My bias.

I am convinced that fly color can be important, but more so in the summer time than in the winter. My theory is that in the warmer months many, many more aquatic insects are active and hatching. Most steelhead rivers in the northwest have a great variety of aquatic insect species, with a broad spectrum of colors, shapes, and sizes. Because of this, I use a much wider range of fly sizes and colors, and change flies more often in pursuit of summer steelhead.

Remember. I am fishing two flies on the leader most of the time. When I change flies, winter or summer, I leave "an old reliable" tied on virtually all the time — as determined by time of year, particular river, and my experience —but will switch up the second fly. It is rare that I will experiment with both flies.

Make no mistake, fly pattern — design, color, and size — is extremely important. I have a lot of confidence in the flies I use. They have been time-tested, and I always try to tweak and fine tune effective fly designs when I create subtle variations of them at my fly tying vise. Rather than devote much time to changing flies, I focus on keeping the flies in the water, drifting relentlessly through areas that might hold a fish. When I reflect on many steelhead fishing days, I realize that my clients (or me) were two casts away from being skunked. Make a thousand casts in a day, maybe only one or two will find a biting steelhead. And, you never know when lightning will strike. So, above all else, keep your flies in the water.

I had a father and adult son team from Minnesota on a high water January day on Oregon's Siletz River. We had drifted almost ten miles of river. When we were within 100 yards of our take out point, the son hooked a steelhead. After the battle and release of the fish, they resumed casting. We were almost on the boat ramp — the last cast of the day when Dad tied into a big bulldog of a fish. The steelhead wanted to run hard down the river. I could have followed it but there was no way I could fight the current to make my way back upstream to the ramp. We would be committed to another hour and a half on the river, as I would have to push hard on the oars — no fishing — to reach the next take out. We would make our last stand — win or lose — at our current location.

Because the water was high and the current swift, we had no place to go. Moreover, it was not feasible, because of brush and nature of the shoreline, to fight the big steelhead from any place other than in the boat. My novice fly-fishing Dad refused to put forceful resistance on the fish, and I was reluctant to tell him to do so. If he broke

the line as a result of my suggestion, I would definitely get the blame for the loss. The day would end on a disappointing note. No matter what other good fishing memories had been created earlier in the day, they would be psychologically overwhelmed by these final minutes. I was going to let him fight his own battle, though I did offer cheerleader support and little reminders to keep the rod bent hard against the fish.

As the struggle continued, I realized other boaters were anchoring upstream on the far bank waiting for us to clear the way for them to eventually row to the take out. With the position of my boat and the taut path of the fly line, the ramp was perfectly blocked. Three boaters and their passengers impatiently watched from a distance, waiting for the fish to be lost or netted. How do I know they were impatient? Because when my guy landed the fish after 20 minutes, the boaters who rowed across the river to trailer up their boats did not have a congratulatory word to say. Only silent scowls about the inconvenience that had been caused by a 10-pound native buck that stubbornly refused to be caught in a reasonable amount of time. However, I had happy clients and photos to commemorate the fish and the moment.

Keep your fly in the water.

Winter, Normal Water Flows

At "normal" water levels, most of my steelhead rivers can be negotiated without problems, assuming the oarsman is skilled. Even with two oversized clients, I can usually make a clean run the entire day, negotiating rapids and hazards without incident. Additionally, I can back ferry my drift boat in many locations, holding the boat stationary near productive steelhead water for as long as I choose without risking a torn

Parasites on steelhead are not uncommon.

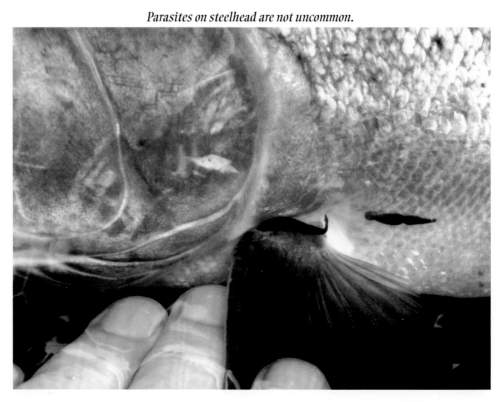

Mark Hoffman puts the wood to a winter steelhead with attitude. A good bend in the rod
helps keep a barbless hook secure in the fish's jaw.

rotator cuff. There are more holes to fish, than at high water or low water. And, finally, the fish-holding locations are better defined, more readable. They can be more easily pinpointed as to their exact location.

As for the downside, normal, good water conditions encourage the highest number of anglers to go fishing. The decisions made throughout the course of the day to linger in any one fishing spot, letting other boaters pass to fish in front of us, or pick up the anchor and stay ahead of most other boats, are critical. These high angling pressure days can also be high anxiety days for a guide wanting to maximize steelhead opportunities for his guests. The river is my chessboard, and across from me are a dozen players all conspiring to beat me, competing without consciences to catch the steelhead we might catch.

I will start out by moving down the river, bypassing the first holes, knowing they've already been fished. Perhaps by good anglers; perhaps by mediocre ones. I will never know, and it doesn't really matter. Many boat ramps are at state or county parks so there is often access for anglers on foot. They will command many of the first prime fishing runs. I usually opt not to invade their domain. Most are a surly lot, with no

love for boaters who disturb their fishing water. They are a competitive nuisance to me. I am the same to them. *Hasta la vista!*

If I approach boats as they linger to fish, I try to gauge if they will stay or run. If they do not see or hear me approaching, I try to blow on by. If they hurriedly pull anchor to chase me, I know I have a horsefly that I will have swat at some point during the day. I will either seriously outdistance them, or I'll game them into giving me plenty of room if they are determined to lead the way down the river. I know the psychology. If they are determined to lead, I will make sure they will be forever looking over their shoulders looking for me. They are torn between wanting to linger and fish at a good location, or fish it hurriedly or bypass it altogether to be the first to the next fishing hole downriver. It's always a chess game. If I encounter inexperienced or unknowledgeable anglers, they can do whatever they want with little concern from me. However, if they are competent and knowledgeable about my waters, I will need to deal with them. If I am lucky, they will be a short-term problem. If I am unlucky, it will be cat and mouse all day, as with my loud, drunken friends mentioned earlier.

Once I have created separation between the boats in front of me and the boats behind me, we can focus on serious fishing. I will tend to linger in those good steelhead runs where I can see back up the river for a long ways above us, sometimes a quarter of a mile or more. If a boat comes into view, I have the option, with plenty of time, to decide to stay or go, to linger, or pick up the pace. This, in light of how our fishing success has gone to this point. I am not so anxious if we have hooked some fish. If I have a Honey Hole I am determined to fish, I will push down the river long before the boat behind gets near. The greater the distance between a following and me boat, the less the likelihood they will try to overtake me. When I get beyond the next bend in the river and out of view, they will not know if I pulled up to fish or if I kept pushing. Should they try to chase me for such a long distance, they know that they will be passing up a lot of fishable water. They have no clue whether this water was fished effectively, or even fished at all. More chess moves. Linger to fish, or run.

The best thing that can happen to a boat that is chasing me or whom I am trying to pass, is that they hook a fish. Now, they must take time to land the fish. If they photo the fish and or kill it for the BBQ, all these activities take time. Additionally, where one fish is caught there can be another biter in the same hole. So, more time is consumed when the anglers stay in an attempt to hook a second or third steelhead. Good for them! Ciao, Baby!

On the other hand, it can be we who are delayed by fighting, landing and photographing fish. This is a problem…but a good one. If boats in front of us missed this biting fish, they will miss others. The guide's anxiety level subsides a little, and confidence grows a bit. I try to make sure that such happy moments are photographed. Guests will be able to view and re-live the moments once the images are sent to their computers, if they do not have a record on their own cameras. I am always happy to use a client's camera to save the memories. (It is utterly amazing, though, how often client camera batteries have gone dead with no replacements at hand.)

Winter, Low Water

Low water, for me, is a flow level that do not allow for easy passage of a drift boat down the river. It's not necessarily unsafe (though it can be on some rivers), it's just that there will be plenty of shallow water in which to hit rocks or get stuck where the best passage through an area is only a couple of inches deep. When I get stuck, I usually have to get out of the boat and push it through to deeper water. Sometimes it may require my guests to exit the boat. This is not boating for sissies. If you have a *wooden* boat, forget low water. The abrasion and rock kissing will take a serious toll on the beauty and structural integrity in a short time period.

My aluminum boat will take a pounding in low water. I may get some dents and scratches, but I will not puncture it. No scars, no glory. This is my very favorite aspect of extremely low water: many boaters will not float these sections of the river. It's work, and it's hard on your boat. Many times the clients must get out of the boat so the oarsman can bang through a riffle or rapid. Sometimes I request that my guests help me push the boat through a shallow stretch. We literally plow the river. Many boaters and their passengers do not wear boots or waders. They will not make it down the river at crash-and-boom flows. Now that is just too bad. *Auf Wiedersehn, mein herrs!*

In addition to banging and clanging my boat down the river, low is virtually always clear water. Clear and low demands special weapons and tactics: light fluorocarbon tippets, smaller flies, longer casts, neutral-color clothing, and minimal boat noise. Stealth is of paramount importance.

Most often, I will use a 3X fluorocarbon tippet testing 8lb. I will fish almost exclusively egg patterns, sizes 8 or 10. Casts up to 40 feet may be necessary, which is a long distance for nymph fishing methods.

Experience has shown that even though the water may be in the upper 30's to lower 40's, steelhead, especially in heavily fished rivers, will tuck up into foamy whitewater pockets to escape detection. When the water is cold, the fish prefer slower currents. But, constant harassment from boats and anglers may force them to the only cover they may be able to find in shallow areas: whitewater pockets where flows are definitely quicker. Once-deep holding runs at normal water flows may be only four or five feet deep. This does not afford enough cover when the current is minimal, the water is as clear as gin, and angling pressure is high.

There are some holding lies I can approach rather closely, even at very low water. You may be surprised at what you can find in whitewater pockets and fast current edges. Steelhead that hold in such locations seem not to be extremely wary. Steelhead here tend to get solidly hooked, too. They seem to take with an aggressive boldness when hidden in the whitewater. In addition, the fly often is drawn into the corner of the fish's mouth by fast currents that wash the line and leader downstream quickly. Once in the jaw's corner, the fly stays stuck. Checkmate!

If you use a strike indicator, make sure you adjust the distance between it and your flies. Sometimes as short as three feet. You want the strike instantly telegraphed. Be careful not to use too much weight on your leader or fly. If you snag your fly and must disturb the pocket to retrieve it, you may have lost a great opportunity. I will fish with just a little weight to begin, then, add more if I never bounce the stream bottom, and feel I am not getting the flies down to the fish's eye level.

Returning home from fishing farther up the Oregon coast on a Monday in February, I traveled the highway that parallels the Alsea River. Initially, I had no plans to stop to fish. The water was extremely low, and I figured even a few anglers would have already harassed the steelhead in the area I traditionally fish on foot. Since the weather was beautiful and I had no pressing appointments in Corvallis, I decided to enjoy a few hours of practicing my casting, with little hope of success. I had my MP3 player with some great music to keep me company as I tracked along the river.

My usual favorite holes were deadly low, with little of their normal depth and current speed. With no one in sight, I got into my casting rhythm and sang along to some of my favorite tunes. Heaven help me if I was discovered singing by one of my students or friends. No doubt, they would have rushed to my assistance, thinking I was in pain or screeching for help, not singing. I made some wonderful casts and drifts for a couple of uninterrupted hours as evening approached. I had but a couple of runs to fish before I had worked my way back to my 4-Runner. Before me was a deep chute where most of the river coursed quickly towards the far bank. The depth was good — maybe four feet — but the current was too fast to get a good drift down the heart. I put my first cast along the far

Ice can be nice…for thinning steelhead crowds.

129

Jay Nicholas readies his leader on a Siletz winter morning. Carrying a waterproof camera can "capture the moment."

current seam, where the fast current edge met slack water. Much to my startled surprise, my line stopped in mid-drift. As I came up tight, I felt the throb of a fish on my hook. "If God was one of us…Just a slob like one of us…Just a stranger on a bus…"I was singing along with Joan Osbourne as I battled the big steelhead buck in a fast current. "Tryin' to make His way home, back to heaven all alone…"Now I'm starting to think about the crappy knot I'd tied in the egg pattern I had just recently tied when I'd broken my tippet. It was the kind of knot I always warned my students and clients about; the kind of clinch knot that does not have enough turns as it is being created. The knot had slipped a bit too much when I pulled it tight. It had pulled so far down the tippet that there was no tag end remaining for me to trim. Soon I may be staring at the dreaded curly-cue tippet end sans fly. I hadn't seen one on my own line for many years, but I expected the fish and I to part company any moment, and there would be the sad evidence of my carelessness held by my wet fingers before my sad eyes.

Fortunately, God helped me a little before he got on the bus to make his way home. Through a miracle (a minor one in the Big Scheme), I slid the 30-inch hatchery buck onto the beach before my knot parted.

No need to make another cast. I sang myself back to my truck, and all the way home, too, with Billy Idol, Radiohead, Ray Charles, and The Eagles. Rock on!

Sight-Fishing

Low water provides the best opportunity you will have to see steelhead in their environment and observe their behavior. This is more easily accomplished on foot than it is from a boat. Standing in a boat *above* the water the only fish behavior you will usually observe is flight, as the steelhead dashes for cover. On foot, you can approach from *downstream*, coming up from behind the fish facing upstream into the current. A would-be observer stands too high in a boat and is drifting from upstream, too easily seen by wary fish. Boat noise can also prematurely announce your arrival.

If the water's surface in which you spot the fish has a bit of chop or froth to it, you have an exponentially better chance to approach and angle to the steelhead. Much can be learned as you gauge and adjust your casts, track the drift of your fly, and watch the fish's reaction, or lack thereof. Your fly usually takes longer to sink than you assumed. The cast usually has to be a little longer than you thought to have it drift where you want it. And, usually your fly has to drift much closer to the steelhead than you realized in order to get its attention.

For those fortunate enough to operate their two eyes independently of one another, it is necessary to keep one eye on the fish at all times. When you look away to tend a tangle, adjust the weight or indicator, or change flies, the fish may disappear. You need to visually track the fish at all times. They tend to blend very nicely with their environment. Such camouflage helps them survive. So, if the steelhead changes location, you had better be looking. Fishing with a partner who is willing to watch the fish while you are distracted by other things is of tremendous aid.

Fishing two flies enhances the chances that at least one of them will eventually drift close enough to be taken, if the steelhead is a player. Once I am convinced the fish has seen my flies up close a few times, but gotten no biting response, I will change flies. Both of them. Pink, purple, black, metallic green, chartreuse, straw and brown are the predominant colors in my winter fly box.

Be careful of using too much weight. If you snag your flies or weights on the river bottom near the fish, you are almost guaranteed to startle it when you break your tippet. If you do snag, watch the fish, not your line as you attempt to dislodge your flies. Wade slowly and approach from behind as you pursue the fish to its next holding location. You may be surprised as to where the fish will try to hide. Those foamy whitewater pockets that are only two feet deep, thought too small to conceal a fish, can hide some very large steelhead. This can expand your list of likely places to find steelhead, especially at low water.

I remember wading the Miami River on Oregon's north coast at low winter water. I was carefully making my way upstream through a long stretch of river that was no more than knee deep anywhere from bank to bank. Eventually, I came upon a shallow riffle that stretched the entire width of the river. There was only one little pocket which I surmised could possibly hide a steelhead. A large fish, having made its journey up this shallow stretch of stream, exposed and vulnerable to being seen, would have only this one little foamy pocket in which to hide. Because the water was foamy and choppy, I could not see into the spot. It would only take a couple of casts to drift my fly through the heart of this tiny pocket.

I approached from downstream, crouching low, until I was a couple of rod lengths from my target. Kneeling before making my first cast, I wanted to make sure my waving rod tip and I would not be seen. All weight had been removed from my leader because this pocket was so shallow, and I did not want to take any chance that the weight or fly would snag. The first cast was on target. My fly landed just above the pocket and drifted into its heart. I saw my bright green fly line hesitate as it coursed back toward me. I lifted the rod and was fast into a great steelhead that thrashed to the surface of its roily hiding place, then, took off downriver. There was no place the fish could run that I could not follow. Soon I propped my water-resistant camera on shoreline rocks, pushed the timed shutter release a couple of times, and took some poor, but memorable, photos of me and my steelhead before its release.

Extreme Benefits

The varying river flows of the "winter" season present challenges and opportunities for the steelhead fly rodder. In light of the heavy angling competition typical on quality steelhead rivers, especially when weather and water conditions are ideal, it is at the flow extremes where the best opportunities to hook and land steelhead may be found. At high water the steelhead are spread out and some willing biters can eventually be found by the knowledgeable and persistent faith-keepers, no matter how numerous other boats and anglers may be. This assumes, also, some good, strategic "chess moves" as the fishing day unfolds. Low water chess moves are driven more by stealth and observance, than angling competition. And, when a watercraft is used, there must be a gaming willingness to take a boat where a boat should not rationally go. All on board must put up with the necessity of getting in and out of the boat when shallow water demands lifting and pushing it to force a passage downstream. Low flows are the best opportunities for sight fishing and observing fish behavior. One steelhead angler's daunting challenge is another's opportunity to learn, and — maybe — catch a steelhead. Welcome the extremes.

For photographic purposes, this is an excellent presentation of a native steelhead, with minimal handling of the fish.

CHAPTER 12

Typical Summer Steelhead Fishing Days: High, Normal, Low Water

THE MAIN DIFFERENCES WE FIND IN
"summer" season steelhead fishing and "winter" season
are that summer water temperatures are, overall, higher, and the
stream flows stay constant longer through
summer and early fall.

Many of our best summer steelhead rivers in the Pacific Northwest have their flows regulated by dams. Other than the occasional influence of a large rainstorm that swells tributaries and the main river, dammed summer rivers tend to rise and drop slowly making for more predictable boating and fishing.

In late spring and early summer — May and June — water temperatures are often in the 50's, optimal for steelhead comfort and activity. Some aggressive fish may track a fly for a considerable distance to intercept it. Arbitrarily, this may be ten to fifteen feet, whereas the same steelhead may not move six inches at 40 degrees. It is this willingness, driven by water temperature, which makes it more likely for a fly angler to catch a summer steelhead than a winter-run fish.

Warmer water expands the variety of fly-fishing technique opportunities. Whereas I have been plying the river bottom most of November through April, now I can use a floating line in the right situations to fish a shallow-running wet fly or a surface-skating dry fly. Now, I can employ all three fly-fishing methods in a single day. And, if I have the right guests with me, we will use all three for the pleasures of variety and experience. The wet fly offers the thrill of a hard tug as the steelhead takes. The dry fly presents the opportunity for a near heart attack as an oversize rainbow explodes to the surface to inhale the hook. At high sun, it's time to fish nymphs. What a thrill for any angler who can attain The Trifecta: landing a steelhead on a wet fly, a dry fly, and a nymph in a single day. This is the most elite of the elitist steelhead clubs. Very few members. Even if you are not a "joiner", this IS a club to which you want to belong!

So, let's go through three simulated "summer" steelhead fishing days, differentiated primarily by water levels.

Summer, High Water

Late spring rain and snowmelt may swell steelhead rivers, even though controlled by dams. Additionally, flows in late spring are purposely kept high to keep rivers cool for the successful downstream migration of salmon and steelhead smolts who are journeying downriver toward the sea. There is a water temperature threshold above which *Ceratomyxa shasta*, a parasite that will kill many fish, especially hatchery-reared salmonids, more easily victimizes the young migrating steelhed in the Pacific Northwest. So increased water releases from dams in spring keep water temperatures lower in an attempt to minimize mortality by *Ceratomyxa*. By early June, in a typical water flow year, the smolts have departed the rivers and entered their new salty domain. Then, many dam-controlled rivers will experience reduced flows and a subsequent water temperature increase. This will be the advent of "normal" water flows, followed by the low water of mid summer and early fall.

The high water of the early "summer" season on many steelhead rivers, limits bank and wading access. High flows, also, spread out the steelhead so even skilled anglers in boats cannot find them all. Boating anglers who do not put in much

fishing time in high water will usually have trouble consistently locating fish because they are not lying in "normal" water places. Anchoring or holding the boat stationary with the oars can be a problem as the force of the current pushes the boat downriver. Many areas of fishing interest can only be quickly fished before the boat is swept downstream.

It is an art to anchor a driftboat in the best position from which to cover the likely steelhead water. It's not as easy as it might appear. Think of parking a car on an icy street, headed down a steep hill. If the boatman parks too far left or right, he will have to lift the anchor to reposition the boat. With

Larger stonefly species may spend three years in the nymphal stage, and are available to be eaten year-round.

four hands this is more easily done: two to row, and two more that simultaneously pull the anchor rope. During the lag time between committing both hands to pull the anchor rope and, then, getting back on the oars, the boat can slip downstream. Even a strong oarsman may not be able to pull back upstream against the current. If the boat was initially anchored too far downstream to begin with, it may be too late to attempt repositioning for the same reason. It is best to get your anchored boat position right on the first attempt.

If we start the fishing day early, my guests and I begin with fishing wet flies before the sun is directly on the water. If I have two anglers, both will be in the front of the boat, one casting left, the other casting right. We will seek water that is shaded, no direct sunlight where the flies will be swimming. Depending on the particular section of river I have chosen, this could be the smooth, even flow of a tailout, or a choppy, narrow run. If the piece of water is not too choppy, and I think we are the first anglers to fish this particular spot, I may give one or both anglers the option of skating a dry fly. I prefer to fish dry flies only where the fish have not been recently harassed. If we work the water with dry flies, I may — if the current allows — row back upstream to fish the area again with wet flies. If the boat traffic is heavy, I may decide it best to push down the river, especially if there is an excellent location I am determined to fish. If I decide to push on, I must also think ahead of what I will do if another angler is fishing my intended target when I get there. One must always be thinking two or three chess moves ahead, with Plan B and Plan C already formulated.

If my next stop is located in direct sunlight, we are fishing nymphs deep. I choose flies according to what has worked well for me in years past, same time of season, same water conditions. If this is my first day with today's clients, I allot time to have them practice getting the right drift of the fly at the periphery of the target-rich environment. I do not want my guys or gals practicing where they might actually get a strike, and, then, blow it by not responding to the strike, or not responding properly. Done that. Don't like the outcomes. Too many memories of lost opportunities. Once I am convinced my guests can follow a few simple directions, then I will take a chance, putting them in position to cast to a steelhead.

Not for the beginning boater—Jeff Elston expertly picks his way through a whitewater minefield.

Nymph fishing is a mass of details, as I have said before. It is impossible for a beginner, or — heaven help me — a "veteran" whom I must deprogram, to get all the details right on every drift and hook set. I scrutinize every cast and drift. While I coach and encourage, I often monitor the tone of my voice. I do not want to put someone in tears early in the day with information overload and a drill instructor's demeanor. My clients will shed enough tears during the day on the opportunities missed and the Big Ones who escape. There may be some tears of joy, too. So, let's save those tears.

I must mention at this point, a strange statistically impossible event that I see at least once every fishing day. When my guests are finally instilled with the cast / drift / hook setting basics, they settle into a nice rhythm. Everything is peachy. Now it's just a matter of time until someone hooks a fish. The final tests are persistence and focus. I can rarely predict when a strike will come. Upon entering the highest probability, target-rich environments, I offer friendly reminders about rod position, casting angle, good drift of the fly, and smooth hook set. Inevitably — EVERY day — an angler will look at something other than their line or indicator when a steelhead intercepts their fly. In a beautiful river environment, there are many intriguing remarkable sights: birds, animals, spacious riverfront homes, waterfalls, and river scenery. The timing of the sightseeing is critical though. If the flies are in the heart of fish-holding country, you dare not look away, even for a second. That's right, not even for a second. When you do, at least once during the day you WILL miss a fish-hooking opportunity. By the time I "enthusiastically suggest" setting the hook, it is usually too late. There is too long a lag time from the moment I utter "Set the hook!", until the command is translated into swinging the rod tip in a tardy attempt by the angler to set the hook. Most anglers, I think, do not fully appreciate how hard a good fishing guide has worked for hours to bring them to this moment. Outwitting other anglers, rowing hard with precision, holding the boat against the current in exactly the perfect casting position, and constantly offering reminders and encouragement have not been enough. Still, the emotionally healthy guide has to temper his disappointment and frustration, knowing the same thing will happen at least once on his next trip, too. It will happen at least once every day, guaranteed.

If you are a devious client, and would take delight in watching your guide go into a seizure, merely say five little words about the missed strike: "It was probably a rock." At this point, I look away for a moment so they do not see me roll my eyes. After regaining my composure, I, often, respectfully ask my client to "hit the rock again". It is very rare that they do, BECAUSE IT WASN'T A DAMN ROCK! After most realize they lost a fish-hooking opportunity, I say something like "Hmmmm…How about that . . ." Then, I pull anchor to move on. If I am very careful, the muttering under my breath is usually undetectable.

Steelhead strikes are valuable. Many days I've reflected to myself, "We were one or two strikes away from getting skunked. Amazing." Two anglers can easily make a thousand casts a day between them. Maybe only one or two evoked a steelhead to bite the fly. If the strike is missed, it could be the entire ball game. A single fish landed compared to zero landed can be the difference between a lousy day and a great day for the angler. I have had many one-fish-landed days where the angler caught the best fish of his lifetime. It just takes one steelhead, especially for a novice, to make our trip the most memorable fishing day he's ever had. This also enhances the chance I will have subsequent guided fishing trips with this fisherman. As I write this paragraph I am recalling a guided trip I had two days ago on which an angler — a nice man and attentive student — landed his first steelhead ever on a rainy, high-water winter day. He had missed several other opportunities, but finally put all the pieces in place to slide a beautiful steelhead into my landing net. Like him, I am thrilled by his accomplishment. I feel a sense of karmic justice when good things happen to good guys. He sent me an email early the next morning thanking me for my efforts, and recounting his enjoyment. On top of these, he was looking forward to our *next* fishing trip together. Nice! A happy client who wants to fish with me again.

Now let's contrast that with two anglers who had fished with me three days before I penned this section. I worked just as hard for them against heavy currents of high water to put them in position — after several missed strikes — to each solidly hook a steelhead. One man landed a super 9-pound hatchery hen that he kept for the BBQ. It was an exciting battle, including having the fish run under the boat on three occasions. Enjoyably memorable, from my standpoint. His angling companion was not as lucky. He lost his steelhead after a brief battle, but at least he had fooled the fish into taking the fly, he detected the strike and set the hook well. The fish just made a clean escape. So it goes.

At day's end, the angler who lost his fish expressed his gratefulness for my efforts. The angler who landed his first steelhead ever never even had the courtesy to say good-bye. He climbed into his car, closed the door, and waited for his companion to drive him home. I am at a loss to figure out some people's behavior. Reminder to self: the only behavior I can control is my own…most of the time. The exception is when I hear, "It was probably just a rock."

Because there are fewer fish-holding locations at high water, I am forced to look hard for fishable areas. I literally try to examine the entire river from bank to bank, seeking out any little nook where a fish might be resting. These spots can be quite visually subtle. They do not appear to be much until I put my boat almost on top of it. Then I notice how the swift current has slowed a tiny bit creating a quiet pocket just big enough to rest a traveling fish. If the water level is six inches higher or lower when I fish it next, new holding areas appear while others disappear as the currents have changed. Yesterday's good holding water may be to slow or too fast today, or not quite deep enough for a fish to feel safe. Water clarity can change too. If the water rose a few inches on a heavy rain or dam release, the water may become slightly muddied. If it has dropped, clarity can increase greatly, requiring longer casts to stay away from the fish, lighter tippets and smaller flies. Little detailed adjustments in tactics and tackle will be the difference between success and failure.

Summer, Normal Water

Normal water flows often present me with the greatest challenge to a successful fishing day. At these times, the greatest number of anglers will be on the river. Bank anglers will have good access in certain areas, sometimes lining up shoulder to shoulder. When I float my boat through such locations, I have my anglers reel in their lines so we can pass the horde quickly. It is like running a gauntlet. Many of the bankies (Yes, I'm one at times myself, so don't get too excited if you sense I've used the term disparagingly.) keep casting even as we drift by, landing their baits and lures within inches of my boat. Kind of like trying to hit a moving target. Some, no doubt, resent boaters floating near or over their fishing water. Often, I just smile and nod as the casts continue to land nearby. "You bastards…"

At normal water flows of late spring through mid summer, most of my steelhead rivers are comfortably negotiable by experienced boatmen. Known routes through tricky rapids are maneuvered without incident. And, because of the combination of fishable, negotiable river flows and vacation time, steelhead rivers get crowded.

Additionally, late spring through summer, the weather in the Pacific Northwest is usually quite pleasant. More people want to spend time outdoors, including fishermen. There is no dealing with winter temperatures and the rain and snow of the winter season. So, the fishing masses ask around in internet chat rooms and call telephone hotlines to discover where I am fishing, then plan their river activities to harass me. At least, it *seems* that's what they do.

Let the Games Begin

If we launch my boat early enough, before the sun is directly on the water, or in shaded areas, we will normally start the day by casting or trolling wet flies. Either method — casting or trolling — can be effective and fun when the angler can experience the thrill of a hard strike when a steelhead grabs. If we troll the flies, letting them hang tight in the current downstream of the boat, I control where the flies swim or hold. When using this method, it is the guide doing the fishing in large part. If I have good casters in the boat, I usually suggest they cast while I back ferry the boat against the current holding it stationary, or drop the anchor. We start by casting short — within twenty feet — then lengthen subsequent casts until I sense that my guests have reached their comfortable maximum casting distance. The boat is then moved to the next casting position where the routine starts again. Angle each cast across and downstream at about a 45-degree angle. The wet fly swings until it ends up directly downstream of the angler. Hold it there for a count of five. After the five-count, strip two feet of fly line from the reel. Cast again, and repeat the procedure. The path of the fly has is moved two feet farther from the angler on each successive cast. In my experience, a steelhead will strike a *well-presented* wet fly the first time it swims into their proximity. A second identical cast of the same length rarely, if ever, solicits a strike.

Some of my guests are willing to risk a heart attack. If one or both of the anglers for the day have the skill and desire, I

A late-summer buck wearing the colors that will attract the girls at The Big Dance.

will set them up to skate a dry fly. I am much more inclined to do this at normal and low water flows than at high water. Higher water usually means lower water temperatures and more current and depth. I have fewer locations to fish and greater difficulty holding or anchoring the boat to remain stationary. Locations with smooth surface currents, as opposed to choppy, riffly water, are my preferences. Choppy surface currents tend to sink the fly. The right cast in flat water — like a tailout above a rapid — will wake the fly nicely in a sweeping arc. There will be no doubt when the strike comes. I remind my guys not to react to the strike until line is pulled from the reel. At this point, the fish has turned right, left or down, drawing the hook point more securely into the mouth or corner of the jaw.

Though it is possible to fish a wet fly on a *sinking* fly line, once the sun is on the water, it is nymph time. Not having eyelids so as to be able to squint, the steelhead much prefer to retreat to the depths and stay low in the water I prefer to fish, which you might recall is seven feet deep or less. Cast the nymphs or egg patterns upstream, allowing them to sink, and then drift naturally with the current. My job is to coach my anglers to make necessary adjustments during the drift, such as mending the line, and lifting and lowering the rod tip, to insure the drift of the fly is slow and "natural". Additionally, I try to keep my guests focused on what they are doing so a precious strike is not missed.

In deeper water, say deeper than 6 feet, or water with a choppy surface, the fish may be suspended off the bottom. It is possible to fish too deep for suspended fish. The weighted nymph can actually drift too far beneath them to create any interest. There are times I will shorten the distance between my flies and a very buoyant strike indicator, suspending the

flies two to three feet off the river bottom. Jig fishermen do exactly the same thing in the summer time: suspend a feathered jig underneath a float, so the jig drifts several feet above the bottom. Even a fish lying near the bottom will often rise several feet to intercept a jig or fly when water temperatures are in the fifty to low sixties Fahrenheit range.

Strategic Maneuvers

Because "normal" river flows tend to bring out the maximum number of anglers, especially on the weekends, I am constantly confronted with the question posed in a 1982 tune by The Clash: "Should I Stay or Should I Go?" Coincidentally, the album that contained The Clash's only number-one hit was entitled *Combat Rock*. It could just as well been called *Combat Fishing*. That is what it feels like some days when fishermen are everywhere, standing or anchored in many of my favorite areas. *Should I go or should I stay now?...If I go there will be trouble...If I stay it will be double...*Many anglers are hackers with few clues, so I may decide to wait for them to leave. Human psychology, however, often comes into play as they observe me waiting for them to clear out. Some anglers will stubbornly stay put just to ensure that I cannot slide into position to fish the waters they have just pounded to no avail for two hours. *So you got to let me know...Should I stay or should I go?* It is very common for stubborn anglers to hold their positions, even though they are ready to leave, until I drift downstream below them. Then they will reel in their lines and depart.

However, the game may not be over. If it is doable, I will move to the river's edge, jump from the boat, and pull it back upstream to access the water that we were temporarily forced to bypass. If I've correctly assessed that the departed anglers were unskilled, used a less effective fishing method, or took the wrong approach to fishing this particular piece of water, we will, more often than not, hook a steelhead. Sometimes, two or three. Oh, that feels good! My guests think so, too.

If I approach a good location about lunchtime that has other anglers where I want to be, I pull into the shade to dine with my crew. I wait and we watch while making pleasant conversation with my clients. Where exactly are the anglers positioned in relation to where I know the steelhead to be holding? Are they covering the likely water effectively? Are they using effective methods and fishing well? All these will determine how much time we spend fishing this same water after lunch. Maybe we do a "drive by", spending little time as we fish it on the run. Or, if I have determined the water was relatively untouched, we may linger.

During lunch, I am also looking upstream for approaching boats that could affect my decisions. Even though my guys are still eating, I may announce I am pulling anchor to slide down the river a bit. This doesn't interfere with their lunching. The idea, if the anglers below have moved down, is to station the boat in the near proximity of our first after-lunch fishing location. If the boat behind us continues down past us,

Katie Zajicek is determined to win this battle. And, she did.
Photo by David Zajicek.

they should, out of courtesy, *I hope*, not fish the water in our immediate vicinity. If I suspect they may cast to our intended target, I will pick up a fly rod and make some ineffective casts into the area that my dining guests will soon fish. I cast far, attempting to push the approaching boat wide of our water. It takes a boatman willing to risk chastisement if he allows his boat to drift through the water I am "fishing". All during this, my guests are continuing to dine, converse, and enjoy the scenery. It's not always important for me to trouble them about the game of chess being played to enable them to hook a steelhead or two after lunch.

There are days when I cannot escape the river traffic. At such times, the best strategy can be to fish every piece of open steelhead water thoroughly, as if no one had touched it. My

hope is that we will fish better flies with better technique than those who fished before us. In addition, there is always the chance that a fish previously not in the mood to bite a fly has changed its mind by the time we arrive. On such busy days on the river, I am constantly reminding myself that I am doing my best in light of circumstances beyond my control. Doing my best needs to be reflected in how I interact with my guests. I cannot afford to indulge in discouragement, though this would be my tendency at times. My attitude and conversation must be upbeat and encouraging, always offering the hope that a steelhead can be hooked on the very next cast. Such a cheery disposition is certainly much easier to maintain if we have already hooked three, four, or six fish already that day. To hook more will be pure gravy. But, as I tell my clients, one of my goals is that each angler in my boat would hook a steelhead on every cast. An impossibility, of course, but it expresses my level of effort throughout the entire fishing day, whatever the circumstances. My people need to know that I have used every trick, every clever strategic move in my arsenal to maximize their chances of hooking a steelhead on every cast they make. I want them to know no other guide could have given them a better effort than me. I want to know at day's end in my own heart that no guide gave a better effort today than I did.

While "normal" water flows can, in many ways, present the greatest challenges, they present the greatest learning opportunities. When the competition for good fishing water is fierce, a determined angler or guide will experiment and make discoveries. I try new, previously overlooked fishing spots. I try new flies, or maybe fish time-tested patterns in subtly different ways. We fish familiar steelhead holes from new or "odd" casting positions. In the process, a few new bits of treasured information may be revealed. Most experiments bear no new revelations. Kind of like panning for gold. Eventually, if you persist, a few nuggets are found.

There is a well known steelhead hole — let's call it Fish Camp — on one of my favorite rivers that can produce five or six hook ups in a given day. This is a good number for the entire fishing day, let alone a single fishing spot. However, there are days this same spot will produce zero strikes, even when the water flow and temperature are perfect. I cannot predict day to day if my clients will hook five, zero or something in between. More than any other single steelhead hole I fish, this one baffles me most. I have fished it at every conceivable water level, angle, time of day, light conditions, and all fly-fishing methods. I think I know it well, fishing it perhaps fifty times every summer steelhead season for the last ten years. Fish Camp seems to get less and less dependable as a regular steelhead producer. I cannot know for sure, but I suspect that this particular holding area changes in subtle but significant ways from season to season. While there are expanses of bedrock and large boulders in this

Since there are no steelhead in Virginia, Matt Cooper comes out West each year to fish with brother Andrew on the Rogue. Photo assist by Andrew Cooper.

spot, there is, also, a substantial portion of the stream bottom covered with smaller stones, fist size down to fine gravel. It is easy to envision high water shifting the smaller rock changing the contours and preferred holding stations for the steelhead. However, the pool has always remained deep enough throughout its majority that it should still hold fish on a very regular basis. The current velocity and structure are good in many portions of the run, along with good, fly-fishable depths. I have seen preferred fish-holding areas relocate from year to year as the bottom shifts a bit, and even day to day as the river level fluctuates. However, until recently, I was able to find the correct casting position and flies to hook fish here regularly.

During the 2006 fishing season, Fish Camp was my nemesis. It looked good and "fished" well. I had a couple of good anglers who had consistently caught steelhead here in seasons past. On this trip, however, the steelhead took them to the woodshed for a beating. If there were fish in this hole, they absolutely refused to bite proven flies presented in an effective manner. And, the problem was not the fish counts. The number of steelhead in the river was good, so we could not use the "no fish in the river" excuse. Hmmmmmm…

Though we caught the occasional steelhead there that season, Fish Camp became my Problem Child in 2006. Often, I pondered this piece of water at night before falling asleep. The one little detail that kept circling back to me was that most of the fish we hooked were by accident. That is, my guys were hooking fish at the end of their drifts as they readied to cast again. What few fish we were getting were taking the fly as it was ascending on a tight line at the end of the drift, or as the fly was hanging tight against the current. Because the fish

were taking unexpectedly outside the heart of the "most likely zone", I often missed locating the exact location of where the steelhead struck. Therefore, I needed to pay closer attention to discover if there was a very well defined, consistent sweet spot. And, there was.

On subsequent days in Fish Camp, when maybe we got a fish, or maybe we didn't, from the upper end and middle portion of the hole, I found a tiny location off the end of an exposed piece of bedrock at the lowest end of the hole that always seemed to hold a fish. It was very difficult to get a natural drift of the fly from where it was necessary to anchor the boat. If I got the boat into optimal position, the clients had only a single opportunity to make the right cast before the boat was swept down the river by powerful currents. So I had to resign to fish to the sweet spot long enough until somebody finally got the right drift. It was, then, just a matter of persistence and faith. As long as the daily water levels did not fluctuate significantly, we had a guaranteed strike every time we anchored at the lower end of Fish Camp. The moral here, then, is that even if you think you know a pool intimately, subtle changes from winter high-water events can occur in the physical environment that will reposition holding fish. Last year's Sweet Spot can move, or even disappear completely.

River Fluctuations Within the "Normal Flows" Range

A few inches of change in a river's level can cause fish to relocate in certain favored fishing holes. A few inches may not be significant to move all steelhead into or from most good fishing locations in a river, but it *will* affect some. Whereas most anglers will not perceive that two or three inches of river flow up or down can be significant, an astute and experienced angler knows it. These affected locations are those that have flows and depths that are right on the cusp of water depth being too low or too high; or the current velocity being too fast, or too slow.

At a spot I call High Banks, the current velocity is barely adequate to get a good drift of the fly early in the summer season. It is at the lower limit of current velocity. Any slower, the leader and fly barely move. The fish seem to have too long to examine the fly, or the delay between the interception of the fly and the angler perceiving the strike is too long. The strike is missed. A few inches of flow drop changes this hole completely.

At a tiny pocket I call Runaway, I need to exit the boat in order to hold it in position with my feet wedged into the rocky stream bottom in order for my guests to fish. My anchor will not hold here at normal water flows. Most days I am barely able to hold the boat steady without losing my footing as I stand in swift water more than waist high. A couple of extra inches of water is usually too much for me to restrain the boat

After spawning in the fall, dead chinook salmon are a rich source of nutrients returned to the river.

as my studded felt soles, even with my heels dug in, slide and slip until I finally have to jump back in the boat, forced to bypass this productive little pocket.

In summary, normal summer conditions can be both the most challenging and most pleasant days of the entire fishing year. The water flows are at their best, the weather is optimal, the flowers are in bloom, and the birds are singing. If we can put our flies in enough productive water during the day, we will most likely catch some steelhead to add to this halcyon mix.

Summer & Fall Low Water

I love low water. Whitewater steelhead rivers become much more challenging to negotiate safely in a drift boat late summer and fall. Average (or prudent?) boaters will not run certain sections of these rivers because of dangerous whitewater rapids. Of course, I seek out these sections. If I am confident I can get

through these hazardous waters without putting my clients at unreasonable risk, I want to run parts of the river where others will not go to cut down on the angling competition.

Decreasing the fishing competition when the water is skinny is particularly critical because the fish-holding areas are well defined and easier to find. The fish are concentrated in the fewer prime locations where the water depth, current speed and structure provide comfort and cover. Also, these fish are more prone to be disturbed since the only way to travel through a certain piece of water may be to run a drift boat or raft right through the small areas where the fish are holding. At higher flows, many fishing holes can be skirted. The boating angler can refrain from getting too close to the water he wants to fish. Low water presents fewer such choices.

Part of my low-water game plan, too, is to avoid popular bank access areas. Bold and or foolish waders can mess up a lot of fishing water. River locations I fished at high or normal river flows might now be eliminated as fishable possibilities because decreased flow has significantly altered the depth and/or current velocity. I will linger longer in other prime locations, knowing we often now have less water to fish.

Because many of our Pacific Northwest steelhead rivers also have fall Chinook salmon runs, dead-drifted egg flies can be particularly effective come September, October, and November. Even though they do not have to eat on their upstream journey, steelhead can get a little giddy about salmon eggs bobbing along the stream bottom, set adrift during salmon mating activity. In the low, clear water of early fall, a 3X fluorocarbon tippet may be necessary to fool wary steelhead who have survived months of fishing onslaught by anglers who would kill them if of hatchery origin. Native fish which have been caught a released a few times will be cautious, too.

For wet-fly and dry-fly action, the famous October Caddis (*Dicosmoecus atripes*) is hatching late September through

Imitations of caddisfly larvae and pupae will catch summer steelhead, especially in September and October with the hatching of the October Caddis, genus Dicosmoecus.

Patterns imitating adult Dicosmoecus caddisflies can draw surface strikes when skated over the right steelhead.

October. This is a large, active insect that can excite trout and steelhead alike. Fishing three stages of this insect's lifecycle can be effective. In the dim light of morning and evening a skating dry fly or damp wet fly can trigger some explosive strikes from aggressive steelhead who cannot deal passively with the thought of a fast swimming pupa or dancing, darting gyrations of the female egg-laying adult. These active movements of this insect are, apparently, an irresistible invitation for certain steelhead to attack.

Fishing an imitation of the October Caddis larva or pupa dead-drift under an indicator can be deadly. Pair the caddis with an egg pattern, and you have a tempting fall season duo. I can almost visualize a willing steelhead being confused by the choice. *Egg or caddis? Caddis or egg? Can I get both at once?*

However, I have touted the October Caddis and salmon egg patterns big time, do not ignore the other flies in your box. Know that savvy anglers (like those reading this book) are fishing these flies, too. Sometimes an excellent choice of flies is to present the fish with something that they have not seen today. Steelhead may have tiny brains but you are dealing with the Best of the Best when it comes to survival. They have made it this far in life, eluding predators and hazards that would end their lives early. Though I have a former guide friend who insists these fish are "stupid", I choose to show them more intellectual respect, especially on those days when I am able to fool very few…or none. On a day I get outwitted by "stupid" fish, where does that put me on the IQ scale? Ouch!

Just as I do during low flows of winter, there are times in late summer and fall I must extricate myself from the boat to plow it through the shallows.

There's also the occasional high-impact kiss from a nasty rock that fails to move when it sees me coming. Every couple of years I take my boat to a shop that does metal work to have them give my aluminum workhorse a facelift. With rubber hammers and tools from The Inquisition, I have the dents and serious dings smoothed out a bit until the next inevitable collision.

High-speed, shallow water can be a seriously underestimated hazard. It seems every whitewater steelheading boatman has to learn some rowing lessons the hard, dangerous way. One time I had three clients in my boat in the low water of October on the Rogue River. My dear friends for this particular day are not small men. As they read this, they will know for sure it is about them that I write. They know I love them dearly, so they will not be offended when I tell you that two of them would have been a good load in my boat at low water. Having made it down miles of river without incident, I was rowing us down a long, very fast, shallow riffle. I was tracking the boat toward the left bank in preparation for fishing a fast-approaching hole in the middle of the river. If I do not pull left with enthusiasm, my boat will go dead center over the spot to be fished. I had performed this maneuver in this particular spot literally hundreds of times, but never with this much weight in the boat. In this moment, just sitting a couple of inches deeper in

the water made a dangerously significant difference on my approach toward the left side of the river. With my boat mostly sideways to the swift current, I clipped a rock smaller than my head nestled among fist-size stones and gravel only a few inches from the surface. Hitting the rock knocked everyone off balance, and all our combined weights shifted hard left. The left chine (the lower edge of a drift boat where the side meets the bottom of the boat) dug into the bed of smaller rocks in the shallows tipping the boat onto its side.

In a panic moment, you never know how someone, including yourself, will react. As the boat rolled onto its left side, in a heartbeat I was able to step left out of the tipping craft, catch and hold the right gunnel (the top edge of the boat running from the bow back to the stern) as a weightlifter would position to do an overhead press. I prevented the boat from completely turning over upside down. As my guest in the rear of the boat exited unharmed, I found plenty of adrenalin-driven strength to push the boat back over to its upright position with the two men still in the front.

We were extremely lucky. No one was injured. No rods broken. The only piece of gear lost was a single fishing glove that floated away into the depths far below us. A maneuver and a rock I had dealt with flawlessly for years all of a sudden combined to become a serious hazard which I failed to anticipate. In subsequent years, I think of this incident every single time I make my move left to fish the Big Eddy on the Rogue.

Like all water conditions, fishing and boating the low water of late summer and fall has competitive advantages and river-running disadvantages. Because some boaters will smartly avoid the crowds and river hazards, I will welcome the opportunities that result, and find a way to deal with the downside challenges. In so doing, I will become a better angler and smarter fly-fishing guide.

Love Those Lazy Guides

Sometimes I think of sending "thank you" cards. I cannot help but love guides that make me look good in front of my guests. Short of taking a bullet for them (it is too hard to row my boat with a bleeding hole in the chest), my clients know I will go to extremes to provide maximum opportunities for them to hook a steelhead. If they have hooked 99 fish for the day, I want them to know I will row my skinny arms off looking for number 100.

On an overcast summer morning, two clients and I were fishing Lower Lunch on the Rogue River. As we began fishing the area, another drift boat slid down the far side of the river. An elderly client in the second boat had hooked a steelhead, so the guide anchored the boat near the bank in knee-deep water. It was easy to see that the man playing the big fish was not very experienced. He would not put much pressure on the steelhead when he needed to do so. Every time the fish got near the boat, the guide would stand with the net in a weak attempt to capture the fish. Even though the guide was wearing

shorts, he refused to exit the boat in very shallow water to net the old man's steelhead easily.

How long did it take the lazy guide to finally net his client's fish? (Yes, I know I just used another split infinitive…) Long enough for my clients to hook three steelhead, and land two of them. We were within a stone's throw of the other boat during all this action. The clients in the other boat saw us hook three fish. They couldn't help it. All this did two beneficial things for me: The other guide did not have a chance to interfere with our fishing, since he was anchored on the far bank, allowing us to find three biting steelhead. Secondly, the guide made me look good as my clients observed how I will do anything to net their fish quickly. This affords them more fishing time, more opportunities, and more steelhead landed in a day.

In Review

As always, the cornerstone strategy is to keep the flies in good steelhead water. Potentially productive water, that is. If there is adequate depth with reasonable water speed and structure, I have my guests casting as I drift down the river from one anchorable location to the next. Occasionally we pick up a steelhead "on the run". If we can find a bonus fish once or twice every fishing day, that is significant. On the other side of the coin, I warn my anglers not to be casting into unproductive or snag-dangerous water we must traverse. I hate losing fishing time by breaking off flies in water that has absolutely no chance of holding a biting steelhead. So, my typical advice

chatter through marginal expanses of water goes something like this: "Cast left…Now, turn and cast right…Back to the left…Okay, reel in the flies for a moment while we drop through this slot…Strip out line. Cast left…Lift your rod tip to get your flies off that snaggy ledge…Good. Cast right. A little farther on the next cast…Mend your line and hold the rod tip high…Here comes a boat. Reel in the flies and let's blow down the river a ways…Blah, blah, steelhead, blah, blah blah…Did you hear the one about the guy and his monkey who walked into a bar? The guy orders a beer, and the monkey decides to…blah, blah, blah . . ."

How long to stay in any one location is always a pivotal decision. Sometimes, the large number of bank anglers and boaters force me to cover every open piece of fishable water, even if the fish-catching potential there is marginal. We take our time, fish thoroughly and fish with focus. Maybe we change flies; maybe we don't. If it is an exceptionally good run, we may fish it a second time. Maybe from the other side of the river; maybe with nymphs instead of wet flies, or vice versa.

Delays will happen, and I must cope. Tippets will break and flies will be lost. To save and make sure it is done right, I prefer to personally tie on the new tippet and flies. Bathroom breaks are necessary. And, my competitive sense of urgency as we push down a crowded river is usually not a healthy thing to spread to my guests. Yes, fishing is our chief focus, but civility, good cheer, and a little tranquility are necessary ingredients to a pleasantly memorable summer steelhead day.

CHAPTER 13
Bushwhacking Your Way to Steelhead and Solitude

ARE YOU WILLING TO GO WHERE TRAILS
are few, the brush is thick, and thorns abound to catch a steelhead?
Will you ford fast water, crawl over logs, crawl under logs, deal with your rod tip
getting repeatedly caught in the brush and limbs you are plodding through
in order to fish waters few will try to approach?

Can you endure re-tracing your grueling steps for two hours at the end of the fishing day to get back to your car? Can you deal with the possibility that you may not have seen or hooked a single fish for all your efforts? If so, you are the rare fly angler. Maybe small coastal stream steelhead fishing is for you.

Reiterating, the Number One obstacle to your steelhead fishing success is other anglers. Escape to where others will or cannot go, and you have eliminated the constant aggravation of other fishermen competing for your water and your steelhead. It is possible, in fact, likely, that you will not see another angler all day.

Overcoming tough terrain can put an angler into productive steelhead water that others cannot or will not reach.

As I begin to write this section, steelhead sleuth Jason Mariner and I have just fished four streams on a recent outing. On the first three of the four, we saw not a single other angler. For seven hours, we crashed brush, waded swift deep water to reach the opposite bank, risked the unplanned swim, and made hundreds of casts, some of which left our terminal gear in the trees. Jason smashed his knee with enthusiasm when he stumbled, wading in murky water. We climbed, crawled, jumped, and, occasionally, cursed the deciduous jungle, which is coastal Oregon. (Let me tell you, Lewis and Clark were REAL men beyond my wildest imaginings to venture through the rain forests of the Pacific Northwest.) And, for all our efforts, I was fortunate enough to hook and land one magnificent native hen that Jason taped at a click less than 34". One strike between us, for what turned out to be an eleven-hour fishing day. For me it was a great day owing to the fact that I was fortunate enough to encounter one willing fish that fought me valiantly for more than twenty minutes, all the while trying to keep my rod tip out of the brush and overhanging tree limbs which begged to aid the fish in its escape attempts.

On our final stream of the day, no bushwhacking was required. Late on that March day, we drove onto a paved parking lot along a very accessible steelhead stream, hoping few anglers would be out after 4 p.m. on a winter day. We found six anglers casting through the two short stretches of river we wanted to fish. Ah, easy access means a frustrating fishing mess. What a stark, unpleasant contrast to the other three waters we had just come from.

Seeking Out Small Steelhead Streams

Virtually all Pacific Coast streams that have a direct feed into the ocean will have winter steelhead in them. With the exception of a few free-roaming hatchery strays, the vast majority of the steelhead will be native fish. From year to year, their numbers will fluctuate. Some waters may find only a few dozen fish ascending them to spawn in any given winter. Many may get only a few hundred steelhead for the year. Despite the sparse numbers, it can be obvious in small waters where big fish will seek refuge. Much of the stream is too shallow, too fast, too exposed for a steelhead to linger. Locate those few areas that can comfortably hide a big fish, and you have a chance.

Many years ago, I often patrolled a little river on the Oregon Coast not too far from Tillamook. It is special because it was there that I caught a winter steelhead on the fly that eventually evolved into my Caballero, Veiled Assassin and Gorman Bead Egg patterns. The fish was caught in the very first pool I ever cast the fly. This steelhead was particularly memorable, too, because it quickly found a deeply submerged limb and swam under it. I realized I was in trouble when I saw my fly line go directly from my rod tip straight out into the pool in front of me holding the limb, but my fish was down the river more than fifty feet jumping and thrashing at the surface like a frog on steroids.

I ran into the heart of the pool to discover the problem, noticing for the first time the large submerged limb. At the risk of flooding my chest waders, I managed to get my toe under the limb and lift it toward the surface as the fish continued to go berserk. With my rod in the downstream hand, I plunged the other arm as deep as I could to grab the limb. Lifting the limb and wriggling a submerged rod tip, I managed to free my fly line. What luck! Even luckier, the steelhead stayed on my hook, and I eventually beached the native buck that was very near 30".

Low water is my favorite time to fish this small river. Many places are no more than knee deep from bank to bank. Gear anglers seem to shun this condition, which is good. I have no competition as I cross from one side to the other to best approach any likely fish-holding pocket. As I search for fish in low water, it is like trying to find a few oases in a vast desert.

One angling situation I remember quite fondly was walking upstream through a large expanse of shallow, fast water when I came upon a little tumble of whitewater that extended all the way across the stream. Surveying it closely, I spied one tiny pocket of deep green water that was barely big enough to hide a steelhead. The pocket might have measured three feet wide by four feet long. All water surrounding it was shallow, foamy and fast. To get an accurate cast that would drift through the target pocket, I crouched low as I moved into short range. I was on my knees as I made the first cast. My Mini Caballero landed just upstream of the target, then drifted into it, dead center. As I watched my fly line drift back to me, I soon saw it hesitate. I felt nothing, but I suspected something. Could be caught on a rock, or…maybe a fish intercepted my fly. As I raised the rod tip to tighten the line, I felt the throbbing headshake of a fish that knew something was wrong.

In a heartbeat, the native hen was waking through the shallow water below me at high speed. As it ran, I followed. It swam through areas that were so shallow its back was out of the water. It never ceases to amaze me that big fish migrate and hold in water that can be nothing more than a trickle. I love playing steelhead in a big river, but it does not match the experience chasing a strong specimen as it charges through shallow riffles and small pockets kicking up a waking spray

with its tail as it seeks run my line around or under any possible obstacle that will win its freedom. Not all battles are won by the fisherman, but I managed eventually to hold this fish long enough for a couple of self-taken delayed shutter release photos.

The point I am trying to make here, is that many anglers will find it hard to believe big steelhead will inhabit such small streams. Or, if the know steelhead do enter these streams to spawn, they do not believe they can be caught in low, clear conditions. And, indeed, they can't if you do not take stealth to the maximum and fish a fly the size no bigger than a bumblebee. Camouflage is not just for hunting four-legged animals. Red caps and red fleece tops make for eye-catching photos on big steelhead rivers, but dressing like a bush and fishing from your knees is often necessary at low water on a tiny steelhead stream.

As for a bushwhacking "tool", I look for a stick on the forest floor that is smooth to my hand, about 2" in diameter, and two feet long. I can beat down or push aside branches and vines in my path. Such a tool is cheap, effective, readily available, and I can discard it without littering the landscape.

Is There a Doctor in the House?

As you might easily surmise, bushwhacking in challenging terrain has inherent dangers. It is easy to twist an ankle, wrench your back, or break a bone while in the wild. There may be no

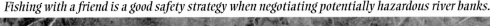

Fishing with a friend is a good safety strategy when negotiating potentially hazardous river banks.

The rewards for bushwhacking can be significant.

one within miles to help an angler in trouble. Cell phones may be useless. There may be no nearby roads. If it's a typical cold, rainy day during our Pacific Northwest winter, an emergency situation can be compounded by the threat of hypothermia.

It is best to bushwhack steelhead streams with a friend. If nothing else, a companion can tell the authorities where to find the body. I make it a point to assure my friends who accompany me on such adventures that if the fishing is good not to be in any hurry to report my demise. They will have worked long and hard to bust their way through tough topography to find good steelhead fishing. If I'm dead, there's no rush. "Catch one for me," I say. And, of course, I remind them my attitude and actions toward them will be the same if they should precede me in making the Last Cast.

The Discovery Process

To discover out-of-the-way streams that hold steelhead, I would recommend starting by thumbing through the fishing regulations booklet put out by the state or province in which you live. Most are broken into regions. Select a region in which you wish to fish. Look for streams that are listed, and the regulations given. Some streams hold steelhead but are closed to fishing, and, may not be listed in the regulations. In Oregon, this usually means that a stream not listed in the regulations handbook is not open to steelhead fishing. Therefore, you can immediately eliminate unlisted streams from your search list.

Listed streams may have narrow windows of when the season is open to legal fishing. Some waters have special regulations, like lure and fly-only, no bait. Many steelhead streams have only certain sections that are open to fishing. You must discover these sections and landmarks that define them. The uppermost reaches of many streams, where steelhead spawn and are vulnerable to harassment, snagging, or poaching, are usually closed to all fishing the entire year. Once you have discovered a stream to explore, make sure you know the regulations.

If some idiot writes a magazine article about some little remote steelhead stream, stay away from it. The same goes for steelhead streams betrayed on chat room fishing blogs, where some full-of-himself braggart is in search of eager groupies wanting to know more from this self-ordained guru. Too many fit, young-gun steelhead addicts will use these sources as a treasure map. When you get to these streams, no matter how hard to access, the number of anglers there to spoil your fishing experience may disappoint you. That is, unless you are looking for a social experience, where you can chat with other fishermen as you *watch* them fish.

In addition, remember, the more accessible a stream is, the more anglers will be there to join you in the search for its fish. Generally, the more you have to suffer to access the steelhead, the less the competition from others, especially the lazy or faint of heart. I smile when I think of those of my advanced years — over 50 — who will not venture where I go for fear

Yes, the steelhead is still on the line, and Jason Mariner eventually landed it. Bold wading sometimes comes with a chilly price.

they will die of exhaustion, a heart attack or, at the very least, risk a shattered kneecap or broken ankle. As with most of Nature, steelhead in solitude goes to the fittest that are willing to pay the price. Bushwhacking is mostly a young man's game… and, for those old guys with an adventurous heart.

Wading Criminals

Wading a river along private property, even though you entered the stream at a public site, can be problematic. Most anglers assume that once they have entered a river and do not touch the shore, or stay below the mean high water mark, that they will not be considered guilty of trespass. In Montana, this is true, but in Oregon and most other western states, for the most part, this is not true. Some landowners, as I understand it, have the stream bottom included on their property description, which means they pay property tax on their portion of the riverbed. So, they may be duly upset about you wading / walking on *their* property.

Some years ago, I remember an irate property owner who wanted a fisherman cited for trespass because the angler was wading a portion of the North Fork of the Alsea River that bordered his property. Even though the sheriff and state police refused to charge the angler with trespass, the wader's life

was miserable until it was finally determined that no citation would be issued.

In another incident on the upper McKenzie River in Oregon, a landowner wanted to bar boaters from dropping their anchors on the river bottom bordering his property. The landowner eventually lost that one, but, again, all parties involved lived with worry and anger for awhile.

If you find yourself in such a situation, consider hanging your head, looking remorseful, apologize for your ignorance, and promise never to do it again. Then, uncross your fingers and leave quickly.

As I said, Montana has a liberal access law allowing waders to stay below the high-water mark and wade right through Ted Turner's property. I have a Montana fishing friend who legally accesses one of Turner's ranch streams not too far from Dillon. Though Turner's hired hands verbally harass my friend, he just smiles and nods in such a way that conveys that the thugs in cowboy hats should all go on their merry ways and have intimate relations with the nearby cattle and buffalo. At a distance, he can be heard to bid them adieu with a goodbye that *sounds* like, "Stuck shoe, and Ted Turner, too!", or something like that.

Once my Montana friend — let's call him Rick — and I legally waded down a small stream and had some memorable fishing. We finished at late evening. The mosquitoes were coming out. So, we decided we would take a shortcut across some property that neither of us owned to escape the biting swarm to safely reach our car. With car in sight, we popped out of some tall willows we thought had hidden us to climb a wire fence that separated us from our truck. Like a jack-in-the-box popping up in front of us was a rancher with a camera aimed at us. Busted! Seems we were not the first to have used this shortcut. It is one thing to be caught when you are 14 years old. Youth is always a solid excuse. However, when you're thirty-five you really don't have a good excuse for trespass. At least we couldn't think of one at that moment. So, we had our red-faced pictures taken and the rancher told us he would add us to his wall collection of offenders who would face trespass charges if caught a second time. Cleverly, he had also photographed our vehicle and license plate. Good move.

Keep Your Anchors Up Where I Can See Them, and Move Slowly Away From the Fishing Hole

On the northern Oregon coast is a small stream with a steelhead hatchery on it. Public access is extremely limited on the very short distance from stream mouth to hatchery, less than a mile. When the fish are running in big numbers late fall and winter, every rock has *two* anglers on it. Near the hatchery, there is a couple hundred feet of public access and if you fish there, you will make many new friends if you wish. With a shoehorn, you can wedge yourself into the line of your new angling acquaintances. You will naturally introduce yourself to the stranger who is touching your left shoulder and the one leaning against your right shoulder. And, just like the famous Rockette Dancers of Radio City Musical hall fame who synchronized perfectly their kicks to the right and their kicks to left, you quickly learn to coordinate your cast and drifts with the rest of the angling chorus line. 1-2-3 cast left. Drift 1-2-3-4. Lift and reel. 1-2-3 cast left. Lift and…Casting a *fly* rod with this group will enable you to work on your verbal jousting and self-defense skills.

On this stream is a prime piece of private property which I got to fish for a day. This land was seriously guarded. Literally. There was a "watchman" who patrolled the property at all times during daylight hours. The watchman carried a camera. It was used every day to periodically take pictures of the cars and their license plate numbers parked in the public parking lot near the hatchery. If trespassers were sighted and confronted, there was hope of discovering their identity by tracking them back to their car. Once done, a trespass report would be filed.

The 100 yards, more or less, of private riverfront property gave access to some ideal steelhead holding water. My friend and I caught steelhead to the point that it was almost boring. Virtually all were fish bound for the nearby hatchery. Steelhead hatched, raised and released with the use of public dollars. To have exclusive access to this public resource as they cross through your private property is a sweetheart deal! It

What price are you willing to pay to get to the fish?

reminds me of how no one in Merry Old England could hunt in the King's forests. Peasants enter at your own risk.

While pillaging this stream's abundant and un-harassed (except by us) steelhead, a couple of resourceful anglers in pontoon boats were discovered by the camera-bearing sentry to be drifting the river through our property. They immediately had their pictures taken. Then, the guard on duty approached them to tell them they were entering private property and they were forbidden from touching the shoreline, wading in the river, or even dropping their anchors on the stream bottom. All these would qualify as trespass, and would be prosecuted. All these rules and the threat were spoken in a smiling, pleasant tone.

As the men progressed downstream with the current, the watchman paralleled them, walking the stream bank at the same pace of their drift. It did not take long for the floaters to leave this coveted section of river. Because of the nature and current speed of the river, they could not hope to safely fish without dropping their anchors to free their hands from the oars long enough to make a cast.

Oh, there was one more little challenge that the boaters had to deal with. Don't ask me about the legality of this, but at the lower end of the property was a slightly elevated wire fence that spanned the entire width of the river. Fish had no problem swimming underneath it since it did not extend to the stream bottom. However, it was definitely an obstacle and hazard to anyone floating the river. The sentry allowed the men to temporarily trespass to clumsily negotiate the fence. I am guessing this was the last time these two guys made this float.

This was a very fascinating day of steelhead fishing from many standpoints. This little strip of riverfront property could easily generate many thousands of pay-to-access dollars in a steelhead season for the privilege of catching a publicly funded resource. I wish I had such a sweet deal!

In Oregon, fish and wildlife laws are primarily enforced by a division of the Oregon State Police. Each school quarter during which I teach a credit Steelhead Fishing class at Oregon State University I invite a member of the Oregon State Police, fish & wildlife enforcement division, to speak to my students about what these troopers do, give an update on new fisheries laws, and answer questions.

One of the questions always posed concerns public access along streams and rivers that border private property. All of the troopers who have spoken in my class over the years say the same thing on the topic of river trespass: It is an issue open to interpretation, a gray area as it relates to trespass and the law. There have been several proposals before the Oregon state legislature to liberalize stream-access laws, perhaps adopting guidelines similar to those of Montana. So far, such proposals in Oregon have met defeat. However, the troopers all agree that if you get into a situation where you cannot safely proceed up or down a stream you are wading, unable to safely return from where you came, you may legally "trespass" on private property to avoid potential injury or death.

I remember getting into such a situation on the Rogue River. To reach the far side of the river and some good fishing, I waded across a treacherous rapid. I did so from a public access point. Foolishly, I had risked going for a dangerous swim through huge standing waves hiding giant boulders. Kissing a huge rock at high speed might make for a bad memory, assuming I survived it to have a memory.

After catching and releasing a good steelhead, it was time to get back across the river to my vehicle and head home. In spite of protests from my ego, I admitted to myself it would be doubly foolish to attempt negotiating the rapid a second time. I knew of a shallow section of river that extended the entire width of the stream. However, the far side of the river where

A great combo: Girls and steelhead. Marcy Gorman shows her husband how it's done.

I would cross was all private property lined with riverfront homes.

After wading back to the roadside of the river at the shallow crossing, I scouted the best route between a couple of homes to make a run for it. However, before I took my first sprinting step, a woman appeared in the yard of the nearest home. After a cheery greeting from the lady and asking about my fishing success, I explained my predicament. She understood, and kindly invited me to walk across her property to reach the highway.

Even if you don't get an invitation from the landowner as I did, the Law will sympathize with your need to cross private property, even without permission. You might risk a tongue-lashing and name-calling from the landowner, but it seems a small price for personal safety. Pray the property is not patrolled by an unleashed Doberman with a bad attitude.

Rewards and Challenges

Bushwhacking can pay off for the steelhead angler rugged and determined enough to do it. It has inherent risks and dangers, which, if successfully overcome, add to the satisfaction of catching a steelhead or two where others fear or are too lazy to tread. A good plan and a companion are major plusses, especially if the plan includes a camera, and your friend takes a photo of *you* with *your* steelhead. Booyah!

CHAPTER 14
A Typical Steelhead Day Fishing on Foot

THOUGH I USE A BOAT FOR VIRTUALLY ALL
of my steelhead guiding, I stay on foot for most of my personal
steelhead pursuits. I imagine most of the readers of this book will do the same,
because of budgetary restraints or lack of boating skills.

Growing up in western Oregon, rain is our constant companion nine months out of the year. As a grade school boy I was attracted to mud puddles. More than once I succumbed to the urge to run full speed through every one I could find. The higher I kicked the water, the better. The idea of being soaked head to toe, to the great displeasure of my mother, really appealed. Bizarre behavior in retrospect. I loved being in water. I still love being in water.

Smoke from a distant forest fire dims the sunrise on the Rogue River.

In his book, *A River Never Sleeps*, Roderick Haig-Brown wrote "…fishing is just an excuse to be near rivers." I use fishing as an excuse to be *in* rivers. There's something intimately wonderful about being in water. Maybe, for me, it goes all the way back to the womb, suspended in fluid, warm, safe, and comfortable. I must have had an enjoyable stay. In some sense, rivers are my comfort zone. However, my semi-submerged experience is not complete without a fly rod in my hand.

To me, fishing big steelhead rivers such as Washington State's Skagit seems like casting in a flowing ocean. I crave more angling intimacy. My preference is for smaller steelhead rivers, those that provide me the opportunity to wade and cross on occasion. I want bouldered pocket water. Lots of it. I want approachable channels and bedrock ledges. I want an abundance of runs and little pools overhung by streamside trees. If I go for an unplanned swim, my feet will soon find the bottom again.

Small steelhead streams allow me to separate myself from the pack. Boats can't float these because an abundance of shallow water or insurmountable obstacles such as fallen trees or impassable little falls. Because there may be serious bushwhacking, trailblazing on hands and knees, and challenging wading situations, most anglers will not venture into certain portions of a river. Because there is an abundance of easy-access areas on most western steelhead rivers, the majority tend to migrate to these sites. I'm happy for them. And, it is my wish for them that they catch the occasional steelhead to reinforce their behavior. In the meantime, I will be upriver somewhere with scratched arms and torn waders fishing quite contentedly by myself or with a companion who, too, enjoys suffering for a little solitude… and a few undisturbed steelhead.

There is something oxymoronic about hooking BIG fish in a little river. I'm talking about streams you wouldn't call rivers, thirty to fifty feet across in most locations. With stealth you can almost get on top of the steelhead here. Unlike most rivers, you have the opportunity to occasionally see a fish before you cast to it. Once hooked, odds are good you will have to chase the steelhead through a downhill obstacle course of boulders, limbs, deep holes, and fallen trees. If I'm lucky enough to run down the steelhead the game is not over. I don't use a net. Besides being inconvenient to carry, part of the challenge is to successfully tail the slippery fish or gently slide it to the edge of a sloping gravel bank. The fish has a tremendous advantage; they win most of the time. Good for them. I never begrudge them victory. In this environment most are native. The hatchery fish are downriver where they are more easily accessed by the angling hordes up to the point they finally ascend the hatchery facility's fish ladder.

At day's conclusion as I pick up the well-travelled access roads again, making my way back to my 4Runner, I often encounter other anglers as they move from one fishing spot to the next. I greet them with a smiling "Hello". It's natural for them to ask if I've had any luck. My favorite current reply is: "You know I made some really good casts today, and I'm hoping to hook a fish or two tomorrow." This is all very truthful. Then, I follow up immediately with "How did you do?" I always wish them "Good luck!" And I mean it.

I'm amused at my sister Joann who's an excellent steelheader, totally focused and quite successful for someone who doesn't fish but a handful of times in a year because she leads a very responsible life, unlike her big brother. After catching a steelhead or two from my boat, she has a stock reply when someone queries "Any luck?" She smilingly responds "No. No *luck*." Rightfully or wrongfully, Joann attributes fish caught to planning and skill, paying way too much tribute to her brother's efforts. Quite amusing. I'll take all the luck that comes my way, and beg for more.

Today's Game Plan

The following is the recounting of an actual day on the stream for me. It's quite typical of many of my personal steelhead fishing trips.

Because it was Spring Break, late March, I determined I needed an early start. My stream for the day is too accessible for my liking, but the chance at a larger-than-average native steelhead is what spurs me on. I drove a back route to come in on the *upper* river. Most fishermen will be driving the highway that accesses the lower river first; they, then fish their way upstream. So, with a little luck, I'll have time to fish several spots before most other anglers reach my starting location.

Location 1

The first run on the river I chose to fish is very accessible. It's located at a large turnout with an easy trail that many fishers familiar with this stream know about. I can get to it and fish it quickly. I'll be in and out and gone before anyone arrives. If my plan works — and it doesn't always — no one will even realize I have fished it.

I travel with my fly rod set up in advance. The fly line and leader are strung through the guides; the fly is tied on, and then held at the hook keeper. When I'm at my destination I merely lift the rod out the back window of my 4Runner and I'm ready to fish. No time spent getting my rod assembled, stringing it, and fumbling to tie on a fly. Such simple tasks can turn into frustrations when you are in a hurry, so I have it done in advance. This is what a commando must do. I'm on a mission.

At Location 1, I move straight to the heart of the run, about half way between the top of the potentially-productive water and the bottom end. The lower half has the optimal current speed at today's water level. By starting in the best water first I've guaranteed, as best I can, that a rude angler can't step in below me while I'm fishing the portion with the greatest likelihood of catching a fish. This only has to happen a few times to you before you learn this valuable lesson. If the

inconsiderate fisherman who cut you off catches a steelhead in the water you were about to fish, that memory will be with you forever!

I start by casting my egg imitation into the deep channel just beyond my rod tip. I roll cast it upstream, well above my standing position. I am fishing a floating fly line with an indicator. Several split shot serve to get the fly down quickly. As it drifts with the current I mend the line when needed to make sure the egg does not drift too fast. I follow the indicator with my rod tip. Successive casts move the line a little farther from my position as I try to methodically cover all the water where a steelhead my hold. Once I've covered the entire width of the channel in front of me I move downstream about a rod length and repeat the procedure.

When I moved to my second casting position downstream from my starting point my indicator went down. As I set the hook and came tight, I felt the familiar throb of a struggling big fish startled by the sting in its jaw. After a few seconds I could see the twisting flash of my steelhead four or five feet under the surface. A moment later, more line ripped off my fly reel as my prize sprinted toward the lower end of the drift into the shallow tailout preceding the rapid below me. If the fish managed to drop into the rapid I'd have to chase it through an obstacle course of boulders and wood debris. The outcome favored the steelhead. So I attempted to turn the fish. To do this I rolled my rod to a horizontal position with the rod tip a few inches above the water. I bent it hard against the steelhead,

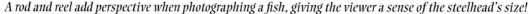

A rod and reel add perspective when photographing a fish, giving the viewer a sense of the steelhead's size!

trying to lower the fish's head and lead it back my way. There's no guarantee this maneuver will work, but most of the time it does for me. Experience tells me how hard I can bend that rod against the fish before my tippet breaks. The drag on the reel has to be set correctly; too little drag, the fish may force me to chase it through dangerous shallows and around line-breaking

Small steelhead rivers that cannot be safely boated have greatly reduced competition for the determined angler on foot.

obstacles; too much drag, I risk breaking the line when the fish makes a hard sprint away from me.

The steelhead took me to the lower end of the run several times. Each time I was able to turn the steelhead back. After six or seven minutes I slid the tired 8-pound buck into the shallows in quiet water. He held still long enough for me to extract the hook and take some photos. I cradled him in the shallows for a few moments before fish swam back into the depths.

Where there's one steelhead there can be two. I took up my last fishing position and resumed systematically covering the likely water. In less than ten minutes I hooked a second steelhead. She came to the surface, thrashing and rolling. Water sprayed in all directions until the fish submerged to run downstream. Like the previous steelhead the hen attempted several times to run downstream through the rapid below. Luckily I was able to counter her moves with a low rod tip, rod bent hard. Being a bigger, stronger fish than the first, the battle with this magnificent hen lasted about twice as long. What a specimen!

A few times every season I am fortunate enough to land a "perfect" steelhead: chrome bright, perfect fins, large girth, no battles scars. This female beauty was the best of my winter season. Resting on her side in shallow water for several moments, she cooperated for a few photos. Then it was a mad

sprint into deep water to rest and continue her upstream journey. If my day was not totally satisfying before, it surely was now. I had barely fished a half hour.

On small steelhead streams, tree limbs tend to claim more flies than the river. One way to identify popular fishing holes is by all the lures, flies, baited hooks, and strands of line hanging from overhanging tree limbs that can't be pulled down by anglers. Neophyte angling sleuths trying to locate good fishing water can use an abundance of hooks and lines dangling from any one tree limb as a clue. Because the upper portion of Location 1 has an overhanging limb — festively decorated with colorful lures and lines — I opted not to fish it. I have managed many casts to this area, successfully using a side-arm casting of the fly line, but today I'm not going to risk breaking off my fly. The time it would take to re-tie my leader and tie on my fly would throw me off my game plan, and adversely affect my psyche. I know myself well enough to know it's best to move on today. The downside risks overwhelm the upside potential. And, after all, I've landed two great fish and photographed them. Life is good.

Location 2

My second destination is accessed from another large roadside turnout. There are a series of pools and runs here, but the water today is a bit too high for all but two to be fishable. Of the two only one is what I consider a prime location. For lazy or less athletic anglers, accessing this stretch requires a bit more effort than they will or can expend. A steep slippery bank must be scrambled down, and, then, an angler has to scramble over huge streamside boulders and crash through some brush on occasion. Today's best water requires a hike for a quarter mile to it…and back, of course. I figured it was a good second choice while others swarmed the most easily accessible spots.

As I drove downstream I found a few cars parked at pullouts, and more fishermen driving upriver in search of likely water. For a Monday the river was busy. "Why aren't these people at work?" I wondered out loud. I was relieved to discover no one was parked at Location 2. Grabbed my rod and slid, literally, down to the river's edge. Within five minutes I was at the pool of my choosing, high on anticipation since I had hooked a large fish here on my last trip. Cast, cast, cast. I covered it thoroughly. Nothing today.

Though the water is higher than I prefer for the runs downstream, I decided to continue downstream on foot to the next couple of runs. So I started by wading across the river. In many locations, this can be a bit hairy, but it's a great way to separate yourself from other fishermen. The fishing spots immediately below me were certainly untouched. Private property cuts off access from downstream. So I traded solitude and being first for less than prime fishing conditions at the water below. I fished my way down for another quarter mile. As I already knew, not much of the water was very fishable today but it would all be worth it if I hooked just one foolish steelhead. Long odds. And, I hooked no fish. I headed back to the car.

Location 3

It was now mid morning. The river would be crawling with men in pursuit of steelhead, driving up and down the highway, playing musical chairs as they switched fishing holes with the rest of the horde. My next move was more luck than strategy. There was an excellent piece of water downstream no more than a mile. It is easily accessed if you know it's there. I had no illusions about it: someone had already fished it. My hope was that this wide expanse of river had not been fished effectively, and that I might be able to reach and coax a steelhead which others could not. This is the "I – think – I – can – fish-better – than – the – other – guy" premise. I think most male anglers carry this type of pride. You know, kind of like "I'm the best driver on the road." The other bit of luck I needed was to find no one parked at my next destination.

When I arrived at my turnout there was no other vehicle parked there. However, there was a pickup stationed just a short ways from me. Hmmmmmm. Where is that angler? Is he just over the embankment from his rig? Or had he parked way over there and walked into my spot? With rod in hand, I made off in a direct line to Location 3, hope in my heart that I would not see movement on the rocky beach adjacent to my water. But, within fifty yards of my target a head popped up to watch my approach. So, I did a quick U turn; loaded up and drove back upriver, knowing I could very well fish have fished that piece of magnificent water better than the angler who currently claimed it. Male pride: it's a terrible thing to waste.

Location 4

Hunches are not very reliable steelhead success indicators. But as I drove upstream near where I started my fishing day I spied a sweet pool with perfect steelhead-holding water at its lower terminus. I had a hunch, even though I knew most hunches bear no fruit. Ask gamblers who go broke. But the water I gazed upon had it all in spades: depth of six to seven feet; walking speed current; and, a boulder-studded bottom. Even if ten anglers have covered it today I'm making a few casts. I can cover this in ten minutes. Very little time lost if it's a bust.

Besides reaching the fishable water on the far side of a distant current, an angler must successfully drift his fly or lure in a manner that will entice a fish. Most often this means slowing the progress of the offering, to minimize the speed with which it drifts to the steelhead. To the fly fisherman this means mending the line. To review, a *mend* is the repositioning of the fly line as it drifts downstream so that it does not pull or drag the fly unnaturally fast down the river. On the flip side, the repositioning of the line may be necessary so that it does not impede the natural drift of the fly, whereby the fly is actually held back or slowed too much. So an effective fly fisherman reads the drift of his line, and repositions it in whatever way is necessary to get — as near as possible — a slow, natural drift of the fly. This is my top priority when I try to fish better than the angler who preceded me.

At Location 4 the prime water was on the far side of the main current. Casting over faster water into slower water always requires a god mend or two to slow the fly. This is my ace: the good mend. Sometimes I need three or four or ten casts to finally hit the perfect mend in order to get the perfect drift. I don't leave a casting position until I'm sure I've made at least three or four of what I consider "perfect" drifts of the fly.

On at least one of my casts in Location 4 I got the perfect drift. At least, a steelhead thought so. I got a very solid hook set when my indicator bobbled. The bright fish twisted and turned as it came to the surface, tumbling downstream in the current as it did so. The fish took my hook no more than ten feet from the lower lip of the run. From there downstream, the river cascaded into a high-speed falls with nothing but trouble in it for me, and an escape route for my fish. To add to the fun there was an exposed root wad from a down tree dead center in the river just where the falls begins. It was toward this root wad that my fish headed. I laid the rod over sideways in an attempt to turn the fish. It worked…momentarily. After coming back to me a short distance it turned downstream once again. If the fish made it to the root ball, it is Game Over. If it drops down the falls on the far side of the roots its Game Over. In fact, if the fish dropped anywhere into the falls this encounter ends. Checkmate!

The fish was only a few seconds into its second dash toward the falls when I felt my line break against a fly rod I'd bent hard against the steelhead. I just slowly shook my head and smiled. I love these fish! Given a chance they act just like my naughty cats.

Location 5

It's cars and pickups and anglers everywhere. Even saw a pickup from Idaho. Foreigners! All easy roadside water has been fished at least once this morning, so my best hope would seem to be a portion of the river that few anglers will seek out. It's time for some very serious brush crashing, to make a trail where there is no trail. Tedious trekking is work as you crash through brush and over tangles of fallen trees trying to get to the river. Once to the stream, wading back and forth from one side to the other is necessary when the side you just left is impassable because of a cliff face or a dense jungle of thicket that makes it impossible to progress farther without crossing. Depending on the water level and clarity, wading across even a small stream can be harrowing. Studded wading shoes and a wading staff are key equipment. Oops. Today I have left my studded shoes back home in my drift boat. I have only my lightweight stud-free wading models. In many areas bordering small steelhead streams I never, it seams, take the same "trail" twice because trails may not exist. The search for an easier route to the river always takes me on a little different path next time. Occasionally I find one; most of the time I don't. But, this is precisely the reason such streams afford you solitude. The requirement of a little suffering thwarts the faint of heart.

It took me more than fifteen minutes from my vehicle to beat and crash my way to the river. And I knew it would take me longer than that coming out and back to the road because the second part of the journey is uphill. If I hook a steelhead it will all be worth it. Even if I don't hook a steelhead it will be worth it. It is locations such as this that allow me to sing along with my iPod tunes without being overheard, and embarrassed as a result. My favorite tunes sound remarkable better — as does my voice — in such beautiful surroundings.

Today I intersected the river at the top end of a perfect-looking steelhead run. It stretches for more than sixty yards. While the lower half is devoid of overhanging limbs, the upper half is challenging in this respect. Side arm casting is necessary. If one is not very good at horizontal casting, you get very motivated to get better quickly or the limbs will continue to eat your terminal gear. Situations like this make me a motivated, innovative caster. A hooked steelhead under a canopy of limbs is a great reward. Such locations discourage other anglers. An undisturbed fish can be waiting in the tough spots.

A natural water slide for the extremely daring.

As I began my fishing I was constantly on the lookout for fresh footprints. There were a few prints but the edges of the depressions were soft, indicating the passage of some time and rainfall since the footprints were made. Apparently, I am the first here today.

As I rocked and sang to David Bowie, Bruce Springsteen, Bon Jovi, and others I covered the water well with cast after cast. In some portions I probably lingered too long, not quite believing there were no biting fish here for me. After more than an hour I reached a downstream point where I needed to ascend through the jungle to find the road and my truck. I had done no harm to the steelhead at this location. I couldn't quite believe it, but these fish *will* mess with your head. Here was another case in point.

Location 6

I've decided to jump into the fray. I'm going to seek out a few roadside fishing holes that either have a tricky approach or require excellent technique to get a good drift of the fly.

Continuing upstream I took a spur off the main highway. Another vehicle was parked a short distance away. I wandered a short ways through the woods to overlook the river. As I looked into the big pool below the high bank I stood on, I spied a couple of anglers walking back to their car. As I slid into the river to make the deep wade to the far side they watched me. Once in position to fish, I fidgeted with my gear long enough for my watchers to get bored and drive off.

I performed a plethora of long, tricky casts to cover the pool until I eventually left my leader and fly in the tree. After breaking off and re-rigging, I made a few more fruitless casts, and moved to the next run above me.

The next pool had a deep channel that ran right against the steep rock outcropping on which I crouched on to cast. I stayed on my knees away from the water's edge in order to not alarm any steelhead that my be lingering here. If there were any fish in this run I was unable to entice them. I even waded the tailout below to cast from the other side. After giving it my best shot, I moved to the shore and moved to the run above me. This third run had a deep channel that ran against the far bank. To fish it demanded I cast under an overhanging limb with a long piece of monofilament fishing line dangling into the water. My leader kept tangling in the mono hanging down from the limb. Aggravating and frustrating. I'm gone.

Location 7

I decided to try one more roadside, easy access locations. As I parked in a large pullout I observed an angler two long casts away getting into his waders, his rod leaning against his car. While he continues to ready himself, I pulled my rod through the rear window and walked to the river. As I settled in, I looked up to see the same angler power up the highway to another location. I did not intentionally mean to do so, but I may have disrupted his fishing plans. Welcome to the combat zone.

Good traction is essential for the angler on foot. Carbide studs are a big plus in slippery rivers.

The water in front of me had the typical deep channel running along the rock face on the far side. In the middle of the target area was and overhanging bush with line and lures draped from it. I tried to fish around the hazard, but the bush eventually grabbed my hook and refused to let go. Grrrrr!

It was mid afternoon, approaching 3 p.m. I felt my energy waning a bit, but the hope of hooking another steelhead prompted me to fish a couple more places before heading home. So after replacing my leader it was back down the river I went.

Location 8

Strategic thinking: seek out a location that requires a bit of a walk, but one that does not require brush crashing and crawling on hands and knees. With fatigue comes less resistance to frustration. It's been an enjoyable day, even if I don't touch another steelhead. As I'm walking back to the 4Runner I hear a vehicle honking at me. It's my friend and former student Jason. We exchange stories about our day's adventures, and soon decided to fish a spot together off the beaten path where we might find a willing fish or two. I had struggled all day to get some fishing photos I wanted. It's always much easier with a companion. I can man the camera, while Jason tends the fish…or vice versa. So we caravanned to our chosen destination, where slid down a muddy trail and worked our way up the river.

It was hard to know if anyone had fished here before our late arrival. Even if they had, we'd fish better. Jason was up first. He had generously invited me to cast first, but I insisted. Generosity begets more generosity. I'd been fortunate enough to hook three fish today so it seemed right for Jason to begin.

Jason is good at methodically covering steelhead water. While staying away from the river's edge so as not to be seen by nearby fish, he started with short casts, covering likely water near our side of the river. With successive casts he moved his drifts farther and farther from our side of the river. On one cast he extended his drift by pulling fly line from his reel, allowing the current to take his egg imitation far downstream between two large boulders. When his strike indicator briefly hesitated Jason swung his rod tip hard. Fish on! But only

briefly. The steelhead thrashed broadside near the surface to reveal itself as large and bright just as it managed to free itself from the hook. And how coincidental! I was listening to my mp3 tunes through my ear buds when Jason hooked this fish. The Canadian band Loverboy was wailing a song appropriately titled "Turn Me Loose". Ouch.

As is our tradition, when one guy hooks a fish — whether it's landed or lost — then the fishing partner gets to step up to take his turn. As I moved into position to try my luck in the same run, Jason walked downstream a short stone's throw to try different water.

The odds are not great of hooking a steelhead in small water where another skilled angler has just fished, but memories

Better have those carbide studs…and good judgment.

of when it has happened in the past give hope to the second fisherman. There was always a chance that I could get a drift a little different, a tiny bit more enticing than my fishing partner had. Maybe the drift of my hook would be a slight bit slower as it approached an interested, but picky, steelhead. Perhaps my egg color was just different enough to encourage the fish to bite. Whatever the reason, I tricked a steelhead. When I detected the strike I brought the rod tip up swiftly to find that familiar throbbing resistance of a big fish. It turned out to be an instant replay of Jason's encounter. As soon as I got a brief glimpse of a big thrashing fish several feet from the surface — pooof! — we parted ways. It's amazing how such a hard and, apparently, solid hook set is not enough to hold the fish. If the hook had made such solid contact with my finger, face, or ear I could guarantee the hook would be firmly buried to its bend.

Location 9

To end our fishing day together Jason and I made a hairy wade across the stream at a point where I could guarantee no other anglers had ventured this day. The water was swift and deep; deep to the point I had no more than an inch between the water and the top off my waders. It's hard to distinguish sometimes the difference between bold wading and foolish wading. I was a lucky fool this day, staying upright and dry. It remained to be seen as to whether or not my luck would carry over into the fishing of the water we had just accessed.

It had rained periodically through the day. During the late afternoon the fall had become steady. The river was rising slowly and the water was getting some color to it. Too often the fish don't bite well under these conditions. They tend to get restless and continue their journeys upstream toward their final spawning locations. Moving fish don't bite nearly as well as stationary steelhead. So even though we covered some excellent runs and obvious channels, we hooked no more fish. For me it was time for the long trip home, during which time I would replay a number of times the encounter I had with each steelhead today.

Safety with a Companion

This last location prompts me to write a little about safety, especially in isolated areas. Cell phones rarely have reception here. Though I've never sustained a debilitating injury while fishing in locations where I could not call for help, I see the potential for trouble all the time. Drowning, hypothermia, bone fractures, and concussions are a risk every day I fish on foot.

One time my nephew Mark Severson and I were fishing a very remote stream for steelhead in March. That day the rain was relentless. After a few hours of fishing it was obvious the river was rising and getting murky. At that point, we had ventured down the creek more than a mile, crossing from one side to the other more than a dozen times where we encountered impassable terrain. Once the decision was made to make our way back up the stream to our truck, deep crossing points had become deeper and swifter. To complicate matters, the water clarity was verging on muddy. It was hard to make out the structure on the stream bottom where we crossed. Our situation went from challenging to dangerous. "Steelhead Fever" can overwhelm good judgment, and this was a case in point. We luckily made it out unscathed, but I've reflected on our situation that day often. It's smart to fish with a companion. In dangerous river crossings two partners can lock arms to steady each other. First aid can be administered, if necessary. And a partner could seek help from others for his injured friend.

A Final Word

Two advantages of fishing a small river for steelhead are significant. 1) When the water is right and the fish are in the river, it is competition from other anglers which is your biggest hurdle to overcome. Because of fallen trees spanning the entire river width, narrow, impassable shoots, and riffles and rapids too shallow to pass over in a floating craft, boats are out of the question on most small rivers. This eliminates many anglers. 2) For fishermen on foot there are many locations where river crossings are necessary because of the terrain and required approach to effectively fish a particular piece of water. Some river crossings are easy; many are not. "Survival of the fittest" not only applies to fish, but fishermen as well. Get to the steelhead where others won't or can't, but think about safety as you do so.

Reference
Haig-Brown, Roderick. *A River Never Sleeps*, William Morrow & Co., New York, 1946

Before you hook a steelhead, plan a pursuit route if you must chase the fish.

CHAPTER 15
Fish On! Now What?

YOU HAVE WORKED HARD,

maybe even suffered, to get to this point:
there is a steelhead on the end of your line, and it's
not happy to meet you.

Just like snowflakes, fingerprints and girls, no two steelhead battles will ever be the same. Expect varying amounts of running, jumping, rolling, spinning, and sulking. All will test your skill and patience.

Having witnessed a thousand ways a steelhead can win its freedom before you have a chance to see your prize up close and personal, even touch it, I have formulated some guidelines that I recommend you pay heed. If you are my client for the day, I am prone to remind you enthusiastically — for your own good, of course — when a violation has occurred. This is, then, followed by an enthusiastic reminder — for your own good — not to do it again.

Michael's Ten Rules for Fighting a Steelhead

Rule #1:	Let the fish run, and keep your rod tip comfortably high.
Rule #2:	Remember Rule #1.
Rule #3:	Keep your hand off the reel unless you are reeling line.
Rule #4:	Remember Rule #3.
Rule #5:	If the fish sprints *at* you, reel as if your hair is on fire!
Rule #6:	While your rod is bent hard against the fish, focus on Rules #1 & #3.
Rule #7:	The first couple of times you think the fish is tired and can be netted, it's probably not.
Rule #8:	Once the fish is on its side, there is a good possibility it is tired enough to net.
Rule #9:	If I am your guide, be assured I will always net the fish as soon as possible.
Rule #10:	If you lose the fish at any time, it is *always* the guide's fault.

In more graceful terms, think of playing a steelhead as a dance. You and the steelhead are dance partners. The steelhead always gets to lead. Step on her feet (grab the reel handle!); she will slap you and leave, laughing as she goes.

Breaking More than the Rules

I have a good client friend — let's call him Jim — who had trouble remembering Rules 1, 2, 3, 4, and 6. It mattered little how often I reminded him. And, oh, I *did* remind him, often.

I study my anglers closely, looking for tendencies that can cost them a steelhead. It did not take long — maybe only two heartbeats — to peg Jim as a Reel Grabber. If you want to lose a big fish instantaneously, grab your whirring fly reel spool as a steelhead sprints away from you at the speed of sound. Pow! You *will* hear the leader explode!

To the wicked delight of his teenage sons, Jim lost four steelhead, all in exactly the same manner: by grabbing the reel handle, which snapped the line instantly. Though he and I had several discussions before it happened the first time, we had additional discussions after each subsequent episode.

Bob Stansbury knows to keep his hand off the reel when a hot steelhead is tearing down the river.

When Jim's fifth opportunity arose, my new tact was to coach/warn him during every second of the fight. From the moment he hooked Number 5 my eyes were on his hands and my mouth never stopped. If necessary, I was going to seize his left hand if he attempted to touch the reel at the wrong time. I did this for ten minutes or more as Jim the Reel Grabber inched that magnificent fish closer and closer to the boat. There was no way I was going to let him lose this fish. Even as I stepped out the front of my drift boat to get into netting position, my eyes were on Jim's left hand.

With the steelhead on its side, tired, and within only a few feet of the net, I told Jim to raise his rod, and NOT touch the reel. For the first time in the entire fight, I looked directly at the fish, in order to make a clean scoop with the net. In a blink, the fish turned away from the net and made a weak lunge for the depths. Kapow! The leader blew up, and the steelhead faded into deep water. I knew what I would see when I looked up to search for Jim's left hand. His sons went crazy with laughter.

To Jim's great credit, the following summer when we fished together, he hooked five or six steelhead, and landed every one of them. He must have visualized the necessary changes for twelve solid months, because his game was flawless. In subsequent years, I cannot remember Jim ever grabbing the reel again.

If You Were a Steelhead

If you should be reincarnated as a fish, there is a maneuver you should remember above all others if hooked by an angler: sprint hard and relentlessly at the fisherman. The slack line created during such a move sometimes enables the fish to shake free the hook. Because I insist on barbless hooks, a slack line can be particularly perilous.

If the angler has a large reel, or a reel with a large arbor, much line can be quickly spun back onto the reel spool as the fish charges. In an "emergency where slack must be gathered at maximum speed, you must strip by hand the slack into the boat (or water) until the line finally comes tight against the fish. However, a serious problem arises when the steelhead turns to run away from you again. The coils of loose line can tangle or loop around the reel handle, rod butt, the button on your sleeve, or something in the boat. All these are the equivalent of grabbing the reel. The fleeting fly line comes to an abrupt halt. Houston, we have a problem!

Only hand-strip fly line if absolutely necessary. Play a steelhead, or any sizable fish, directly from the reel. An excellent drag is a necessity. Do not "cheap out" on this piece of equipment.

Another way a charging-directly-at-you steelhead can beat you is when you are convinced the fish has escaped because the line is slack. When the angler cannot feel the tug of the hooked fish any longer, it is too often assumed the fish is gone. It seems at least once every good fishing day I have to remind an angler to "keep reeling" though the fisherman thinks the fish has escaped. It has merely swum in our direction, creating enough loose line that the angler has been fooled. If the line is slack for too long, the fish will escape, almost assuredly. Time is of the essence. Reel or strip line until you are absolutely certain the fish is gone.

Now for a little story on the importance of keeping a tight line while fighting a steelhead…

Tight is Right During the Fight

When I owned a fly-fishing shop — The Scarlet Ibis Fly Shop, Corvallis, OR — I published a monthly newsletter. Just prior to a February issue, I decided I needed a new steelhead photo. Norton Young helped me with the layout and creation of the letter, so I suggested he and I take a quick to the Alsea River in search of a photo subject.

The location I wanted to fish was vacant of other anglers, so we were soon into our casting routine, methodically covering the run. We were both using the Hybrid Line System. For flies, we decided we should both use something different, with the hope that at least one of the flies would attract a steelhead.

To maximize our chances, we each fished two flies. I cannot recall what Norton had chosen, but I had a Green King on the point, and a Mini Green-Butt Black on a dropper about 2' above the King.

I soon had a solid strike. The fish pulled hard after the hook set, running up and down the pool. Initially, I made all the right moves and counter-moves. Soon, the beautiful hen was in shallow water. Here comes the "but". But, in my excited haste to subdue the fish, I failed to tire it sufficiently to make a secure grip on it. As I attempted to do so, the hen sprinted back toward deep water. In a futile attempt to turn the fish back to me, I exerted too much pressure with the rod, not letting the fish run away. Instead of breaking my tippet, the fish actually stripped the entire leader off my fly line.

An ideal landing location. A steelhead can be landed without a net by sliding it into gentle-sloping shallows, where the tired fish will usually lay on its side momentarily while the hook is removed.

The steelhead disappeared into the heart of the pool wearing the Green King in its jaw, and trailing the dropper fly and leader behind it. Impatience had cost me. I had no one to blame but the man in the mirror.

After I quieted my emotions and tied on a new leader and flies, I hoped against hope for a second fish. And, though I did not deserve it, shortly I got a second strike. I tightened up. The fight was on. As most would, I vowed to make good on my second chance. No hurried impatience would repeat Act One.

When I finally played the steelhead to the surface, it took me a moment to comprehend the situation I was looking at. Neither of the flies on my leader was hooked in the fish. Unbelievably, my point fly was tenuously attached to the dropper fly being dragged around by the fish I had hooked earlier. I was brining in the same fish that had already beaten me once. If at any time I would lose tension on the line, the two hooks joined together in the same manner, just as you would interlock the forefinger on your left hand with the forefinger on your right, would separate. I had a chance to lose the same fish twice in fifteen minutes!

I surmise that the point fly on my leader snagged the leader trailing from the steelhead, slid along it, eventually grabbing the attached dropper fly hook. A freak accident, for sure. I am certain this will never happen again in my lifetime, but it did happen once. Kind of like winning a mini lottery drawing. I got my newsletter picture.

Countless times, I have had clients sadly drop their heads in despair in the middle of a great fish with a runaway steelhead that had ripped the line from the fly reel at frantic speed. Then, the line went slack. Most, here, naturally assume that the steelhead has escaped because they no longer sense obvious tension and tugging on the line. What they fail to notice is that the line is not *totally* slack. Being ever vigilant, I vehemently encourage the client to "reel like a banshee" on the chance that the streaking steelhead has made a 180 degree turn and is actually charging them. More times than not this is indeed the case, so it is imperative that the angler restore tension on the line ASAP. I love the instant mood changes as the angler quickly transitions from elation to despair back to extreme delight when the fish they assumed to have lost has — magically — been rediscovered at the end of their line. Psychologically, this scenario adds greatly to the joy and appreciation of actually landing the fish. This particular drama insures that this individual steelhead will not soon be forgotten. Its legend will live forever, as this exciting fish tale is told over and over by the angler to all who will listen.

Keep that line tight against the fish until you are absolutely sure a jailbreak has been successful. Do not be fooled by the "U" Turn Maneuver.

big boulders and wood; on foot, the angler can have his downstream path blocked by streamside trees and bushes, or dangerously fast or deep water.

Hot pursuit on foot can be aided by footwear with good traction. Wading boots or wading shoes with synthetic felt on the soles are a good aid, reducing the slipping and sliding on slick rocks. For additional traction, soles with carbide studs can't be beat. However, these are not guarantees against a nasty fall or going for an unplanned swim, felts and studs are quantum leaps beyond footwear without them. I have literally run down rivers chasing runaway fish. If you do so, remember to keep your rod tip high, always keeping in mind what you will do with that rod if you stumble and fall. Occasionally, I've had to toss my rod aside as I am going down after stumbling. Throwing the rod into shallow water or streamside brush usually is better than the impact against the rocks if I continue to hold the rod, while trying to cushion my fall with my hands

Nets with rubber mesh are easy on the fish, and leaders and flies are removed from the net with minimal tangling or breakoffs.

In Hot Pursuit

There are times a hooked steelhead will charge down the river and you must follow to have any hope to land the fish. If you fail to pursue, the fish will either run you out of line and backing or entangle the line on a rock or wood debris. Once a steelhead is hooked it is always prudent to start planning a "what if" pursuit plan. Such plans are usually much more challenging on foot than they are in a boat. My main concern in a boat pursuit is chasing the fish through a nasty rapid replete with

and arms. Needless to say, none of these options are beneficial to landing the fish you are chasing.

When further pursuit is not an option you must try and stop the fish before you run out of line or the fish is about to run through a cataract or into a fallen tree in the river. In these cases, I am moving my rod to a horizontal position very near the water, bent hard in a tight arc against the fish. This is done to keep the fish's head low, and the steelhead as horizontal as possible in the current. When you fight the fish with a high

As the fish tires, it's time to get into position for the scoop.

rod tip, the fish is slightly tilted upward in the water. Because the fish is angled up, the force of the current against the tilted body is magnified; the fish gets more "push" from the current than when it is perfectly horizontal and streamlined. This maneuver does not always turn and stop the fish, but it does sometimes. It is always worth a try when pursuit no longer remains an option.

The Rock-Toss Gambit

There is a very memorable part of Jim Teeny's *Catching More Steelhead* DVD where he wants to coax a steelhead from an unfishable position in the river to a more desirable one. To "coax" the fish he tosses a rock near — but not too near — the steelhead's holding location and prompts it to move to a better location where Teeny can finally cast his fly to the fish. If my students remember any portion of this hour-long film, it is this one particular clip.

On occasion, I have tried this same rock-tossing stunt. However, I've never gotten the desired result. The steelhead always goes to a less desirable locale, or it runs away never to be seen again.

On a pleasant winter day on Oregon's north coast, I was fishing with a former student and friend Greg Shurgar. We were fishing a long run together, with Greg at the head and me about two thirds of the way down. A short cast below me the river took a hard turn to the right and the water velocity increased as the flow continued into a high-speed "S" turn. If a hooked steelhead should run into this "S" turn, it would surely win its freedom. There was absolutely no chance of pursuit because of the raging water and overhanging trees.

When I hooked a steelhead at the lower end of the run, I immediately bent my rod hard to the horizontal, attempting to prevent my steelhead from dropping into the turbulence below me. Of course, the fish immediately dashed downstream into troubled waters. I put the brakes on as hard as I dared; much more tension and my line would have parted. I got the fish to stop in midstream. Unable to lead it back upstream, I

decided on a course of action. I threw a stone downstream of it, hoping to startle the fish into moving upstream again. Greg arrived just in time to watch the show up close.

My first throw was a good one, well below the fish. It budged a little bit, but not much. My next throw would have to be closer to the fish. It was…too close. The stone landed almost on top of the fish. Yikes! It stampeded down the river into the "S" turn and broke my leader. Hard lesson learned… maybe.

Eventually Greg and I changed places; I fished the upper end of the run, while he began anew at the lower position. In less than fifteen minutes, I hooked a second steelhead. I had high hopes of landing this fish because I was seventy to eighty feet above the treacherous water at the very end of the pool. But, my hopes soon turned to doubts as this fish — just as its predecessor — ran to the fast water at the edge of the "S" turn. As before, I bent my rod hard and low, able to stop the steelhead. Unable to budge the fish back in my direction I asked my companion for assistance. I would have him do the rock-throwing honors.

Déjà vu. The first rock did very little. However, just as before, the second rock landed a little too near, panicking the steelhead into sprinting downriver. "Snap!" went my leader. "Adios!" went my fish and hook. "Grrrrr!", or something like that, went Michael.

Old Tightrope Walkers and Guides Use One

A net is extremely useful in securely capturing a steelhead. When I am fishing clients, I always use a net. Landed fish are fun and, for me the guide, profitable. Landed fish are particularly important to a few of my clients who only care about, or even remember, a steelhead that they actually get to touch. Even if the fish escapes in full view right underneath their rod tip, some anglers refuse to "count the fish" as part of a successful day. I remind myself often: the client is always right. Putting the fish in the net EVERY TIME is an important goal for me.

I am a big proponent of rubber-mesh nets. In lieu of cotton or — heaven help us — cheap, hard nylon strands, rubber netting is easy on the fish and fly and leader tangles in the netting are minimal.

Steelhead, like many fishes, have a protective coating of slime over their entire body. This serves as a barrier to the invasion of some parasites and disease organisms. Additionally, it "waterproofs" the fish to maintain the proper balance of fluids and chemistry in the fish with its surroundings. So, the removal of this slime as the fish thrashes around in the net bag before its release can be extremely harmful, even fatal. A captured steelhead that is released may swim away, apparently, unharmed. However, over a matter of days or weeks, it may die.

Besides the net bag, dry hands are also very effective in removing fish slime. It is best to wet your hands before you cradle a fish for a picture or its release.

Another consideration of fish anatomy when netting it is the fish's eyes. Unlike us, steelhead and trout have no eyelids. Imagine thrashing around, twisting, frantically squirming in a large abrasive net without being able to blink or close your eyes. I have no idea if a steelhead feels pain in the eye, but if you have ever had a scratched cornea — I have several times in my life — you know that the pain lasting for days can confine you to the couch. You do not want to move. Even as the eyeball moves against the ultra-soft inner surface of a closed eye, it is painful!

So, let's imagine a panicked steelhead, unable to protect its eyes, thrashing its head back and forth in a hard nylon net. It is not hard to envision (bad pun) scratching damage to the outer eye. Be considerate of these special creatures who have

Cheryl Black knows that patience has its rewards. Note the photogenic lipstick and red fingernails.

overcome tremendous odds against its survival to give you fishing pleasure.

One more significant tidbit. When netting a steelhead, always scoop it headfirst. Bad things happen when you try — as I have in my career — to come from behind the fish, tail first.

The best you can hope for on a scoop from the rear is that the fish swims away from or out of the net as soon as it touches the tail. Because this startles the fish, it will usually find a burst of energy. If the angler is not prepared for this sudden sprint, the leader can be immediately broken, or a lightly hooked fish may throw the fly.

Now, I will tell you what is most likely to happen if you are fishing two flies, which my clients do most of the time. You will really hate this one when it happens, especially if you are netting your friend or client's fish. As you lunge for the steelhead, you may or may not get it partially into the net before it swims away in a panic. It is virtually guaranteed that the hook not in the fish's mouth will snag the netting. You will now witness an instant break off. Question: What kind of noise does a goat make? Answer: Whatever sound *you* immediately utter as this fish escapes is the sound a goat makes.

Remember: Just like a newborn baby…head first.

Make the net scoop once the fish conveys it is getting tired. If the angler puts steady lifting pressure on the steelhead — as the fish, the leader of the dance allows — it will

eventually turn on its side, planing on the surface. At this moment, the angler should attempt to smoothly slide the fish towards the net.

There is always a chance the fish may turn its head down as it nears the net, making another surge to get away. Be patient, and maintain steady resistance. A good reel will do what needs to be done. Let the steelhead have its way for the moment. Repeat the application of steady pressure when the fish turns its head to face you again, bringing it to the surface and sliding it on its side toward the net.

If someone is netting the fish for you, do not let them rush. I have seen many fish lost by an impatient or inexperienced netter. Lunging at a submerged steelhead that still has plenty of energy will end unhappily most of the time. Remind him not to make the scoop until the fish is on the surface and on its side…And, ALWAYS head first into the net.

Photographing Your Prize

I look often at fishing magazine photos. Most pics involving the fish as main subject are not to my liking, particularly the "grip and grin" variety. With two people — the angler and the photographer — the angler holds his quarry horizontal, with one hand over the wrist of the fish, exposing the back of the hand nearest the steelhead's tail. This is an unimaginative, hackneyed pose. Way too common, and, therefore, not interesting, no matter the size of the prize.

I am not an expert photographer by any stretch, but I know what I like. I like a shot that exposes more of the fish, and is, often displaying the fish diagonally, not on the perfect horizontal. Alternatively, hold the fish with one hand on its side, partially or fully submerged in the shallows. Or, cradle the fish slightly with an open hand underneath it. But, please spare me another "grip and grinner".

If you plan to release a photo fish, do not hold it out of the water for very long, especially on a hot summer day. How long would it be comfortable for you to be held underwater to have your picture taken immediately after some very vigorous exercise? Consider submerging the fish after a few quick photos before taking more pics. Make sure your hand does not interfere with the movement of its gill covers while it "breathes".

Wet your hands before holding the fish to minimize the amount of protective slime removed from its body while you hold it.

To insure we get a few hero shots of my more inexperienced clients with their fish, I ask to hold the fish for them during the first couple of photos. The angler holds the fly rod and net, while I cradle the steelhead for maximum exposure. We then rest the fish in the net so it can respire and rest before the client holds the fish for a couple of pictures. One of us, then, will submerge the steelhead so it is facing into a gentle current. This is another photo opportunity: the release. Holding the fish barely subsurface allows for the possibility that the lens will capture an interesting and pleasing image. If you are the camera operator, keep shooting. Hope you get ONE good shot.

This is a Net-Free Zone

There are times I opt not to use a net for my personal fishing. It may be inconvenient to carry a big net when I am on foot, or I desire the challenge of landing a worthy fish without the advantage of a net.

When I fish without a net, I scout for places to slide a steelhead into the shallows, or onto a gradually sloping beach. Experience has taught me to discover such locations before I actually hook a fish. You always need a game plan for every detail from start to finish to successfully landing steelhead on a consistent basis.

Every angler, I think, has to go through certain experiences in the early stages of his or her angling career whereby hard lessons are learned. One of these is the loss of an excellent fish as you near the end of a memorable fight. There is a natural

A hatchery steelhead is taken home to be the guest of honor at a BBQ.

A steelhead will signal when it is exhausted enough to be landed when it turns on its side at the water's surface.

tendency to subdue a fish before it can be reasonably landed. It has too much remaining energy and fight to be safely beached, grabbed, or netted.

Without a net, patience is doubly important. It is only when a steelhead finally rolls onto its side, and I can lead it with the steady pressure of a bent rod and tight line, that I try to grab the fish. I try to grip it securely in the narrow region just above its tail. This is the steelhead's "wrist", even though it is nowhere near the fish's hands. Strange.

Once I have secured the fish by the wrist I push or pull it to an area where I will disengage the hook for release, take its photo, or do what is necessary — assuming it is of hatchery origin — to ready it for a trip home where it will be the guest of honor at a BBQ.

For a quick release, I slide the fish into a few inches of water, place my rod carefully on the shore or under my arm, and slide the barbless hook free. If the fish is exhausted, and this is most important in the warm waters of summer, I hold the fish upright facing into a slow current until it swims away without assistance.

Getting a photo, especially fishing alone, can be tricky business. I actually try to get my camera ready before the fight has ended completely. Once the fish is tired, I reach for my camera that is lying on a safe spot near the water's edge. It is all ready to shoot once I put the fish in the shallows or on the beach. Because of wet hands or the possibility of a splashing fish, I always have a small towel with the camera. Often, a tired fish will lie quietly in the shallows briefly, resting on its side. I will take five or six quick photos, and then send the fish on its way, or to its Great Reward. Of the half dozen pictures I take, I hope to get one good shot. Sometimes, none are suitable.

A great aid to securely dripping a steelhead at the wrist is a glove. Get it wet to minimize the removal of the body slime. It might be a good idea to carry a second pair of gloves on winter days.

In areas I fish that do not lend themselves to sliding a steelhead into the shallows or a nice beach, I use my neckerchief, if I am wearing one. I wrap this cotton cloth around my hand as a makeshift glove. Wet cotton cloth grips like a vise. In a pinch, it works well. If you could get your fishing companion to give you his tee shirt, it will do nicely, too.

Preserving a Harvested Steelhead

Once you have humanely (quickly) dispatched a hatchery steelhead, consider bleeding the fish immediately. This drains the fish's flesh of most its blood, and better preserves the meat for eating. Additionally, the fish is less messy when dressing it for refrigeration or freezing.

On a cool day, I do not worry about leaving a bagged (plastic trash bag) lying on the cold floor of my aluminum drift boat for several hours, especially a fish that has been "bled out". Once lunch is removed from the cooler chest, I place the steelhead on ice, turning it occasionally so both sides eventually contact the ice on the cooler bottom.

The idea is to retain a hatchery fish near the end of the fishing day, but there is never a guarantee that a fish will be landed after lunch. Some anglers put too much pressure on themselves (and me) if they are determined to retain a post-lunch steelhead. Murphy's Law WILL come into play much of the time. Fish can be lost during the battle in an endless myriad of ways. Maybe no fish will be hooked during the last several hours of fishing. Or, the steelhead landed may all be native fish, which must be released. It is personally unpleasant for me when an angler is actually disappointed to discover the beautiful steelhead he or she has landed is native, not of "keep-able" hatchery origin. It takes so much joy out of the accomplishment of having fooled and landed a wily fish on a fly rod. Knowing this, I always recommend that such an angler keep the first quality hatchery steelhead of the day, even if they catch it on the first cast of the day. I *will* find a way to preserve the fish's eating quality, even if it means carrying a second cooler, or displacing a portion of the lunch in the cooler.

Many angling slobs leave the entrails in the water when they field-dress fish at day's end. The most popular place to do so is at boat ramps. Besides being unsightly, it is illegal in Oregon to do so. Oregon Law, as written in the Oregon Sport Fishing Regulations handbook, under the heading of *General Restrictions*, states: "The following activities are unlawful… (to) Dispose of dead animal (fish) carcasses, *or parts thereof*, in Oregon waters."

If you keep an Oregon steelhead and dress it in the field, when it comes to the entrails, bury it or carry it.

A Rhyme to Console

There will always be those times when the steelhead on the end of your line will win its freedom in spite of your best efforts. Years of keeping statistics indicate that the odds are about 50/50. Every angler I know wants to land every steelhead he hooks. Even for those anglers who have hooked a thousand, I will wager there is a little disappointment for any fish that escapes.

All my clients and angling friends have heard me refer to steelhead as Heartbreakers and Dream-Makers. Assuming the role of counselor/psychologist, when a guest is especially brokenhearted at having lost a steelhead before getting it to the net, I, often (poetically: *oft*), try to console them with a little poetry.

> *I hold it true, what'er befall;*
> *I feel it when I sorrow most.*
> *'Tis better to have hooked and lost*
> *Than never to have hooked at all.*

My deepest apologies to Alfred Lord Tennyson…

CHAPTER 16
Think Before You Give Away Your Gold (or Silver)

IN THE SUMMER OF 1896,
Skookum Jim Mason, Dawson Charlie, and
George Washington Carmack found gold in a tributary
of the Klondike River in Canada's
Yukon Territory.

Word of their discovery prompted as many as 200,000 prospectors, by some accounts, to flood the region in 1897 and 1898 seeking to make their fortunes. There were murders, suicides, death and permanent injuries from frostbite and hypothermia. Of 200,000 prospectors, about 400 actually found gold, and many of the 400 frittered away or were bilked of their booty.

A half century earlier, in January 1848, James Marshall discovered gold in the American River at Sutter's Mill, east of Sacramento, CA. By March, word was out. Samuel Brannan, a San Francisco newspaper editor and savvy businessman, loudly

Knowing where to locate excellent steelhead holding water off the beaten track is priceless.

and repeatedly advertised the fact of Marshall's discovery. He had brilliantly set up a store selling prospecting supplies and waited for the hordes to come. And, they did. First from within California; then, Oregon. After an eastern newspaper detailed the discovery, and President James Polk spoke of California's gold riches in an address to Congress, an estimated 300,000 immigrants from all over the world streamed into central California in search of gold. The small town of San Francisco grew from a population of 1,000 people to more than 20,000 residents in two years! Sutter's Mill — private property — was overrun with gold-crazed squatters who illegally mined John Sutter's property, ate his crops and took his cattle. (Obviously, ancestors of some steelhead fishermen I know!)

On a much smaller, but still significant scale, word of a steelhead "discovery" can create a stampede. Bragging anglers, fishing chat rooms, newspapers, magazine articles and sport show participants trying to drum up business can ruin a good thing. No friends of mine. In fact, anyone who talks about, and freely promotes specific locations on specific rivers I fish, is my adversary. And, make no mistake, I do not view any as a *friendly* adversary. You have made my guiding job harder, perhaps eliminating it on certain rivers. You are a threat to my enjoyment and my livelihood. Remember: steelheading is a Zero Sum Game. There are winners and losers.

The exception to those steelhead locations about which people feel obligated to tell the world are those rivers that are already inundated by the hordes. Oregon's Deschutes is a great example. If one million people know it is a good steelhead river, what does it matter if two million people know? Go to this 100-mile flowing gem in north central Oregon and try to find a rock to stand on and a little quiet solitude August through November. If you love rude, claim-jumping crowds, you will have a great experience. I guided there for 15 years so this is not a casual observation. Those who would disagree can send me all the hate mail you want, but you know the number one problem to enjoying the steelhead experience on that river is numerous inconsiderate anglers and guides. Congratulations if you are a polite, considerate exception to my generalization. I am not talking about YOU, of course.

Oregon's Grand Ronde and Rogue rivers, and California's Trinity are more examples of waters that are/ were primarily the domains of fly and lure anglers who now find the silver-mining masses vying to stake claims on steelhead water where you used to be able to find a vacant rock to fish from, enjoying a slight modicum of fishing peace. No more. It is in the shortsighted nature of people to brag about their good fortunes, unwittingly inviting the hordes to overrun and overwhelm the treasure site.

"Gold Discovery" on the North Coast

In 1982, I went in search of "gold" on the northern Oregon Coast. Chip Goodhue and I headed for the Miami River, north of Tillamook. We were acting in response to a story we had heard about an undiscovered, unexploited claim on that river. As the story went, the occasional angler actually caught chum salmon on a fly.

It was a sunny November day, the 11th, Veteran's Day. As we drove up the road paralleling this small stream exploring for access points, not a single other angler did we see. That can be good, and that can be bad. It is good that we can fish undisturbed by those who would fish our water, but no anglers can mean few or no fish to catch.

Late in the afternoon, I waded in at the top of a promising looking fishing hole and began to drift a purple Woolly Bugger deep along the stream bottom. When the line stopped in the middle of the drift, I found myself battling a large, strong fish, my first chum salmon. In the next hour, I hooked nine, and Chip hooked some, too. We had found the initial vein of the Mother Lode. Subsequent trips produced many fish on a river off the radar of other anglers.

For a couple of fall seasons we shared our discovery with a few close angling friends, creating new fly patterns for this fishery and refining our angling equipment and methods. Life was good. No claim jumpers in sight.

What happened to the fishery, you might ask? By the early 1990's, the returning chum runs were dramatically reduced. I cannot say that the unwashed fishing masses wading with abandon through obvious spawning areas in this tiny river was a large contributing factor to their demise, but I wonder. I cannot say that the unwashed fishing masses snagging with abandon obviously spawning salmon in this tiny river was a large contributing factor to their demise, but I wonder. Eventually laws were enacted which eliminated the taking / killing of chum salmon, and the season was shortened, ending November 15th each fall, allowing the salmon to complete their reproduction undisturbed. Subsequently, the chum runs have rebounded in the New Millennium. The hordes have returned, also, to catch and release these great fish every year during the first two weeks of November.

Hey, Everybody. Fish Here!

I have learned some heard lessons about revealing not-very-obvious locations where steelhead lie. In sad retrospect, I should have foregone fishing these particular spots when other anglers are watching.

There is a very wadeable steelhead run near a large county park. Once upon a time when the world was as it should be, all anglers fished the run, which stretched for more than a hundred yards, from the shallow park-side of the river. Day after day I would watch them cast toward what I knew to be the productive water on the far side of the current. Delightfully, their success was dismal. Their problem was not reaching

the water where steelhead lay. Unknown to them, I suspect, was that they could not get a controlled, deep, strike-inducing drift. The flies moved too fast in the flow, and did not get deep enough to interest the fish. As I drifted my boat through this area, I would float tight against the far bank, away from the anglers on the opposite side. Since we were almost on top of the steelhead, I would have my clients cast short and hold their rods high to get a deep, slow drift. Most of the time, to the astonishment and, often, the dismay of the onlookers, someone in my boat would hook a fish. Sometimes we would hook two fish. This was pride before the inevitable fall.

In this ever-present group of park fishermen was a retired senior citizen who spent just about every day on the river. He was astute, and he was determined. For an older man Mr. Astute was also an able wader. Though he had to walk quite a distance up my side of the river, and the currents were faster and the water deeper on my side, he eventually found his way to the sweet spot which I could not resist fishing in spite of an audience. Astute fashioned a wading staff, and doggedly plowed his way into the correct position to present his fly, just as I had been doing for years without competition. To my dismay, others eventually followed him. My observant competitor shared his bounty with his friends who shared it with their friends. Additionally, other observant anglers stationed themselves on my side of the river to catch the steelhead that I had little opportunity to fish for on subsequent trips. Because of my lack of discipline, in the throes of Steelhead Fever, I educated the fishing public. In turn, they locked me out of this particular

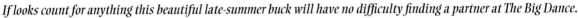

If looks count for anything this beautiful late-summer buck will have no difficulty finding a partner at The Big Dance.

A waterproof point-and-shoot camera makes an underwater fish photo simple, and it's easy on the steelhead too.

fishing sweet spot. Most days on the river, I do not get to fish here because someone is already standing where I want/need to be. Why must the best lessons always be difficult lessons?

Many would take exception to my hard-line view that fishing, especially for steelhead, can be a zero sum game: there is a finite number of fish and too many anglers wanting to catch them. In my most selfish moments, if I could, I would catch every biting fish in the river. More accurately, I hope my clients and guests could do so. It is with this attitude that I approach the river every day, every minute on the river. My paying clients know this. They can rest assured, without the slightest doubt, that I will do whatever it takes to put them on steelhead before someone else has a chance to hook THEIR fish. I need not be rude, but I will always play hard, and play to win. That means — given the chance — my guys (or gals) will be catching ALL the fish…though in reality it never works this way. Think of it as a game of chess. I am looking for checkmate on every move. I can wave, and even smile, on the river, but I am looking to knock everyone's king off the board. In addition, I expect that most anglers and guides play with the same outlook, whether they admit it or not.

Wow! Did You See That?

I had a husband and wife team seated in the front of my boat, both fishing wet flies downstream, perhaps forty feet from us. The flies were dangling in the heart of a channel that had produced many fish for me. We were dead center in the Red Zone.

High on our prospects, I happened to look upstream over my shoulder as another fishing boat was just coming into view. Concerned about revealing the location of this obscure little channel and its fish-catching potential, I immediately began rowing laterally toward shallow water to the right of the prime spot. Ooooops! Too late. I had only made a couple of oar strokes when it was "Fish on!"

Now, if you truly want another angler to sit up and take notice of a good fishing spot, do what my clients did in this revealing moment: hook *two* fish! As the approaching boat passed us, they were looking at two bent rods attached to jumping steelhead. Ouch. So much for keeping this hidden vein of silver hidden any longer. I virtually invited the observers into the mineshaft and showed them where to use their picks and shovels the next time they floated the river. And, yes, about half the time since this event, I can count on finding another boat fishing this once-obscure little channel. My bad!

Every angler I get to know well eventually tells me at least one story of regret about sharing a "secret" spot with a friend or acquaintance who, in turn, tells or somehow reveals this sacred place to others. In short order, all such secret spots become well known. In too many cases, angling hordes make it virtually impossible for the storyteller to enjoy his old favorite fishing location. Regret is a sad companion

Remember: Once gone, forever gone. I know that public rivers are public resources for public use. I cannot lay claim to them as my private playground. But, I can wish it.

CHAPTER 17
Prepare to Define and Defend *Fly-Fishing*

THIS SEEMS LIKE A SIMPLISTIC,
unneeded topic to cover: What is *fly-fishing*? I guarantee
you will be confronted by Absolute Moralists who will try to convince
you that only their designated fly patterns and techniques
qualify as *real* fly-fishing.

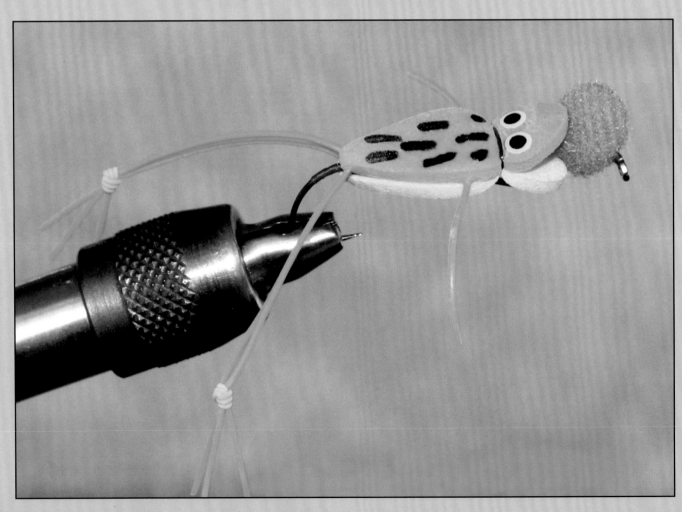

Any straying from the One True Way can make you a deviant. Your challenge, then, is to think about and be prepared for those who would look down on you and your methods as unsporting, even unethical. This, in spite of the fact that you pursue steelhead with a fly rod, fly reel, fly line, and legal fly pattern.

It is nymph fishing — the deadliest and least understood of the fly-fishing methods — that creates more controversy than issues dealing with wet or dry flies. If you get seriously involved in nymph fishing methods for steelhead, put on your body armor and strap tight your helmet.

Note the positions of the hands to present the fish for a photo.

Umpqua Nymphing Show

Years ago, in the late 1980's, I saw an amazing demonstration of the effectiveness of nymphing for steelhead. It was on the "camp water" section, near Steamboat Creek, on the North Umpqua River. A well-known Northern California angler and his female companion hooked nine steelhead taking turns fishing from the same midstream boulder. It was early afternoon on a cloudless summer day. The sun was directly overhead. The early morning wet-fly anglers who fished before the sun hit the water had given up hours ago, and would return in the evening after the water was again in shade. Like vampires, they had no use for, or faith in, fly-fishing for steelhead in the sunshine. At that point, in my steelhead fishing evolution, I subscribed to the same belief: fish for steelhead only when the sun is not directly on the water. The exhibition of effective nymph fishing for steelhead that day was a turning point in my steelheading efforts. I did not turn my back on fishing wet flies and dry flies for steelhead, but I discovered I could utilize nymph fishing to catch fish even when the sun was high. My hope for successful steelhead fishing expanded from three or four hours a day, to all day.

The following morning I watched the Californian angler catch a bright steelhead as I stood on the Mott Bridge. A short time later, I met him as I walked the river bank. After congratulating him on his fine catch, we talked a little about his method and his flies. He utilized a floating fly line, long leader, strike indicator, and a small weighted nymph. He showed me the simple black fly on which he had just landed the fish I witnessed. Besides its simplicity, I was amazed at the fly's small size. It looked like an ordinary #12 trout fly.

Though I had caught countless trout on nymphs many years prior to this encounter, I had no understanding that steelhead which do not need to feed on their spawning migration would actually eat a fly simulating a real food item. I was now a believer.

Since no one was now on that special mid-stream rock from which yesterday's show was given, I waded to it, and stood there overlooking a very tasty channel of dark green steelhead water. I found a black fly in my box that was larger and of a different design than I had been shown, but it was the

Absolute Moralist Glo Bug

1.

2.

3.

4.

5.

When does a fly become a fly for the Absolute Moralist?

nearest imitation I had. Using the same nymphing set up and method I had employed effectively for trout, I actually hooked a steelhead. I was a little shocked. Though I did not hook another that day, I knew I was on to something good.

Shame on You

In May 2009, I stumbled onto a fly-fishing blog that had a number of interesting photos on the homepage. Among others, there was a pic of a Glo Bug (a popular and well-known egg pattern) and a second photo with a package of strike indicators. The caption adjoining these photos was "This is not fly-fishing." Hmmmm.

The 2010 Oregon Sport Fishing Regulations definition of an artificial fly: *"A fly is a hook, dressed with conventional fly tying materials. The affixed materials may be natural or synthetic. Tied in conjunction with other materials, the following items may be part of the fly: wire (lead or other metal) used for weighting the fly, dumbbell eyes or beads (metal, glass or plastic). A fly is not a hook to which sinkers, molded weights, spinners, spoons or similar attractors are attached."* A Glo Bug is made entirely of synthetic yarn and thread, two mainstream fly tying materials. A Glo Bug mimics a real trout and steelhead food item: a fish egg. It fits the definition in my state.

At what point would a Glo Bug become a "real fly" for the blogster above? What if I added a tail? Not enough? Then I will add a hackle. Still not acceptable for a holy purist? Then I will put wings on it. So now, not only do pigs fly, but so does my egg.

As for strike indicators, here we go!

Satan Created the Strike Indicator

A strike indicator is a floating device or material attached to the leader by which an angler can detect a strike when he observes or suspects a fish has intercepted his flies. When the indicator hesitates, bobs, dips, or zooms, the hook is set. Indicators are commonly made of cork, fly line, foam, yarn, and plastic. They come in a broad variety of sizes and colors. A few fly lines have tip sections that are a different high visibility color from the main line. An angler focuses on the bright tip section to detect a strike. The butt section of a leader can be made of bright green, red, or orange material to act as an indicator. Because the strike or interception of a deeply submerged fly can be very subtle and brief, strike indicators are a LEGAL and effective means employed by most nymph anglers to detect a fish bite.

Nymph fishing methods are my specialty. For fly anglers at all skill levels, nymphing can enable them to catch fish when other methods fail. As I wrote earlier, fishing nymphs and egg patterns effectively is a mysterious art to many anglers, including veteran anglers I have fished with over the last thirty years. This method is often the difference between having a mediocre fishing day and a fabulous one. Some days, nymphing is the line between good fishing and being skunked. This method and the fly patterns used create the vast majority of

the Absolute Moralist buzz as they chastise the unwashed fly-fishing masses about the rights and wrongs of what constitutes True Fly-fishing.

To my knowledge, the only river in the entire western USA that prohibits strike indicators is Oregon's North Umpqua. However, Glo Bugs are legal there…at least through 2010. More on this river a little further along in this chapter.

Much controversy, also, arises from the fact that under many fishing conditions it is imperative that a fly must be presented deeply, near the stream bottom, in order to entice a steelhead to strike. Incorporating lead wire or lead eyes into the fly, or securing split shot to the leader are the most

The spawn of Satan.

popular ways to sink a fly quickly. An additional aid is to use a sinking fly line. Even where these methods are legal, a few fly anglers will disparage some or all of these "sinking aids" as "unsporting" or reprehensible. Motives vary, but an air of moral authority is a common thread.

The first time I encountered an Absolute Moralist was during the reading of a steelhead book written in the 1970's. The author advocated using flies uncontaminated with lead wire under the dressing of the body, and no metal eyes could be used to sink the fly either. Instead, sinking flies should be sparsely dressed and tied on a hook as big as a ship's anchor in order for them to gain depth during their presentation to the steelhead. The "pure of heart" fly angler would not ever consider using lead in or on the fly, and certainly no weight on the leader.

I crossed paths with the author on the Deschutes River in central Oregon years later. That morning the native rainbow trout preferred a heavily weighted stonefly nymph in fast water. If the fly had little or no weight, it was virtually impossible to get it into the trout's zone of interest. When the Ab-Moralist saw worthy trout being caught all around him while he was fishless, the sight (humiliation?) was, apparently, too much for him to bear. I witnessed the man stoop to putting split shot on his leader. And, yes, he started hooking fish, too. So much for his Moral Code.

Got Religion?

Nymph fishing — generally, drifting a fly as naturally as possible with the current near the stream bottom — is the most effective of fly-fishing methods much of the time, be it for trout or steelhead. (It is discussed in detail in another chapter.) This technique — with rare exception for steelhead — requires the fly to be drifted deeply and slowly to the fish. The deeper and faster the water, generally, the more weight must be added to the fly or leader. Ah, you may say, why not use a fast-sinking fly line? My reply will always be the same: a floating fly line with weight in the fly or on the leader is S-O-O-O much more lethal. So deadly, in fact, that I personally know of two anglers who now refuse to fish nymphs or egg patterns (fished like nymphs) for steelhead, and they look down on those who fish as these two once did; they got religion, in a pejorative fly-fishing sense. To these recovering nymphers, only dry flies and wet flies are moral. In addition to these two keepers of the One True Faith, I have heard of others through my network of fly-fishing clients and friends.

None for Me, Thanks

Some of my fishing clients disdain nymph fishing. Most of them do not know how to effectively fish this method so they don't like it. They continue to slander the method *until* their companions outfished them. Then, they are suddenly willing to have me show them how to fish this technique. Once they catch a few fish, the prejudice magically disappears. Hmmm.

Other angling guests refuse to nymph fish if it involves heavily-weighted flies, indicators, or split shot on the leader because a standard fly casting stroke cannot be safely used. So, what it comes down to for them is whether or not they can make a reasonable standard over-the-head fly cast with the system. I might, then, pose the question as to whether or not a *roll cast* is an acceptable activity in their conception of "fly-fishing." If they can't easily perform this maneuver with a one-hand rod, is it now acceptable if they can successfully roll cast the nymphs with a switch or two-handed rod. Wait. Oh, no! Nymph fishing with a two-handed rod?

I not only lead many guests to the Slippery Slope, I give them a push.

Can't We All Just Get Along?

Over the next couple of years, the word was out. I watched more anglers adopt nymph fishing for steelhead on the North Umpqua. Many were successful. Because of their effectiveness in hooking steelhead throughout the entire fishing day in very popular steelhead runs, apparently other fly anglers — indignant Absolute Moralists? — who disdained nymph fishing for steelhead, or, perhaps, were unknowledgeable about this method, found they could not hook as many fish in the evening as they had been accustomed. It seems that many of the potential evening biters had been stung by a nymph hook at mid day. Uhh Ohhhh. Somebody may be bent on seeing justice done was not happy. The paradigm for steelhead fishing

The indicators went down, and it was fish on for both Chuck Beck and David Zajicek on the Siletz River.

the North Umpqua had changed, and not for the better. As a result, some nymphers found their vehicle tires slashed.

Now I am not saying there was an epidemic of ruined tires, but it only takes a few instances and a lot of talk to spread the message. The couple of instances I know about personally may have been the work of a serial slasher, not an organized group of crazed anglers shouting and wielding knives.

Currently (2010), there *may* be more restrictive steelhead fly-fishing regulations than those on the "fly-only" section of Oregon's North Umpqua River. However, if there are, I don't know where that would be. Only one *unweighted* fly may be used, where in the rest of Oregon, an angler may use as many as three flies, and weight in the fly is no problem. The use of a strike indicator, used by most nymph anglers, is against the law, too, on the North Umpqua.

You are a law breaker on the North Umpqua for using a strike indicator. However, on the 31 miles of fly-only section of the North Umpqua *"Any type rod or reel permitted, but no metal core lines and no added weights or attachments to line, leader or fly (including, but not limited to, strike indicators) except non-fly monofilament lines may have a casting bubble or similar floating device."* So, strike indicators are illegal for an angler using fly-fishing gear, but someone casting a spinning rod and monofilament line can attach a plastic bubble or float to their line! A plastic bubble or float is an excellent strike indicator. This is little like restricting a bow hunter to using

only 12-inch arrows, while giving rifle hunters no restrictions in the same hunting area.

A proposal was made to effectively eliminate nymph fishing on the North Umpqua. The proposal found very little opposition, and was adopted by the vote of the Oregon Fish and Wildlife Commission. That's how the system works.

Letters and comments received by the Commission concerning a proposition for an angling regulations change are available to the public. I obtained copies of some of the written comments for the North Umpqua change. I remember in particular one from an angler who was now a reformed nymph fisherman. He wrote of how he had hooked an inordinate (in his mind) number of steelhead on nymphs. So many, he contended, it seemed unconscionable in retrospect. How unsporting of him to hook and "torture" so many steelhead! He was sorry for his sins, and wanted to impose his newly found morality on other fly anglers who would fish the river. Rumor has it this man still wears a hair shirt and whips himself in repentance every day he fishes for steelhead. *Mea culpa, mea culpa, mea maxima culpa.*

So, do not be surprised if you find yourself defending the flies you use for steelhead, especially if they have weight in or on the body. If you choose to use split shot on your leader where the law allows it, be prepared for someone who might tell you "It's not really fly-fishing." If you drift a nymph or egg fly under an indicator, you are in clear and present danger of being scolded or mocked by "The Enlightened". If you choose to respond, think through, in advance, what you might say. If you don't have conviction in your equipment, flies, and methods, merely ask yourself these: Is it legal? Is it sporting? Does it give me enjoyment? Answer "yes" to all these and conviction is yours.

Finger-waggers beware! Not everyone is as enlightened as you. If some of the fly-fishing equipment, flies, and methods you disdain are legal, remember that some of us are not soliciting your opinion; so keep it to yourself. I know some anglers with time on their hands who might seek you out on the river just to aggravate. They might be inclined to fish three Glo Bugs with lead eyes under a beach ball indicator with a Spey rod, right in front of you. To hear you rant will be their pleasure, the louder the better. ☺

We Are Much Too Civilized for That!

I had a client in the fall of 2009 who related a story of his friend who took a guided steelhead trip down the Deschutes with a well-known outfitter. It was a multiple-boat affair involving at least four *paying* clients. After a morning of fishing wet flies, the sun was high and everyone took a break to dine and rest. Almost everyone…As the story goes, one paying guest decided to rig a nymph rod to continue fishing steelhead. As he was about to proceed, one of the guides chastised the *paying* client, "Oh, no. *We* don't do that on *our* steelhead trips."

It's hard to imagine the condescending guide received a gratuity at the conclusion of the event. What are the odds these anglers will use this outfitter again?

I May Have Saved the Best for Last…

Spey rods with indicators.

I think I just heard a collective groan from various quarters, as some horrified anglers placed their hands in front of their eyes and turned their heads in fright. Somewhat similar to the reaction when the Phantom of the Opera takes off his mask. The crowd shrieked and averted their eyes.

Follow my line of thinking. Many popular wet flies cast on two-hand rods are heavily weighted. So, what is wrong with fishing a weighted nymph in lieu of a weighted wet fly?

What if you slipped a two-inch piece of highly-visible fly line (with the braided core removed) up onto the leader as a strike indicator? When cast, the caster would not even know it was there. Is that acceptable? What if you slipped a Corkie the size of a pea onto the leader, instead of the hollow hi-vis fly line? What about a clump of synthetic yarn the size of a nickel? A quarter? A silver dollar? A beach ball? Is it legal? Is it sporting? Do you enjoy it? If yes to all, then to the Absolute Moralist an outspoken angler might suggest, "Shut your pie hole unless someone asks you."

Stay low to the water when lifting a steelhead for a quick photo.

CHAPTER 18

Are You Willing To "Cowboy Up"?

THE AMERICAN COWBOY OF THE
late 19th century seems to epitomize all that many of us admire in a
man or woman: independence, self-reliance, resourcefulness,
courage, the ability to overcome adversity without
whimpering about life as "unfair".

Even though today's collectivist progressives may disdain him, I suspect the cowboy is secretly admired by them, too. A Byronic hero: publicly scorned, but privately envied.

I see the cowboy's admirable traits most obviously demonstrated today in amateur athletes (rarely professionals), small business owners, good fishing guides, and *successful* steelhead anglers. All dwell in an extremely competitive environment. Most will not succeed in their quest, falling by the wayside as they lose another race, close the business, give up on steelhead, or are unable to satisfy their fishing clients who take their business elsewhere.

Here's a little test. Choose the best answer.

1. A cowboy riding his horse on a narrow, precipitous trail encounters a coiled rattlesnake determined to block his path will a) scream like a little girl and ride for home b) close his eyes and hope the snake goes away c) try to reason with the reptile d) hope someone else will come along and deal with the snake e) organize a committee to study the problem f) none of the above, little cowpoke

2. A businessman (or woman) is steering his business through a severe economic turndown in a competitive market. He encounters uncertainty and misfortune determined to block his business success. He will a) scream like a little girl and drive for home b) close his eyes and hope the downturn goes away c) sit quietly catatonic d) hope someone else will come along and deal with the problem e) organize a committee to study the problem f) none of the above, little cowpoke

3. A good steelhead guide riding his drift boat into a harrowing whitewater rapid encounters a nasty, jagged boulder determined to block his path. He will a) scream like a little girl and row for home b) close his eyes and hope the rock goes away c) try to reason with the rock d) hope someone else will come along and remove the rock e) organize a committee to study the rock f) none of the above, little cowpoke

4. A frustrated, wannabe steelhead fly angler cannot catch a fish, or lucks into only the occasional steelhead. He should a) give up, go home, and sell his gear on eBay b) take up golf c) Shut up, suck it up, and Cowboy Up, little cowpoke

I am going to trust you did well on the quiz, and have set yourself with the American cowboy's state of mind. Assuming so, read on.

Steelhead Fishing Reality Show

There are three realities: 1) perceiving the world and our circumstances as we *think* they are, but aren't (a delusional, secular socialist / progressive); 2) perceiving the world and our circumstances as we *hope* they are, but aren't (a fearful ostrich or delusional, secular socialist / progressive); and finally, perceiving the world and our circumstances as they *truly are* (a smart cowboy and/or successful steelhead guide or angler). A reality-based fishing guide *real*-izes witty conversation sprinkled with jokes and fish stories under beautiful skies surrounded by a magnificent river environment, and the client sharing the fishing experience with friends and family, will rarely compensate for no fish caught. At day's end, the single most important item on every client's checklist — even though he may deny it — is how many steelhead were hooked. Maddeningly, for too many, it's how many steelhead were actually *landed*. And, I know that my hoping very hard that their outlooks were more benevolent does not change this fact of fishing reality a tiny bit. Gotta get real, and stay real.

Knowing the ultimate pitfall of guiding — not catching enough significant fish to please the client — I "cowboy up" every day on the steelhead river. This is never a casual approach. I anticipate and plan for adversity: weather, water flows, and intrusions by other river users, uncooperative fish, clients unable or unwilling to take directions necessary to catch a fish, and clients not psychologically geared to the usual demands of successful steelhead fishing. Reality tells me most days my resourcefulness and confidence will be tested.

The Fishing Guide as Steely-Eyed Gunfighter

For almost two decades, I have tried to outsmart the stock market to grow my retirement investments. Studying and researching potential investments harder than anything I ever did through graduate school, I have dedicated, literally, thousands of hours. Anyone who watches The Market and his investments too closely is sentenced to living on an emotional roller coaster. One day is elation; the next is hell.

An aspect of investing I continued to ignore for too many years is the emotional control necessary for the investor (me) to maintain his sanity. Whenever I encountered articles, chapters and whole books addressing the topic of emotional evenness, I totally ignored them, underestimating its importance. Motivated by sleepless nights, learning to successfully deal with the short-term mountaintop highs and valley-floor lows of my retirement investments has assumed top-priority importance.

The same analogy applies to steelhead fishing and guiding. On one hand, I need to learn all that can be discerned about steelhead behavior, reading rivers correctly within a vast universe of water flows, secret flies, effective techniques, and the right equipment; it is a totally different matter not to succumb to the emotional havoc inherent to the pursuit of steelhead. For some of us, self-doubt may be sent into hibernation for a while, but never is it completely eliminated.

Analyze This

*Lord, please give me the strength to
change the things I can,
The ability to endure the things I can't,
And, the wisdom to know the difference.*
— The Prayer of St. Francis

Having to deal constantly with temperamental fish and temperamental clients, being "skunked" usually ranks near the top of a fishing guide's daily fears. At the start of a two-week stretch of late winter, guided fishing in the not-too-distant past, I had three guests fish with me for three days. The river was extremely high, but clear. There was no doubt that steelhead could easily see the flies that were drifted into their

Sometimes Steelhead Fever and common sense collide.

zone. I was confident we would catch steelhead even though it was obvious by the lack of anglers on the river that not many shared my faith. On top of my confidence, my guests were upbeat, persistent, and grateful for my efforts. We WERE going to catch fish! And we did, on all three days. I could never predict where or when during the fishing day, but we netted at least two steelhead every day, and hooked others which escaped. Self-doubt was not an option.

Following these halcyon days, fishing marginal water conditions, a long-time client and his friend arrived to fish with me for three days. We are two hours into our first eight-hour fishing day when my client friend is lamenting the possibility of being skunked. After reminding him the day is young and we had been in this same situation during many fishing days in the past, he seemed encouraged. However, in less than thirty minutes, he commented again that he was on track to go fishless. To add to the pressure I was starting to feel, he remarked that "this is the reason we're here," referring to putting a steelhead in the net. Granted, at the moment I was probably overly sensitive, this repeated comment seemed to totally disregard the fact that the day was cloudless, the river scenery magnificent, and my boating and guiding efforts were the best they could be. My only comment at this point was, "I will try harder." I did not know exactly *how* I was going to try harder, but if there were a way, I would try

to discover it. Short of capturing a steelhead and placing it on the hook, I was at a bit of a loss.

At 3 o'clock in the afternoon, six hours into our fishing day, my guest in fear of being skunked hooked a fabulous steelhead. After putting up a memorable fight that took us several hundred yards down the river, I was able to slip the beautiful hen into the landing net. Photos commemorated the moment. I reminded the doubting client that his patience and persistence would be rewarded. This message stuck with him…until the next day.

We were further into Day 2 than the previous when skeptical guest again started in about being skunked, though his companion had already hooked and landed a steelhead. I reassured him of my faith in him to hook a fish by day's end if he kept making good casts. By day's end, he had landed two. Again, I tried to point out the lessons of patience and persistence.

It's mid afternoon of Day 3. I have already heard the "I'm going to get skunked" line several times AGAIN. It's after 3 p.m. In the midst of a weak moment, my client is doing a good job of convincing me, even though I have not been blanked on this river for many years. Just before 3:30, my guy sets the hook into another excellent steelhead. Fight, fight, net, and photos. We still had two hours to fish. I chastised myself silently for doubting.

A few days later, I had two brothers, R and E, same river, high water. E was a first-time fly-angler. He's in pursuit of a moody *winter* steelhead with a fly rod. Brother R had fished with me a couple of times previously in the winter, landing his first steelhead ever on a fly a couple of months earlier. Both had great attitudes, just happy to be learning about fly-fishing on a beautiful river. They, also, realized the effort I exerted to row them into fishing position on a swollen river. I was doing my best to reward them for their faith and appreciation of me.

It's after 4 p.m., and no fish landed. Even though a few steelhead had been briefly hooked, clients seem to forget about opportunities and only remember fish that make it to the net. It may not be "fair" or "right", but it seems that only landed steelhead count towards a day's fishing success. It is *landed* steelhead that best ensures clients return to fish again.

Cut to the ending. Novice brother E lands his first winter steelhead on a fly. Veteran brother R lands a two-salt, six-pound beauty. How could I ever doubt? As they say in infomercials, "And, that's not all!" R puts another spectacular nine-pound native hen in the net to end the day. Almost seven hours — no fish landed. Then, three steelhead in the last hour and fifteen minutes. Go figure.

The Guide on Reconnaissance

Before my next clients were scheduled to fish during the same time-frame continued from above, I had two days to write another portion of this book and/or go fishing. On the first day, driven mostly by the guilt of being a writing slacker, I sat for hours composing at my laptop. Just before noon on my second day, I made the decision to launch my boat for some steelhead reconnaissance. With my mp3 player blasting in my ears, I was rowing down the river by 12:30 p.m.

The first spot at which I anchored was a suspiciously good-looking run where I had never caught a steelhead. But, at high water, it had "The Look". Having tied on a couple of egg patterns that had worked for my clients during the past week, it took me exactly two casts to hook my first steelhead of the day. I brought the bright little hen to the boat, admired her briefly, and then, sent the fish on her way. After a couple dozen more casts, I sang myself down the river toward my next stop.

My next destination was the edge of a fast chute that had produced two steelhead in quick succession for one of my guests the week before. I had fished this same locale four times with clients since the two fish episode. We did not touch another fish in those attempts. Maybe today would be different. It took a few more than two casts but I quickly found myself connected to a jumping sprinting steelhead that headed straight into the chute, and through the rapids. I was looking at my fly line backing by the time I pulled the anchor to pursue.

When fishing alone in a drift boat, it's most useful to have three hands when chasing a fish: two hands to man the oars, and one hand to hold the fly rod. I rowed a few strokes to position myself for the oncoming whitewater drop, then cranked on the fly reel to gather line as I sped toward the slowing fish. Row, row. Reel, reel. Row some more. Reel some more. I dropped through the final waves, then, let the boat go where it wished. As the current speed decreased and the water shallowed, I released the anchor. It did not take long to realize the steelhead had toasted my leader, breaking off both flies during

Sometimes two hands are not enough when fishing alone.

its escape. The excitement diminished any disappointment. The fish had beaten me fair and square. I have always admired a resourceful win by a worthy adversary.

I re-tied my leader and flies, and rocked on to location #3, a narrow channel immediately above the next big rapid. Staying well away from the fishable water, the anchor came down again. After five minutes, or so, I was about to give up when I made a cast that did not appear to be too different from many of the others I had already thrown. But, apparently, there was some little nuanced change in the drift that encouraged a previously reluctant steelhead to bite.

The silvery hatchery hen made a great move to start the game: she charged the boat, creating slack line. When using barbless flies — which I do — this maneuver can often win a fish its freedom. The swiftness of the current, however, kept tension on the line, preventing the hook from being dislodged. It was a visual treat to watch the fish do battle in the shallow water near the boat. All during the fight, it never strayed very far from me. Soon, the fish exhausted itself. I held the rod tip high with my right hand, and scooped the fish into landing net with my left.

Three anchor drops; three steelhead hooked. Why was angling success so easy today? Same water level. Same flies fished in the same old spots with the same technique. Different angler…It came back to me, as the realization has many times, that successful steelheading is always a game of small details. There are little nuances in the cast, the drift of the flies, the position of the rod tip, and the fine-tuned awareness of what is happening during the fishing process, that all contribute significantly to consistent success. I fear that some of these details are so minute that they escape detection. That is, an experienced angler may make tiny adjustments to get the "perfect" drift of the fly that will trigger a strike from a steelhead that the average angler would not be able to coax. Additionally, exceptional anglers stay focused on the task of fishing. When the strike comes, a great angler *anticipates* that it is coming. It's an intuition born of experience. The great angler slows the drift of the fly with a subtle mend in the line, when the average angler thinks is drifting perfectly already. Conversely, the exceptional angler does not over manipulate the drift of the line and fly, making needless or detrimental adjustments. Also, what the average, or even good, angler may think is too subtle to be a fish strike, or worse yet, presume the fly was caused to hesitate by "a rock", the exceptional fisherman always assumes is a fish, looking for any excuse whatsoever to set the hook.

Experience takes time, even with a good mentor helping you. I do my very best to coach my clients on the river. I constantly banter about technique, focus and awareness, and I am aware that I can annoy some of my guests by repeating myself often. But, when the Moment of Truth (the strike) comes, I have tried to prepare them for it. If a client gets only one or two strikes in a full steelhead fishing day, I want them to make the most of it. I want them to be successful in hooking a fish or two (or three, or ten), so they will learn and enjoy, and, oh yeah, hire me to take them fishing again and again.

Let's move on to spot #4 during my fishing day. This was a run where, due to circumstances thrown my way by Murphy's Law, I had been unable effectively fish with clients in the last week and a half. The currents are swift and tricky, so positioning boat in an effective location is a challenge. Biting fish can always be found in this spot IF the angler can be held in place long enough to finally get the right cast. This day it took me less than a dozen casts to make the right one. Fish on!

The steelhead screamed line off the reel, headed downstream with purpose. I lifted the anchor to follow. When I

A strategy of stealth may include camo threads.

reached quiet water a hundred yards downstream, I dropped the anchor, made my stand, and fought the steelhead all the way into the net. After a few brief moments of admiration, I sent the fish back into the river.

Locations #5 and #6 held high hope for me. Unfortunately, the fish showed this spoiled man no love, so it's on to Les's Ledges. One portion of this long, irregular channel had "saved the day" several days in the last week. Another High Hope location.

To get to this channel I had outrun a couple of drift boats that had decided to linger well upriver and out of sight. However, before I could be too pleased, a jet boat full of anglers was cruising *up* the river right at me, deviously sliding into the water I was about to fish. Though I am tempted here to rant on about the noise, wake, pollution and the violation of tranquility perpetrated by powerboats on small rivers, I will merely say I held my ground and began to fish.

In the same portion of the Ledges that my clients had hooked steelhead in recent days, I was fortune enough to do the same. It turned out to be the biggest of the day. As my audience in the powerboat watched, I drifted into quieter waters with my fish in tow. Things were good for the first couple of minutes. I got a close look at this wonderful steelhead. I could clearly see my egg fly in its upper jaw. Then, the hook came out, and my rainbow denizen slowly sank into the depths.

I turned up the volume on my mp3 player, and drifted downriver with a few last locations in mind. Though I fished these well, I got no cigar. In two and half hours at midday, my tally was five hooked, three steelhead landed. Gratifying, but almost too easy. Why couldn't my attentive, studious clients do the same? Ultimately, the same old answers circled back to me: experience, focus, attention to, and execution of, the fishing details. For the beginner, or a veteran "expert" diligently trying to change his bad fly-fishing habits, these are all fed by persistence and faith.

Tested Faith…Again

My last client came in to fish the final two days of my extended stay. He is a good nymph angler because I trained him from

Ground Zero. No bad habits, good focus, sound technique, and a great attitude. What a treat for me. Because of my personal fishing experiences from the day before, my confidence was high. I forgot about being humble in my state of confidence. Steelhead can be harsh, merciless taskmasters.

On the first day, my good and attentive guest caught two steelhead in the latter half of the day. He had fished well, and was pleased. On the other hand, the results had not matched my expectations. Maybe tomorrow would live up to my expectations. I really wanted it for my client friend. I wanted it, perhaps, too much.

Though I tried to conceal it, my friend noticed my frustration that he was not hooking numerous fish. He kindly reminded me that he was having a great day, and that he knew I

A good angling guide will do what is necessary—within reason—to get his clients to the steelhead.

was trying my best to get him into fish as I had done so many times over the years. So, instead of relaxing a bit, I actually was more determined to row harder and fish smarter to get this deserving man into a willing steelhead. However, just like in the Wide World of Dating, he who presses too hard to impress the girl usually hurts his chances. He who *needs* to find a biting steelhead will be slapped across the face by Miss Murphy's Law.

On this day, Murphy showed up in the form of numerous boats and bank anglers. It seemed that everywhere I wanted to fish someone was already there. When I dodged the drift boats, the bankies and powerboats found me.

Trying to take to heart some of the sage advice I had often repeated to my clients, I was reminded — AGAIN — not to give up until the last cast is made. So, I had my client keep his fly in the water even in areas I had never caught a fish, seen a steelhead caught, or even heard of a steelhead caught there. Again, my pathetic silent prayer: "I know I'm doing a poor job of Cowboy-ing Up, but please, God, just one suicidal steelhead."

We were running out of fishing time and water as we drifted through what I deemed to be mediocre steelhead water. The area where my client's fly was drifting was too fast and shallow. Apparently, a willing seven-pound steelhead did not know this as it grabbed my friend's hook. On top of this, the fish put on a tremendous, memorable fight that took us down the river on a merry chase that ended happily with it safely in the net. Lots of photos memorialized the memory of the fight and all the combatants.

The day ended with big smiles all around and another lesson in tested faith and persistence. Remember. The game is not over until the Fat Lady sings and the last cast is finished.

Don't Expect Steelhead Justice

One February morning on the Alsea River I covered one of my favorite fishing runs quite thoroughly with a couple of proven flies. Before I left, though, I wanted to switch flies and fly lines to make another pass through the area. About this time, an angler with a spinning rod casting a large spinner asked if he could make a few casts. Since I had to re-rig, I agreed to his request.

The man had made several dozen casts before I was ready to fish again. As I stripped out line to begin my next round, the angler said he would make "just one more cast". It was a good cast — he hooked a fish. MY fish! He played it well, beached it, and happily wandered down the trail with his prize. If I said I was happy for him I would be telling a whopper. My joy in his "victory" did not increase over the next thirty minutes during which I made many excellent casts to no avail. Life isn't always fair, and neither is steelhead fishing. Therefore, I do my best to deal with such situations, just like a cowboy who wakes up with a rattlesnake in his bedroll — treat the bite, learn from the incident, and saddle up.

Having dry clothes in a waterproof bag tucked into your backpack is smart for winter fishing.

One More Test of Faith, Little Buckaroo

One more story to illustrate a couple of points about persistence, patience and faith…

It was mid April, the tail end of the winter steelhead season on the rivers I fish. I was locked into the date by my client's schedule. The river level was good, and the weather for the day was occasionally rainy. It was all systems go.

My client for the day was definitely experienced. He was a fly-fishing veteran. I knew this would be a problem. It ALWAYS is with veterans not having gone through my "training program"! Like trying to teach an old dog new tricks, long-time fly-fishermen are locked into the bad habits formed over years of using poor or ineffective techniques. They cast too far and too often. Loose coils of line are everywhere, but especially tangled on gear in the boat, or underfoot. These guys mend line at the wrong time in the wrong way, and too often. When the drift of the fly should end to be re-cast, the veteran is determined to feed more line through the rod guides to extend the drift beyond its effective range. Veterans waste a lot of valuable fishing time. In addition, they are unable to take suggestions for any significant length of time before they immediately revert to wasting fishing time again. In short, with rare exception, these "experts" are unteachable. On top of incorrigible fish, I have to attempt to help an incorrigible fisherman. They may be nice people with good intentions, but they seem unable to help themselves. Try as I may, after more than a quarter of century of guiding, short of shock therapy and a frontal lobotomy, I have not found a way to de-program these anglers. However, I must admit to entertaining training fantasies that involve cattle prods and dog shock collars. Now back to the story.

My client, a good-natured and conversational man, was thrilled to know we would be nymph fishing for steelhead. This was his realm of fly-fishing expertise. And, as the day unfolded, it was evident he had done quite a bit of nymph fishing. He could handle a fly rod and understood casting mechanics. That's good…kind of. Downside: cast too far, mended too much and ineffectively, and persisted in lengthening the drift of the fly by shaking additional line through the rod guides. At the start, experience told me we would be on the water for eight hours, but effectively fishing for — maybe — three hours. Please, God, let me find some suicidal steelhead.

By early afternoon, my experienced nympher had had two confirmed brief encounters with steelhead. In both cases, in spite of my constant reminders, his continued employment of poor line management skills had cost him the chances to solidly hook and hold a steelhead. All I could do was continue to offer encouragement "it could be the next cast" which would produce a willing-to-commit-suicide fish.

We are now about 180 seconds from the boat ramp for takeout. At most, my guest has three casts remaining for his day before the river's current pushes the boat through the last water with any hope of hiding a steelhead. Though my hope had departed, lightning struck. My veteran nympher was fast into a big steelhead that revealed its impressive dimensions as it rolled to the surface. After frantically gathering loose coils of fly line, my guy was lucky enough to get the fish on the reel. It was hallelujah time! My client's persistence had paid off in creating a dramatic end to the day. After having made hundreds

A high vantage point aids greatly in spotting resting steelhead.

and hundreds of casts for eight hours, it all was coming down to what may have realistically been the last cast of the day.

It is not good for the angler when a steelhead persists in rolling and thrashing. You want it to swim normally. Maybe it swims away at high speed, or charges the boat, but these things are manageable. But, a rolling thrashing fish is trouble. Often, these troublemakers tangle in the leader, or worse, are impaled somewhere with the second fly.

Apparently not applying undue tension on the line, my guest was too quickly parted from his beautiful prize. The steelhead had broken off, tangled in the leader; I am sure, by its unsportsmanlike antics. My guest was greatly disappoint-

ed, as was I. But, fortunately for me, he wasn't disappointed enough not to give me a nice gratuity as we said good-bye for the day. He congratulated me on my upbeat, encouraging attitude in the face tough fishing, which made me feel especially good. On top of this, he wanted to immediately book another guided steelhead trip.

Persist, persist, persist. Fish hard right through the last cast. You never can predict what will happen. Moreover, if you can, be happy while you do it. Strangely, steelhead days can be both disappointing and gratifying.

Each season I have three or four occasions where anglers in my boat will hook a steelhead on what is intended to be the

If you can keep your head when all about you are losing theirs…
If you can trust yourself…
If you can wait (wade) and not be tired by waiting (wading)…
If you can meet with Triumph and Disaster,
And treat those two impostors both the same…
If you can force your heart and nerve and sinew
To serve your turn long after they are gone…
If you can fill the unforgiving minute
With sixty seconds' worth of distance run,
Yours is the Earth and everything that's in it,
And — which is more — you will know what it means
To "cowboy up", my son.

More apologies for tinkering with Rudyard Kipling's fine poem "*If*".

A Closing Note for Cowboys

Fly-fishing for steelhead — if I may be so audacious — is an allegory of Life. Every day has its challenges, even for Bill Gates and Brad Pitt, and the world's greatest steelhead fisherman/guide, whoever he may be. Observe, learn, persist. But most of all, persist.

Not everyone is cut out to be a consistently successful steelhead fly angler. Most do not have the necessary mind set. You know, like the tenacity of an angry pit bull clamped on a mailman's thigh. Maybe you are happy in the casual pursuit of the world's most fabulous freshwater game fish. If the rain is falling, you will wait to fish when the weather is nice. When the river is high, you will wait for more suitable flows. If you don't get a strike in the first two hours, there is yard work to do and football on TV…and laundry to fold, and ruffled-sleeved shirts to iron.

On the other hand, there will be the cowboys with fly rods making a thousand casts today with frozen fingers and rain dripping down their necks. And, every now and then, their rod tips will be bent hard against a magnificent fish that others would not, could not, and should not catch.

Giddyup!

last cast of the day. Now and then, it is the only fish of the entire fishing day for that fisherman. After hundreds and hundreds of casts in an eight-hour stretch it may all come down to the final swing of the bat. It is a valuable lesson for all that witness it, including the guide. The memory and retelling of the last-cast fish serves to keep hope alive. Hope and persistence — all cowboys have 'em.

So, an integral part of the Cowboy Up process is keeping the faith, even when the outlook seems bleak — keeping hope alive may enable you to find a biting steelhead when it seems none will be found. Just as in Life, you *will* be tested. Expect it; welcome the challenge.

SELECT STEELHEADING BOOKS
FROM FRANK AMATO PUBLICATIONS

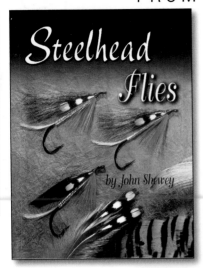

Steelhead Flies
by John Shewey

Fly-Fishing for Pacific Salmon II
Les Johnson & Bruce Ferguson
With Pat Trotter
Foreword by Russell Chatham
Artwork by Ron Jenkins

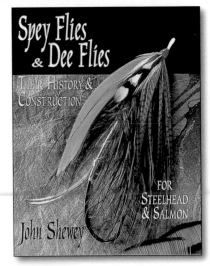

Spey Flies & Dee Flies
THEIR HISTORY & CONSTRUCTION
FOR STEELHEAD & SALMON
John Shewey

Two-Handed Fly Casting
Spey Casting Techniques
by Al Buhr

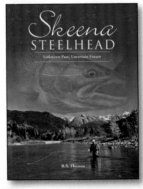

Skeena STEELHEAD
Unknown Past, Uncertain Future
R.S. Hooton

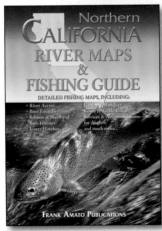

Northern CALIFORNIA RIVER MAPS & FISHING GUIDE
DETAILED FISHING MAPS, INCLUDING:
• River Access
• Boat Launches
• Salmon & Steelhead
• Run Timings
• Insect Hatches
Fishing Techniques
Knots & Tackle Guide
Services & Accommodations
for Anglers
and much more...
FRANK AMATO PUBLICATIONS

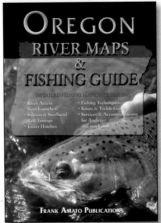

OREGON RIVER MAPS & FISHING GUIDE
DETAILED FISHING MAPS, INCLUDING:
• River Access
• Boat Launches
• Salmon & Steelhead
• Run Timings
• Insect Hatches
Fishing Techniques
Knots & Tackle Guide
Services & Accommodations
for Anglers
and much more...
FRANK AMATO PUBLICATIONS

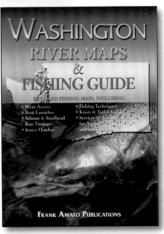

WASHINGTON RIVER MAPS & FISHING GUIDE
DETAILED FISHING MAPS, INCLUDING:
• River Access
• Boat Launches
• Salmon & Steelhead
• Run Timings
• Insect Hatches
Fishing Techniques
Knots & Tackle Guide
Services & Accommodations
for Anglers
and much more...
FRANK AMATO PUBLICATIONS

Steelhead FLY TYING GUIDE

Babine
A 50-Year Celebration of a
World-Renowned Steelhead and Trout River
Pierce Clegg & Peter McMullan
Foreword by Mark Hume
Artwork by Dave Hall

FLY-FISHING COASTAL CUTTHROAT TROUT
Flies, Techniques, Conservation
LES JOHNSON

THE COMPLETE ILLUSTRATED DIRECTORY OF SALMON & STEELHEAD FLIES
CHRIS MANN

Ask for these books at your local fly/tackle shop or call toll-free to order:
1.800.541.9498 (8-5 P.S.T.) · WWW.AMATOBOOKS.COM

184